JOURNAL OF BIOSOCIAL SCIENCE

Supplement No. 7

BIOSOCIAL ASPECTS OF SPORT

Proceedings of a Galton Foundation Conference held in London 26–28th March 1980

Edited by

BRUCE TULLOH

M. A. HERBERTSON

ALAN S. PARKES

GALTON FOUNDATION

CAMBRIDGE, ENGLAND

1981

© Galton Foundation 1981. No part of this publication may be reproduced or stored in a retrieval system in any form or by any means without the permission of both the Galton Foundation and the author.

ISBN 0 907232 02 7

Typeset by Lindonprint Typesetters, Cambridge
Printed in Great Britain by Spottiswoode Ballantyne Ltd
Colchester and London

CONTENTS

	Page
Foreword	iii
Contributors	vi
Opening of Conference	1

Sport and society

Social bonding and violence in sport. ERIC DUNNING	5
The role of the media in sport. CLIFF MORGAN	23
Discussion	27
Comment. JAMES WALVIN	29
Women and sport – social aspects. MARGARET TALBOT	33
Comment. ROSEMARY PAYNE	49
Discussion	52

Sport and health

Sport and personality. J. E. KANE	55
Comment. BRUCE TULLOH	69
Sport and physical health. E. JOAN BASSEY & P. H. FENTEM	71
Sport and mental health. MAURICE YAFFÉ	83
Comment. DAVID RYDE	97
Discussion	98

Factors in performance

The biological basis of aptitude: the endurance runner. CLYDE WILLIAMS	103
Comment. W. L. STEEL	113
Sex differences in athletic potential. ELIZABETH A. E. FERRIS	117
Comment. MOIRA O'BRIEN	129
Selection and training as they affect factors of performance. JOHN F. CADMAN	133
Comment. KEVIN HICKEY	143
Discussion	146

Hazards of sport

Injuries and physical stress. JOHN E. DAVIES	151
Comment. GREG McLATCHIE	159
Discussion	161
Use and abuse of drugs in sport. ARNOLD H. BECKETT	163
Comment. RON PICKERING	171
Comment. WILF PAISH	175
Discussion	177

Trends in sport

Citius, altius, fortius? JOHN WILLIAMS	181
Discussion	187
Whither sport – the next decade. G. C. LAMB	191
The international scene. TOM McNAB	197
Discussion	201
Closing of Conference. ROGER BANNISTER	203
Subject index	205

Organiser
PROFESSOR SIR ALAN PARKES

Advisory Panel

MR JOHN CROOKE	DR PETER SPERRYN
DR JOHN DAVIES	MRS MARGARET TALBOT
DR ELIZABETH FERRIS	DR VAUGHAN THOMAS
MR RON PICKERING	MR RAY WILLIAMS
MR BRIAN REES	DR MAURICE YAFFÉ

Secretary
Mrs Jacqueline A. Sheriff

FOREWORD

Few will disagree that the development of sport on a universal scale has been one of the great social forces in the 20th century. The protagonists of sport stress how much sport offers: a chance of physical and mental self-improvement, the release of powerful emotions, social interchanges, or merely the feeling that occasionally the human body is free and in command of itself, despite the increasingly mechanical demands of work and society. For a sufficiently affluent country, sporting success offers a unique chance of promoting national prestige before the world's press and television. But to achieve such ends athletes and their coaches are tempted to cast to the winds the 19th century notions of fair play and of sport as an educational force and, instead, turn sport into what has been described as 'the moral equivalent of war'. So sport, potentially a force for good, both individually and internationally, is, like many of man's institutions, threatened by individual ambition and greed, by national politics and by international conflict. The Olympic Games in Munich were the scene of irrelevant and appalling murders and the Moscow Olympics were compromised by Russia's invasion of Afghanistan. The abuse of drugs, such as anabolic steroids, by athletes who will seemingly pay almost any price for success, is a continuing scandal.

I firmly believe that scientists from many fields can study some of these problems in an objective way and can clarify the complex issues involved. This book records the efforts of many experts who hold the health of sportsmen in higher regard than national prestige. They believe that at a certain point the scientist cannot avoid reflection on some of the moral and ethical dangers many of which, ironically, are the results of scientific progress. They have suggested in this book insights which should help to build a better and saner future for sport at all levels and in all countries.

ROGER BANNISTER

CONTRIBUTORS

Chairmen

Roger Bannister, Consultant, National Hospital for Nervous Diseases, London
Christopher Brasher, Olympic Correspondent, *The Observer*
G. A. Harrison, Professor of Biological Anthropology, University of Oxford
Olive Newson, Senior Executive Officer, Sports Council, London
Ray Williams, Centenary Officer, Welsh Rugby Union, Cardiff
Peter Sperryn, Medical Officer, British Amateur Athletics Board

Speakers

E. J. Bassey, Lecturer, Department of Physiology and Pharmacology, Nottingham University Medical School
Arnold H. Beckett, Professor, Chelsea College, University of London
John F. Cadman, Director of Coaching, The Hockey Association
John E. Davies, Medical Adviser, Sports Injuries Clinic, Guy's Hospital, London
Eric Dunning, Senior Lecturer, Department of Sociology, University of Leicester
P. H. Fentem, Professor of Physiology, Nottingham University Medical School
Elizabeth Ferris, Medical Officer, Modern Pentathlon Association of Great Britain
Kevin Hickey, National Coach, Amateur Boxing Association, London
John E. Kane, Director, West London Institute of Higher Education
Dick Jeeps, Chairman, Sports Council, London
G. C. Lamb, International Rugby Referee and Chief Executive, Badminton Association of England
Greg McLatchie, Senior Registrar, Southern General Hospital, Glasgow, and Consultant to Martial Arts Commission, London
Tom McNab, Sports Consultant, Broadcaster, Writer, British Bobsleigh Coach
Cliff Morgan, Head of Outside Broadcasts Group, BBC Television, London
Moira O'Brien, Reader in Anatomy, Royal College of Surgeons, Dublin
Wilf Paish, National Coach, British Amateur Athletics Board
Rosemary Payne, Principal Lecturer in Education, Director of School of Psychological Studies, Birmingham Polytechnic
Ron Pickering, Broadcaster and Lecturer, Former Amateur Athletics Association National Coach
David Ryde, Chairman, Medical Commission of the International Table Tennis Federation
W. L. Steel, Director, Department of Physical Education, University of Manchester
Margaret Talbot, Senior Lecturer in Human Movement, Trinity and All Saints College, Leeds, and Chairman, Leisure Studies Association
Bruce Tulloh, Biology Master, Marlborough College, Wilts
James Walvin, Senior Lecturer in History, University of York
Clyde Williams, Senior Research Fellow, Department of Physical Education and Sports Science, Loughborough University of Technology
John Williams, Director, Farnham Park Rehabilitation Centre, Farnham Royal, Bucks
Maurice Yaffé, Senior Clinical Psychologist, Department of Psychological Medicine, Guy's Hospital, London, and Psychological Adviser, Medical Subcommittee, British Olympic Association

OPENING OF CONFERENCE

DICK JEEPS

*The Sports Council,
London*

Today sport is very much in the news, especially sport and politics which have been part of our agenda and diet for a few weeks now. This aspect of sport is not scheduled for this programme but it will no doubt arise in discussion and it emphasizes the topicality of a conference on sport.

I would first like to give you a little of the history of the Galton Foundation. It is a charitable trust established in 1968 for the promotion of biosocial science and named after Sir Francis Galton, a pioneer in the scientific study of man and, very relevant to us here, interested in sport and a member of the Alpine Club. In 1884 Galton initiated an anthropometric laboratory which was the forerunner of the Biometric Laboratory of University College here in London. He also confirmed earlier investigations on the permanence of fingerprints from youth to old age – so many people here may have cause to remember Sir Francis Galton.

May I say to Sir Alan Parkes, many congratulations on having gathered together so many household names and so much talent as speakers and advisers. Many of those names are in daily contact with the Sports Council and with the world of sport and, on behalf of the Conference, I say thank you for setting up this entire interesting programme. To the participants and the audience, I guarantee a very interesting and informative next three days. If I could relate topics from the programme to the work of the Sports Council I believe that these are the sort of issues that we at the Sports Council are very much in touch with daily and I feel very honoured that as Chairman of the Sports Council I have been asked to open this Conference.

This afternoon we are to hear about Sport and Society. I believe that is what we at the Sports Council are mainly concerned with, as illustrated by our slogan 'Sport for All'. Our aims are simply to increase participation and to improve standards of performance with the elite within our governing bodies of sport. Tomorrow your programme is Sport and Health; that is why we promoted the 'Come Alive' campaign and why we have an equal working relationship with those governing bodies of sport whose first concern is not fierce competition but rather general fitness; in particular, it is why we are keen to see the right kind of coaching and management in sport in this important area for health and psychological well-being.

Factors in Performance is another one of the topics. I would like to ask some questions. Do we use the knowledge available to the best advantage? Do we compete on equal terms with our main competitors? Do we discover all of our talent? Do we use the resources available to us to gain maximum benefit for our performance?

Later you are to discuss Hazards of Sport. The Sports Council is very well aware of the drugs scene. Our investment with Professor Beckett and others some two years ago on testing equipment for drugs was something over £200,000 and that is very topical at the moment when you look at one or two of those people who have been proved positive within certain spheres for taking drugs in sport but who seem to have been redeemed by those that govern their sports. So perhaps there is the question should we be in this drugs scene at all, or should other people in it be as convinced as we are about it? Those of you who witnessed England playing Wales at rugby would hardly say that one of the objects of playing sport must be for fun and enjoyment and this leads into the next theme about injuries and treatments. I believe they are all a part of a sportsman's life and there certainly were a few players injured during that particular match.

If we could look at trends in sport and so to the future, that is to the end of the 1980s and into the next decade, I believe that Conferences such as this provide the platform for comment from the experienced practitioner to ensure an approach to the future that will be informed, soundly based and of sufficient vision. Never let us sit back applauding our past efforts and successes. Let us make sure that we surge into the future when the young of today will be the operators. Let us make sure that they will be applauding their forebears. I appreciate that the past has been the springboard and I believe that, like you, I am all for taking off into the future. I hope that this Conference by discussing many of the benefits and trends in sport as well as some of the hazards and problems, will highlight sport's importance within society today, and if it does that it will then help us to win the case for a proper and realistic place for sport within the country's economy.

I wish you a most successful Conference. I say to all your speakers enjoy it and I have much pleasure in declaring your Conference open.

I

SPORT AND SOCIETY

Chairmen: G.A. Harrison and Olive Newson

Biosocial Aspects of Sport

SOCIAL BONDING AND VIOLENCE IN SPORT

ERIC DUNNING

Department of Sociology, University of Leicester

Summary. Having set out a provisional 'typology of violence', the question of violence in sport is considered in its historical perspective, with numerous examples. The question of violence in relation to social bonding is then considered and distinctions are drawn between the types of violence inherent in two differently structured societies, the segmentally and functionally bonded. Contemporary football hooliganism is then considered as developing from segmentally bonded elements in present-day society.

Introduction

It is widely believed that we are living in one of the most violent periods in human history, an era in which physically violent assaults of one kind or another are increasing. Indeed the fear that Western societies are currently undergoing a process of 'de-civilization' – with regard to physical violence if not in other respects – is one of the dominant beliefs of our time.

A not insignificant part of this belief is the widespread feeling that violence is increasing in and around sport. Without denying the seriousness of the problems that this raises, it can be suggested nevertheless: (i) that the issues are more complex than seems often to be believed; and (ii) that the ability to undertake successful remedial action will be increased if hasty responses are eschewed and the problem is approached by means of 'the detour *via* detachment' (Elias, 1956); this means temporarily suspending moral judgement, keeping anxieties and indignation in check, avoiding preemptive dogmatism and attempting a cool, hard appraisal based on rational analysis and systematically collected empirical evidence. The foundations for such a detached, empirically-based analysis will be established in this paper. Specifically it is suggested that: (i) the rate of violence in contemporary sport and contemporary society is perceptually magnified in various ways. A distinction will be made between different types of violence and, partly by historical analysis, it will be shown that whilst violence in sport is probably increasing in certain respects, it has also decreased in others; (ii) these different types of violence are produced by different forms of social bonding, that is, by differences in the manner in which human beings are related to one another. The concept of social bonding will be used in its sociological and not its sociobiological sense, i.e. to refer to the social and not the biological production of different forms of relationships. Discussion of whether a genetically-determined 'male bond', of the type hypothesized by Tiger (1969), plays a part in the behaviour is not appropriate here. It must be sufficient to say that the evolutionary inheritance of human beings makes them, relative to other species, heavily dependent on learning and that this is as true of the forms of bonding as it is of human behaviour in general. Consequently, whatever influence genetic endowment may have on these bonds, they are centrally affected by the structure of the societies in which we live. In discussing the influence of social structure on social bonding, the first task is to lay down the foundations for a typology of violence.

Towards a typology of human violence

The types of violence engaged in by human beings, in sport and elsewhere, are diverse and complex but the problem can be clarified by distinguishing between the separable forms and dimensions of violence, of which there are at least eight:

(i) whether the violence is actual or symbolic, i.e. whether it takes the form of a direct physical assault or simply involves verbal and/or non-verbal gestures;

(ii) whether or not weapons are used;

(iii) where weapons are used, whether or not the assailants come directly into contact;

(iv) whether the violence is intentional or the accidental consequence of an action-sequence that was not intentionally violent at the outset;

(v) whether the violence is initiated without provocation or is a retaliatory response to an intentionally or unintentionally violent act;

(vi) whether the violence takes a 'mock' or 'play' form, or whether it is 'serious' or 'real'. This dimension might also be captured by the distinction between 'ritual' and 'non-ritual' violence. Ritual and play, however, can both have a highly violent content;

(vii) whether the violence is legitimate in the sense of being in accordance with a set of socially prescribed rules, norms and values, or whether it is non-normative or illegitimate, i.e. in contravention of accepted social standards;

(viii) whether it takes an 'instrumental' or 'affective' form, i.e. whether it is rationally chosen as a means of achieving a given end or whether it is engaged in as an emotionally satisfying and pleasurable end in itself. Retaliatory violence that is undertaken immediately in response to a violent attack also has a high affective content, that of anger as opposed to pleasure. However, retaliatory violence can also be engaged in rationally and instrumentally as part of a longer-term campaign of revenge.

These distinctions are between 'ideal types' in the sense that the different forms and dimensions of violence, in sporting and other contexts, overlap and can be transformed into one another. Thus, verbal and non-verbal gesturing often precede hand-to-hand fighting in war and their sporting counterparts can be found, e.g. in professional wrestling and ceremonial battle dances such as that of the Maori rugby team. Similarly, a fast bowler in cricket may bowl a bouncer with the intention of merely intimidating a batsman but may strike him accidentally with the ball. Or an act of instrumental violence in rugby or soccer, perhaps engaged in with the aim of neutralizing a key opponent, may provoke retaliation, leading to a fight in which the emotional level rises.

The different forms and dimensions of violence are usually considered as mutually exclusive dichotomies – as simple either–or affairs – but it is more realistic to conceptualize them as poles on a series of continua. Since, moreover, situations usually involve an admixture between two or more dimensions, or one type being transformed into another, it helps to think about the problem by conceptualizing violence as varying around a complex of overlapping and interdependent polarities. Thus, because human rationality and emotions are inseparable aspects of a single whole, violence is never entirely instrumental or entirely affective, but more or less instrumental or more or less affective. It is a question of balances and degrees.

This mode of conceptualization as applied to the problems of violence in sport will be considered in relation first to some general issues and then to the development of modern sport.

Sport and violence in developmental perspective

Although all sports are inherently competitive, only those such as rugby, soccer and boxing where the competition takes the form of mock combat between two individuals or teams will be considered here. That is because an essential element of sports of this kind consists of the ritualized expression of violence and, just as the real battles that take place in war, e.g. the battles of tribal groups such as the Dani of New Guinea (Gardner & Heider, 1974), can involve a ritual component, so the mock battles that take place on a sports field can involve elements of, or be transformed into, non-ritual violence. This may occur when people participate too seriously in sport with the consequence that the tension level is raised to a point where the incidence of hostile rivalry is increased and the rules and conventions designed to limit violence and direct it into socially acceptable channels are suspended; the people involved then start to fight one another in earnest, with the aim of inflicting physical damage and pain. However, the standards governing violence-expression and violence-control are not the same in all societies. And, in our own society, they differ between different groups and have not been the same in all historical periods. In fact, a central aspect of the development of modern sport has been what Elias (1978a) calls a 'civilizing process' regarding the expression and control of physical violence. Central to this process – whatever short-term fluctuations there may have been – has been a long-term shift in the balance between the affective and instrumental forms of violence. This can be illustrated by reference to the development of rugby football.

Modern rugby is descended from a type of medieval folk-games in which particular matches were played by variable, formally unrestricted numbers of people, sometimes considerably in excess of 1000. The boundaries of the playing area were only loosely defined and limited by custom, and games were played both over open countryside and through the streets of towns. The rules were oral and locally specific, rather than written, instituted and enforced by a central controlling body. Despite such local variation, the folk antecedents of modern rugby shared at least one common feature: they were all play-struggles that involved the customary social toleration of a level of physical violence considerably higher than is normally permitted in rugby and comparable games today. An example is the Welsh game of knappan as described by Owen in 1603.

According to Owen the number who took part in knappan matches sometimes exceeded 2000 and, just as in other games such as Cornish hurling, (Carew, 1602), some of the participants played on horseback. The horsemen, said Owen, 'have monstrouse cudgells, of iii foote and halfe longe, as bigge as the partie is well able to wild (wield) ...'. The following extract illustrates that knappan was a wild affair:

> '... at this playe privatt grudges are revendged, soe that for everye small occasion they fall by the eares, wch beinge but once kindled betweene two, all persons on both sides become parties, soe that sometymes you shall see fyve or vi hundred

naked men, beatinge in a clusture together, ... and there parte most be taken everyeman with his companie, so that you shall see two brothers the one beateinge the other, the man the maister, and frinde against frinde, they nowe alsoe will not sticke to take upp stones and there with in theire fistes beate theire fellowes, the horsemen will intrude and ryde into the footemens troupes, the horseman choseth the greatest cudgell he can gett, and the same of oke, ashe, blackthorne or crab-tree and soe huge as it were able to strike downe an oxe or horse, he will alsoe assault anye for privatt grudge, that hath not the Knappan, or cudgell him after he hath delt the same from him, and when on blowe is geven, all falleth by the eares, eche assaulting other with their unreasonable cudgells sparinge neyther heade, face, nor anye part of the bodie, the footemen fall soe close to it, beinge once kindled with furie as they wholey forgett the playe, and fall to beatinge, till they be out of breathe, and then some number hold theire hands upp over theire heades and crye, ... peace, peace and often times this parteth them, and to theire playe they goe a newe. Neyther maye there be anye looker on at this game, but all must be actours, for soe is the custome and curtesye of the playe, for if one that cometh with a purpose onlye to see the game, ... beinge in the middest of the troupe is made a player, by giveinge him a *Bastonado* or two, if he be on a horse, and by lending him halffe a dozen cuffs if he be on foote, this much maye a stranger have of curtesye, although he expecte noethinge at their handes.'

There is ample evidence to show that games of this type were played in various parts of Britain from at least the 14th to the 19th century. This does not mean that they were not played before the 14th century; simply that there is no documentary evidence before that time. Nor does it mean that they died out completely in the course of the 18th and 19th centuries. Ashbourne football and Hallaton bottle-kicking are examples of what some anthropologists might call present-day 'survivals' of the folk tradition. But the existence of one or two survivals is less relevant for present purposes than the fact that the wildness so vividly depicted by Owen is confirmed by other accounts (Dunning & Sheard, 1979). It is what one would expect in a type of games characterized by the following features: large, unrestricted numbers of players; loosely defined and locally specific oral rules; some participants playing on horseback whilst others played on foot; the use of sticks to hit other players as well as the ball; the players being controlled by one another rather than by a referee; no outside body which could be appealed to in cases of dispute.

Not all of these features were present in all cases but most of them were. As a result, such games were closer to real fighting than are modern sports. As Riesman & Denney pointed out in 1954 (cited by Dunning, 1971) modern sports are more abstract, more removed from serious combat. The folk antecedents of modern rugby may have been mock battles in the sense that the lives of the contending groups were not directly at risk and the infliction of serious injury was not their central aim, but the relatively high level of open violence and the opportunity afforded for inflicting pain may have constituted one of the sources of enjoyment. After all, the people of pre-industrial Britain enjoyed all sorts of pastimes – cock-fighting, bull- and bear-baiting, burning cats alive in baskets, prize-fighting, watching public executions – which appear uncivilized by present-day values. Such pastimes reflected 'the violent tenor of life' in Europe during the latter part of the middle ages and which continued until well into what historians regard as modern times

(Huizinga, 1924). They also reflected the comparatively high threshold of repugnance with regard to witnessing and engaging in violent acts which, as Elias (1978a) has shown, is characteristic of people in a society that stands at an earlier stage in a civilizing process than our own. Of course, since the participants ran the risk of receiving injury and pain as well as inflicting it, taking part in a combat game like knappan, hurling, or folk football was not the same as watching a cock-fight or burning cats alive. But, by adding the spice of fear, such a risk may have heightened the enjoyment and, at the same time, been central to the chances for demonstrating masculine prowess in taking as well as meting out hard knocks.

By contrast, modern rugby exemplifies a game-form that is civilized in at least four senses missing from the ancestral forms. It is typical in this respect of modern combat sports more generally. Modern rugby is civilized by:

(i) a complex set of formally instituted, written rules which demand strict control over the use of physical force and which prohibit it in certain forms, e.g. stiff-arm tackling, and hacking, i.e. kicking an opposing player off his feet;

(ii) clearly defined intra-game sanctions, i.e. penalties, which can be brought to bear on offenders and, as the ultimate sanction, for serious and persistent rule-violation, the possibility of exclusion from the game;

(iii) the institutionalization of a specific role which stands outside and above the game and whose task it is to control it, i.e. that of referee;

(iv) a nationally centralized body, the Rugby Football Union, which makes and enforces the rules.

This civilization of rugby football occurred as part of a continuous long-term social process. There were two significant moments in this. First, there was the institution, at Rugby School in 1845, of the first written rules; these attempted, among other things, to restrict the use of hacking and other forms of physical force, and to prohibit altogether the use of navvies, the iron-tipped boots which had formed a socially valued part of the game at Rugby and some of the other mid-19th century public schools. Second, in 1871, the Rugby Football Union was formed, partly as a result of public controversy over what was perceived as the excessive violence of the game and one of its first acts was to place, for the first time, an absolute taboo on hacking (Dunning & Sheard, 1979). At each of these moments the standards of violence-control applied in the game were advanced; first, by demanding from players the exercise of a stricter and more comprehensive measure of self-control over the use of physical force, and second, by attempting to secure compliance with this demand by means of externally imposed sanctions.

To speak of rugby football as having undergone a civilizing process is not to deny the fact that, relative to most other modern combat sports, it remains a rough game. Features such as the ruck provide the opportunity for kicking and raking players who are lying on the ground. The scrum offers opportunities for illegitimate violence such as punching, eye-gouging and biting. Given the close-packing of players that the scrum involves, it is difficult for the referee to control. His difficulties are compounded by the unwillingness of the Union authorities to transform touch-judges into soccer-type linesmen, i.e. into officials whose task it is to aid the referee in securing compliance with the rules. Perhaps their reluctance to innovate along these lines stems from their commitment to a pristine amateur ethos which makes them unwilling to model their practice, even in this limited regard, on that of a professional sport. Alternatively, they may simply be underlining the point that a rough game such as rugby in its present form can only be played in comparative safety by civilized men capable of exercising a high degree of self-control.

Nor is the contention that rugby has undergone a limited civilizing development inconsistent with the fact that it has probably grown more violent in specific respects in recent years. It has certainly grown more competitive as is shown by the introduction at all levels of cups and leagues. A game in which, until 1971, matches were organized predominantly on an informal, 'friendly' basis, now has a plethora of competitions in which teams compete regularly for an extrinsic, long-term goal, i.e. for the honour of winning a trophy, as well as for winning each particular match. The demand for such competitions was, in itself, an indication of the growing competitiveness of the game, and, their introduction further exacerbated the competitiveness. Growing competitiveness means that the importance of victory has increased, and this has involved a further erosion of the old amateur ethos; for example, it has diminished considerably the significance of the idea that taking part is more important than winning. It has probably simultaneously increased the tendency of players to play roughly within the rules and to use illegitimate violence in pursuit of success. In short, it seems likely that the use of instrumental violence in the game has recently increased.

This is not to claim that, in the past, the violence of the game was entirely non-instrumental and affective, but rather that the balance between these types of violence has changed in favour of the former. The structure of modern rugby, and the relatively civilized personality structure of the people who play it, mean that pleasure in playing is now derived far more from the expression of skill with the ball, in combining with team-mates and from fairly strictly controlled and muted forms of physical force, and far less from the physical intimidation and infliction of pain on opponents than was the case in its folk antecedents and in the mid-19th century public schools when hacking and the use of navvies were central and legitimate tactics. But the social and personality structures that have given rise to this modern game-form have simultaneously increased the incidence of instrumental violence in the game; players who gain satisfaction from the comparatively mild forms of physical force that are permitted in the modern game and who do not find pleasure in inflicting pain on others, are constrained to use violence, both legitimately and illegitimately, in an instrumental fashion. They do not gain pleasurable satisfaction from such violence itself; it is not engaged in as an end in itself but as a means of achieving a long-term goal, that of winning a league or cup. As such, it is rational and planned in character rather than spontaneous, a deliberate tactic which, in its illegitimate forms, is probably introduced most frequently in game-situations where it is most difficult to detect and control.

How is this apparently paradoxical development, i.e. that a game has grown less violent in certain respects and simultaneously more violent in others, to be explained? It is hypothesized that it is principally a consequence of a long-term shift in the pattern of social bonding, of the manner in which the members of our society are related to one another, and this can be illustrated by reference to Elias's theory of the civilizing process.

Violence and the transformation of social bonds

Elias demonstrates that a civilizing process has occurred in the main societies of Western Europe since the middle ages and he explains it principally by reference: (i) to the establishment in these societies of a state monopoly on the right to use physical force, i.e.

to a process of internal pacification under the aegis of the developing state; and (ii) to the correlative lengthening of interdependency chains or, more crudely, to a growth in the division of labour. The consequences of this twin transformation were first of all evident on the upper classes who were subjected simultaneously to growing social pressure from above and below, i.e. to increasingly effective state control and to pressure from a widening range of lower groups as their dependency on such groups increased with the growing division of labour. Then, as state-formation and the lengthening of interdependency chains continued, particularly as the modern, urban–industrial type of society began to emerge, the effects of this civilizing process gradually percolated down the social scale. Its principal consequence has been a more or less constant growth in the social pressure on people to exercise self-control.

Central to this civilizing transformation has been a change in the pattern of social bonding. This can be described as a process in the course of which 'segmental bonding' came gradually to be replaced by 'functional bonding', i.e. in which the significance of ascriptive ties of family and residence grew gradually less, whilst achieved ties determined by the division of labour grew gradually more important. The differences between these two types of social bonding can be expressed by means of the two polar ideal types shown in Table 1.

These two ideal types are a rather crude attempt to express some of the central structural differences between the societies of medieval Europe and those of modern times. As they are ideal types they are very general and they obscure differences such as those between social classes. They also ignore the existence of overlaps empirically between the two types and, to the extent that it is based on extrapolation from observable trends, the model of functional bonding exaggerates, for example, the degree of sexual equality that has so far been achieved in societies which approximate to that type. But such complexities are less germane for present purposes than the manner in which such types of social bonding and their wider structural correlates produce, on the one hand, a tendency towards violence with a high emotional or affective content and, on the other, a high degree of individual and social control over violence together with a tendency towards the use of violence of a more rational, instrumental kind.

Segmental bonding and the sociogenesis of affective violence

The structure of a society in which segmental bonding is the dominant type is conducive to physical violence in human relations in a number of mutually reinforcing ways. Expressed in terms of a cybernetics analogy, the various elements of such a social structure form a positive feed-back cycle which escalates the tendency to resort to violence at all levels and in all spheres of social relations. The weakness of the state, for example, means that such a society is prey to outside attacks. That places a premium on military roles and that, in its turn, leads to the consolidation of a predominantly warrior ruling class, trained for fighting and whose members, because of their socialization, derive positive satisfaction from it.

Internal relations in such a society work in the same direction. Fighting, with or without weapons, is endemic, largely because in-groups are defined very narrowly and even ostensibly similar groups from the same locality are defined as outsiders. So intense are the feelings of pride and group attachment generated within particular kin and local segments that conflict and rivalry are virtually inevitable when their members encounter

Table 1. An ideal type representation of segmental and functional bonding and their wider structural correlates

Segmental bonding	Functional bonding
Locally self-sufficient communities, loosely tied into a wider, proto-national framework; relative poverty.	Nationally integrated communities tied together by extensive chains of interdependence; relative affluence.
Intermittent pressure from above from a weak central state; relatively autonomous ruling class divided into warrior and priestly sections; balance of power skewed strongly in favour of rulers/authority figures both within and between groups; little pressure generated structurally from below.	Continuous pressure from above from a strong central state; relatively dependent ruling class in which secular and civilian sections are dominant; balance of power equalized by the generation of multipolar controls within and between groups; intense pressure generated structurally from below.
Close identification with narrowly circumscribed groups united principally by ascribed kinship and local bonds.	Identification with groups united principally by achieved bonds of functional interdependence.
Narrow range of occupations; homogeneity of work experience both within and between occupational groups.	Wide range of occupations; heterogeneity of work experience both within and between occupational groups.
Low social and geographical mobility; narrow experiential horizons.	High social and geographical mobility; wide experiential horizons.
Little social pressure to exercise self-control over physical violence or to defer gratification generally; little exercise of foresight or long-term planning.	Great social pressure to exercise self-control over physical violence and to defer gratification generally; great exercise of foresight and long-term planning.
Low emotional control; quest for immediate excitement; high threshold of repugnance regarding violence and pain; pleasure from inflicting pain on others and from seeing others suffer.	High emotional control; quest for excitement in more muted forms; low threshold of repugnance regarding violence and pain; vicarious pleasure from watching mimetic but not real violence; rational recourse to instrumental violence where it is perceived as undetectable.
High degree of conjugal role-segregation; mother-centred families; authoritarian father with low involvement in the family; high separation of male and female lives; large numbers of children.	Low degree of conjugal role-segregation; joint, symmetrical, or egalitarian families; father with high involvement in the family; low separation of male and female lives; small numbers of children.
High physical violence in relations between the sexes; male dominance.	Low physical violence in relations between the sexes; sexual equality.
Loose and intermittent parental control over children; violence central in early socialization; spontaneous, affective violence of parents towards children.	Close and continuous parental control over children; socialization principally by non-violent means but limited, planned recourse to instrumental violence.
Tendency for gangs to form around the lines of social segmentation and for them to fight other local gangs; emphasis on aggressive masculinity; ability to fight the key to power and status in the gang and the local community.	Tendency for relationships to be formed voluntarily and not simply on a local basis; civilized masculine style, expressed in formal sport; chances for more than local power and status; status determined by occupational, educational, artistic and sports ability.
Folk forms of sport, basically a ritualized extension of fighting between local gangs; relatively high level of open violence.	Modern forms of sport, i.e. ritualized play-fights, based on controlled forms of violence but strong social pressure to use instrumental violence.

one another. And their norms of aggressive masculinity, coupled with the lack of social pressure to exercise self-control, mean that conflict between them leads easily to fighting. Indeed, fighting, both within and between such groups, is necessary for the establishment and maintenance of their reputations for aggressive masculinity. The best fighters emerge as leaders and all the members of such groups have to fight in order to feel and prove to others that they are men.

The fighting norms of such segmentally bonded groups are analogous to the vendetta systems still found in many Mediterranean countries in the sense that an individual who is challenged or feels slighted by a member of an outsider group feels that his group honour and not simply his own is at stake. He is likely to seek revenge, not simply by retaliation against the particular member but against any member of the offending group. On both sides there is a tendency for others to come to the aid of the initiators of the conflict. In that way, fights between individuals tend to escalate into feuds between groups, often long-lasting ones, thus illustrating the close degree of identification, under such social circumstances, of individuals with the group to which they belong.

The endemic violence characteristic of such societies, together with the fact that their structure consolidates the power of a warrior ruling class and generates an emphasis on male aggressiveness and strength, is conducive to the general dominance of men over women. In its turn male dominance leads to a high degree of separateness in the lives of the sexes and to families of the mother-centred type. The relative absence of the father from the family, and the large family size which is typical of these societies mean that children are not subjected to close, continuous or effective adult supervision. There are two principal consequences of this. First, because physical strength tends to be stressed in relations among children who are not subjected to effective adult control, it further increases the violence characteristic of such communities. However, the tendency of children in segmentally bonded communities to resort to physical violence is reinforced by its use by their parents as a means of socialization and by the adult role-models available to them in the society at large. Second, it is conducive to the formation of gangs which persist into early adult life and which, because of the narrowly defined group allegiances characteristic of segmental bonding, come persistently into conflict with other local gangs. The sports of such communities – e.g. the folk antecedents of modern rugby – are ritualized expressions of the gang warfare typically generated under such conditions, an institutionalized test of the relative strengths of particular communities which grows out of, and exists with, the perpetual and more serious struggles between local groups.

The positive feed-back cycle by means of which high levels of violence are generated in a society characterized by segmental bonding is illustrated schematically in Fig. 1.

Functional bonding, civilizing pressures and the sociogenesis of instrumental violence

A society based on functional bonding is, in most respects, diametrically opposite to one where segmental bonding is the dominant type. Like the latter, such a society is subject to a positive feed-back cycle but, in this case, the cycle performs, on balance, a civilizing function, serving mainly to limit the level of violence in social relations. However, the structure of such a society simultaneously generates intense competitive pressure and a tendency for rational means to be used in goal-achievement. This combination generates

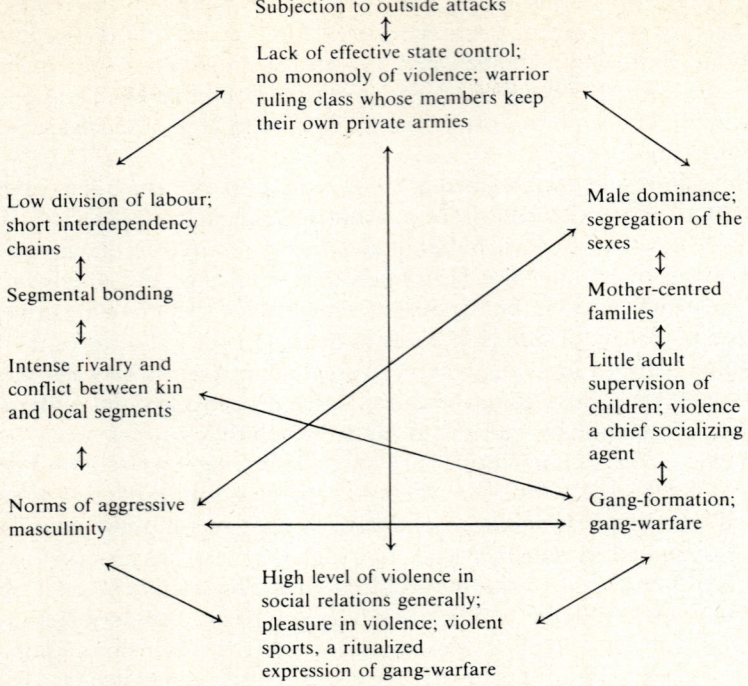

Fig. 1. Social dynamics of violence-generation under conditions of segmental bonding. Arrows indicate main directions of influence in positive feed-back cycle.

a tendency for illegitimate violence and other forms of rule-violation to be used instrumentally in specific social contexts, e.g. in highly competitive combat-sports.

In a society where functional bonding is the dominant type a key structural feature is that the state has established a monopoly on the right to use physical force. To the degree that its monopoly is stable and effective, the division of labour is permitted to grow – i.e. the chains of interdependence in it lengthen – and that, reciprocally, augments the power of the state, e.g. because central control becomes increasingly necessary as the social structure grows more complex. Both the state monopoly on physical violence and the lengthening of interdependency chains exert a civilizing effect. The former exerts such an effect directly by preventing citizens from openly carrying arms and by punishing them for using violence illegitimately, in situations where it claims a monopoly for its own agents. The latter exerts an indirect effect because the division of labour generates 'reciprocal' or 'multipolar' controls (Elias, 1978b). That is, bonds of interdependence allow the parties to a division of labour to exert a degree of mutual control producing an equalizing or democratizing effect which is civilizing for at least two reasons: (i) because the reciprocal controls generated by interdependence are conducive to greater restraint in interpersonal behaviour; and (ii) because a complex system of interdependencies would be subject to severe strain or even break down altogether if some personnel failed to exercise continuously a high degree of self-control. In that way, self-control is an essential precondition for the maintenance and growth of the division of labour.

A society of this type is highly competitive because a complex division of labour also generates a tendency for roles to be allocated on the basis of achievement rather than ascription; functional differentiation diminishes the effect of heredity in occupational placement and augments that of competition. This leads to a general increase in rivalry and aggressiveness in social relations but it cannot be expressed in the form of openly and directly violent behaviour because the state claims a monopoly on the right to use physical force. The dominant standards generated in such a society work in the same direction by decreeing that violence is wrong and, to the extent that such standards are internalized in the course of socialization, men and women come to have a low threshold of repugnance to engaging in and witnessing violent acts.

But, whilst the dominant tendency in such a society is towards a comparatively high level of effective violence-control, coupled with the fact that long chains of interdependence and the correlative pattern of socialization constrain people to use foresight, competitive pressure to defer immediate gratification and to use rational means of goal-achievement means that there is a parallel tendency towards the planned use of violence by ordinary citizens in specific social contexts, such as crime, in sport, and in the socialization and education of children.

Instrumental violence in sport

In a society based on functional bonding, combat sports such as rugby, soccer and boxing form a social enclave in which specific forms of violence are socially defined as legitimate. Such sports are ritualized and civilized play-fights in which the use of physical force is hemmed in by rules and conventions, and controlled, immediately, by officials such as referees and, at a higher level, by committees and tribunals set up by national and international ruling bodies. But, as the competitive pressure in such sports increases, either because their practitioners are competing for extrinsic rewards such as financial remuneration or the honour of winning a cup or league, or because they are subject to pressure to win from the local or national groups whom they represent, there will be a tendency for the significance of victory to be raised and for players to break the rules as a deliberate tactic. As part of this there will be a tendency for them to use violence illegitimately when they think the likelihood of detection is low or where they take a calculated risk that the penalties incurred upon detection will not detract significantly from the achievement of their own or their team's long-term goals.

The positive feed-back cycle by means of which low levels of general violence are generated in a society characterized by functional bonding, together with the tendency for people to resort to instrumental violence in specific situations, is illustrated schematically in Fig. 2.

The tendency towards the use of instrumental violence in modern sport is counteracted by sportsmen being socialized into the dominant values of our society, which condemn physical violence; and because they have a personal interest in controlling the level of violence since they are potential victims as well as potential aggressors. A further complication is that acts of instrumental violence are liable to produce retaliation, either in the form of a spontaneous emotional outburst or as a delayed and calculated act of revenge. Thus, instrumental violence in modern sport is counteracted by general values

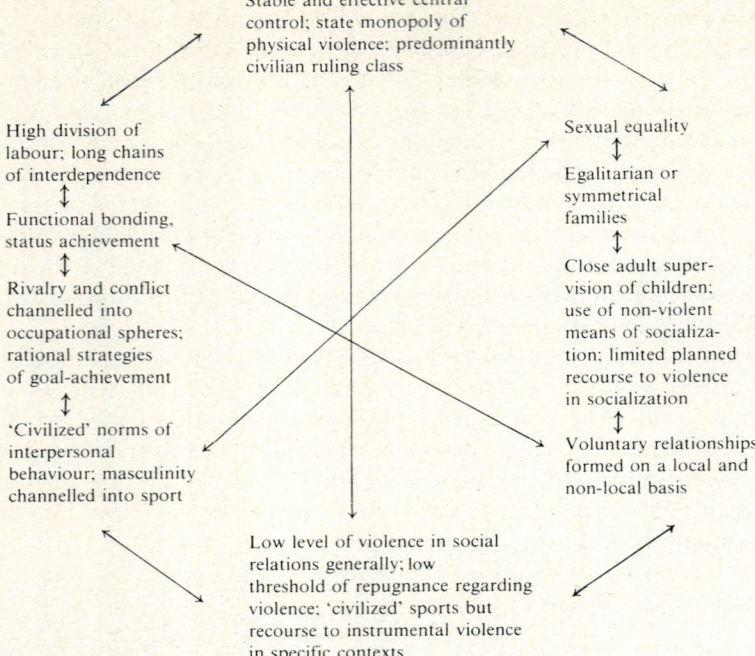

Fig. 2. Social dynamics of violence-limitation and recourse to instrumental violence under conditions of functional bonding. Arrows indicate main directions of influence in positive feed-back cycle.

and sport-specific norms but, because it is liable to provoke retaliation, serves simultaneously to increase the general level of sporting violence.

The discussion so far has been based on an ideal type that exaggerates the degree to which functional bonding has been achieved in modern Britain and ignores the fact that segmental bonding remains significant in certain areas of social life. Two such areas are (i) the continued, and in some cases increasing, significance of national bonds; and (ii) the fact that segmental bonding still seems to be closely approximated in certain sections of the working class. National bonds play a part in increasing the level of violence in modern sport and it is suggested that football hooliganism may be connected with the segmental bonding and correlative masculinity norms of specific working-class groups.

Segmental bonding in modern society and the sociogenesis of violence in sport

Although they unite large groups and are consequently abstract and impersonal, the ties that unite the members of a nation are a type of segmental bonding for two main reasons: (i) because for all except naturalized citizens they are ascribed rather than achieved; and (ii) because they unite people in terms of a specific similarity, the fact that they were born as members of a particular nation-state. As such, national ties form an overall framework of segmental bonding within which the principal development of chains of interdependence and functional bonding has so far taken place. At the same time, they act as a barrier that places constraints against the further development of such bonds. The significance of sport in such a context is largely explicable in terms of the fact that it has come to function as one of the principal media of collective identification. In societies where the state has established an effective monopoly on the right to use physical force, sport provides one of the few occasions on which a large, complex, impersonal and predominantly functionally bonded unit such as a city can unite as a whole. Similarly, at an international level, sporting events such as the World Cup and the Olympics, apart from providing regular occasions for limited international contacts, are one of the few peacetime occasions where whole nations are able to unite. Such contests allow the representatives of different nations to compete without killing one another, though the degree to which they are transformed from mock fights into real ones is a function, *inter alia*, of the pre-existing level of tension between the nation states involved and of the degree to which their members view one another as enemies. Thus extrinsic sources of tension are added to the element of sporting competition. These tensions are further fuelled by the pressure put on representative sportsmen by the mass media and the general public to secure victory on their behalf.

The violence of the England–Wales rugby match at Twickenham in February 1980 is a case in point. It was a match between the representatives of a dominant and a subordinate nation in which: (i) the dominant nation has, for a long time, been deprived of the success – in rugby and other sports – which its members, partly on account of their imperial past, believe to be their due; and (ii) members of the subordinate nation perceive themselves as receiving more than their fair share of the cuts and deprivations to which the British nation overall is currently being subjected. Under such conditions, especially given the build-up by the media before the match and the presence of a large, excited and chauvinistic crowd of supporters of both teams, the chances of a violent encounter were exceedingly high.

Thus, national bonds are segmental in character and, as such, contribute to the occurrence of non-normative violence in modern sport. But segmental bonds also continue to exist, at least in present day Britain, on a smaller, more concrete and less impersonal scale, especially in certain sections of the working class. It is reasonable to suppose that such bonds contribute significantly to the sociogenesis of football hooliganism.

Working class segmental bonding and the sociogenesis of football hooliganism

It is commonly believed that football hooliganism first became a social problem in this country in the 1960s. The following examples, culled mainly from press reports, show, however, that spectator disorderliness at football matches was by no means unknown before the first world war and in the inter-war years:

1885: Aston Villa v Preston North End

> Preston North End were not in any way conspicuous for their rough play, but once during the progress of the match, a disturbance between one of the Preston men ... and Dawson, threatened a pugilistic encounter, which, however, was

avoided by the interference of the officials. Then why the roughs should have congregated round the Preston team as they left the field at the conclusion of the game and hiss and jeer them is a matter of wonder. The attentions of the mob seemed at first to be principally directed to the man who was engaged in the slight quarrel with Dawson, but each of the visiting team subsequently came in for their share of ill-treatment. The Preston men, with commendable courage, turned round upon the crowd surrounding them and retaliated. A free fight quickly ensued, during the course of which several aereated water bottles were hurled into the crowd and smashed, regardless of the consequences. The fight lasted but a few minutes, and the Preston team, with the assistance of the Villa men, made their way to the dressing tent. Not content with this uncalled-for demonstration, the roughs continued hissing and hooting, and it was a considerable time before they left the field, despite the efforts of the few constables of the Perry Barr Division who were present ...

(*Birmingham Gazette*, 11th May 1885)

1909: Hampden Park, Glasgow

About six thousand spectators tore up goalposts, fences and pay-boxes, set fire to them and danced around them in the middle of the pitch. Police, firemen and ambulancemen were stoned, fire-engines damaged and hoses slashed. The police, after throwing the stones back at the rioters, finally cleared the ground at seven o'clock, at a cost of fifty four constables injured and the destruction of virtually every street-lamp around Hampden.

(*Glasgow Herald*, 19th April 1909, paraphrased in Hutchinson, 1975)

1910: Aston Villa v Derby County

I saw crowds of girls about 17 years of age, and also of youths who were in such a state as to be a disgrace to a respectable citizen. Some were rolling about the pavement utterly helpless and seemed to have hardly the strength to do anything but curse, swear and endeavour to sing. I wondered what was the cause of this, and found that it was due to the fact that we had thousands of visitors from Derby to see the cup-tie at Aston. New Street, and particularly the station, was one huge pandemonium of shouting, blowing whistles and other noisy instruments. Certainly, at a low estimate, 30% of the men were drunk or very much the worse for liquor, dragging each other along, arguing incoherently with each other, neither sense nor reason prevailing. No consideration for others – simply pushing and upsetting everyone in their way. Gentle manners and chivalry were conspicuous by their absence. Police were helpless or powerless. Is all this necessary in the true interest of sport?

No respectable person could go over the bridge, but had to go by the subway.

(Citizen, Handsworth, Letter to the Editor, *Birmingham Post*, 11th February 1910)

1930: Queen's Park Rangers v Northampton Town

What threatened to prove an ugly incident at the close of the game between Queen's Park Rangers and Northampton Town at Loftus Road, Shepherd's Bush, was quelled by the prompt action of the stewards and police. During the second half there had been considerable demonstration against Mr. C.E. Lines of Birmingham, the referee, and at the close he was escorted to his dressing room by the police. A large section of the crowd booed, and some missiles were thrown. One spectator seized a plank of wood, and with this cracked the window of the referee's dressing room. A mounted constable then helped to quell the disturbances and the crowd gradually dispersed.

(*Birmingham Post*, 20th January 1930)

1934: Return of Leicester City fans from a match in Birmingham

Everything had gone smoothly from the time of the departure at New Street and it was feared that something extraordinary had happened to cause the train to pull up in such a manner only 300 or 400 yards from its destination. After a thorough search of all the coaches, it was found that the communication cord had been pulled ... it was ascertained that the hooligan element sometimes found on the trips had caused not a little damage to the rolling stock, some of it almost new. Windows were smashed, seats cut and torn, and the leather window straps slashed with knives.

(*Leicester Mercury*, 19th March 1934)

These examples show that football hooliganism is not confined to the 1960s and 1970s. The examples were selected from a large number found after only 6 months of systematic research, and document the occurrence of train wrecking, fights among rival fans, a death, assaults on referees and players, pitch invasion, and commotion in a city centre. Thus, although the scale, fluctuation over time, and balance between different types of spectator disorderliness, and variations over time in the form, scale and intensity of public reaction to it, remain to be determined, some kind of football hooliganism is recorded for every decade since the emergence of soccer in a recognizably modern form.

A recurrent dimension of football hooliganism is the occurrence of physical violence, either in the form of assaults on referees and players, or of clashes between rival groups of fans. Sometimes, such violence involves the use of weapons, either in direct, hand-to-hand combat or in the form of aerial bombardment with missiles from a distance. Marsh, Rosser & Harré (1978) suggest that football hooliganism is a form of ritualized aggression that is not usually seriously violent, except to the extent that official intervention distorts it and prevents it from taking its normal, socially useful and constructive form. They evidently think of ritualized and serious violence as mutually exclusive alternatives, for it is difficult to conceive of throwing coins, darts, beer cans and, as happened at a recent match, a petrol bomb as 'socially constructive ritualized aggression'. This is not to deny the possible effect that official intervention may have on the forms that football hooliganism takes. The segregation of rival fans, for example, has probably increased the incidence of aerial bombardment. But Marsh and his colleagues seemingly wish to deny that such groups evidently want to inflict serious injuries on one another of the kind, for example, caused by coins, beer cans, darts and petrol bombs.

It is hypothesized that such violence – whatever elements of ritual it may contain – is centrally connected with norms of masculinity that: (i) place an extreme stress on toughness and ability to fight; (ii) are different from the masculinity norms that are currently dominant in society at large; and (iii) tend, as a result, recurrently to incur condemnation from socially dominant groups. Such norms are reminiscent in many ways of the masculinity norms which were general in British society at an earlier stage of its development; for example, if the analysis presented earlier in this paper is correct, those which were generated by segmental bonding and its wider social structural correlates.

There are at least four aspects of present-day football hooliganism which suggest that its core features may be generated by segmental bonding.

(i) The groups involved appear to be more interested in fighting one another than in watching football. Indeed, their own accounts suggest that they derive positive enjoyment from fighting and that, for them, ability to fight forms the principal source of both individual and group prestige. Their songs and chants point in the same direction for violence and the symbolic enhancement of their own masculinity and simultaneous emasculation of their opponents are recurrent themes.

(ii) The rival groups appear to be recruited principally from the same level of social stratification, the so-called 'rough' section of the working class. Their fighting is a form of intra- as opposed to inter-class conflict, and this can be explained by segmental bonding.

(iii) The fighting of such groups takes a vendetta form in the sense that, independently of any overt action they may take, particular individuals and groups are set upon simply because they display the membership insignia of a rival group. The long-standing feuds between rival groups of hooligan fans which persist despite the turnover of personnel within such groups, point in the same direction; they are an indication of the degree of identification of particular hooligans with the groups to which they belong.

(iv) The remarkable degree of conformity and uniformity in action that is displayed in the songs and chants of football hooligans. It is difficult to conceive of the members of more individualized groups either wishing to or being capable of engaging in such complex uniform actions and it is reasonable to suppose that the homogenizing effects of segmental bonding may lie at their base.

Sociological research (Bott, 1957; Parker, 1974; Willis, 1978; Wilmott & Young, 1957) suggests that rough working-class communities are characterized by all or most of the following social attributes: more or less extreme poverty; employment of members in unskilled and/or casual jobs, coupled with a high susceptibility to unemployment; low levels of formal education; low geographical mobility except for some males who travel occupationally, for example, in the army or in connection with unskilled work in the building and construction trades; mother-centred families and extended kin networks; a high degree of conjugal role segregation and separation of the lives of the sexes generally; male dominance, coupled with a tendency for men to be physically violent towards women; little adult supervision of children, coupled with frequent resort to violence in socialization; low ability to exercise emotional control and defer gratification; high threshold of repugnance towards physical violence; the formation of street-corner gangs, or adolescent networks, which are led by the best fighters and within and between which fighting is frequent; intense feelings of attachment to narrowly defined in-groups and intense hostility towards narrowly defined out-groups.

The different aspects of such social configurations tend to be mutually reinforcing;

like their pre-industrial counterparts, they constitute a positive feed-back cycle, one of the principal consequences of which is aggressive masculinity. However, these modern forms of segmental bonding are not identical with the pre-industrial forms. Because they are located in a society with a relatively stable and effective state, in which there exists a complex network of interdependencies, the segmentally bonded groups of today are subjected to civilizing pressures and controls from two main sources: (i) from the policing, educational and social work agencies of the state; and (ii) from functionally bonded groups in the wider society.

In short, such groups are subjected to restraint from the outside but much less so from within. Internally, their members remain locked in social configurations that are reminiscent in many ways of the pre-industrial forms of segmental bonding generating acute forms of aggressive masculinity. The intense feelings of in-group attachment and hostility towards out-groups of such segmentally bonded groups mean that rivalry is virtually inevitable when their members meet. And their norms of aggressive masculinity and comparative inability to exercise self-control mean that conflict between them leads easily to fighting. As with their pre-industrial counterparts, fighting within and between such groups is necessary for the establishment and maintenance of reputations in terms of their standards of aggressive masculinity and particular individuals take positive pleasure in performing what, for them, is a socially necessary role.

Football is a natural setting for the expression of such standards because norms of manliness are intrinsic to it; it is basically a play-fight in which masculine reputations are enhanced or lost. Its inherently oppositional character means that it lends itself readily to group identification and the enhancement of in-group solidarity in opposition to a series of easily identifiable out-groups, the opposing team and their supporters. To the extent that some fans are drawn from communities characterized by segmental solidarity, football hooliganism in the form of fighting between gangs of rival supporters is an almost inevitable result.

Football hooliganism is a present-day counterpart to the folk antecedents of modern football, though superimposed on and intermingled in a complex manner with the more differentiated and civilized game of today. Present-day football thus attests to the stage in a civilizing process at which Britain currently stands. On the one hand, the game of soccer is representative of the not inconsiderable advances achieved whilst, on the other hand, football hooliganism and the segmental structures which contribute centrally to its generation, are symptomatic of how far there is to go. The cries of many members of the dominant groups in our society for harsh punitive measures for the control of football hooligans provide further testimony to how comparatively uncivilized we remain. In responding thus to the social hiatus created by the continued existence of segmental bonds in a predominantly functionally bonded society, they help to perpetuate such a division. The only way of eradicating it, and hence of providing an effective long-term solution to problems such as football hooliganism, would be by seeking to integrate segmentally bonded groups into the wider framework of functional bonding, and that would require a truly civilized, egalitarian and democratic approach.

Acknowledgments

Extracts from newspaper reports were kindly made available by J. Maguire and P. Murphy.

References

Bott, E. (1957) *Family and Social Network.* Tavistock, London.
Carew, R. (1602) *The Survey of Cornwall.* London.
Dunning, E. & Sheard, K. (1979) *Barbarians, Gentlemen and Players: a Sociological Study of the Development of Rugby Football.* Martin Robertson, Oxford.
Elias, N. (1956) Problems of involvement and detachment. *Br. J. Sociol.* **7**, 226.
Elias, N. (1978a) *The Civilizing Process.* Blackwell, Oxford.
Elias, N. (1978b) *What is Sociology?* Hutchinson, London.
Gardner, R. & Heider, K. (1974) *The Gardens of War.* Penguin, Harmondsworth.
Huizinga, J. (1924) *The Waning of the Middle Ages.* English translation published by Doubleday, New York.
Hutchinson, J. (1975) Some aspects of football crowds before 1914. In: *The Working Class and Leisure.* Proceedings of the Conference of the Society for the Study of Labour History. University of Sussex, Paper No. 13 (mimeo).
Marsh, P., Rosser, E. & Harré, R. (1978) *The Rules of Disorder.* Routledge and Kegan Paul, London.
Owen, G. (1603) *The Description of Pembrokeshire.* Edited by H. Owen (1892) Cymmrodorion Soc. Res. Ser. No. 1, p. 270.
Riesman, D. & Denney, R. (1971) Football in America. In: *The Sociology of Sport: a Selection of Readings.* Edited by E. Dunning. Cass, London.
Parker, H.J. (1974) *View from the Boys.* David and Charles, Newton Abbott.
Tiger, L. (1969) *Men in Groups.* Nelson, London.
Willis, P. (1978) *Profane Culture.* Routledge and Kegan Paul, London.
Wilmott, P. & Young, M. (1957) *Family and Kinship in East London.* Routledge and Kegan Paul, London.

Biosocial Aspects of Sport

THE ROLE OF THE MEDIA IN SPORT

CLIFF MORGAN

*British Broadcasting Corporation,
Kensington House, London*

Summary. The part played by radio and television coverage of sport in developing public appreciation of sports is covered, and consideration is given to the responsibilities involved in dealing with sports in which violence occurs. The duties of the television producer in relation to the players, the viewers and the sponsors of sport are discussed.

Sport and broadcasting attract more attention and criticism than any other activity, even that of a practising politician, and they are the two subjects on which everybody in this country seems to be an expert. Participation in sport and working in broadcasting teaches one to live with failure, the prospect of which affects everyone from time to time. The relationship between sport and the media is not at all times comfortable. What is written and what is said are not always welcomed by sporting bodies and sportsmen. Occasionally, those who have the singular privilege of writing and broadcasting fall into the trap of creating a brisk market and easily reached satisfaction. Occasionally there is a lack of objectivity and sensitivity but, by and large, the general standard of sports writing and sports broadcasting in Britain is far ahead of every other country in the world.

First, and this may not be apparent to sport, it is a far kindlier press than in almost any other country. Generally speaking, and there are well known exceptions, the British sports writer and broadcaster loves the sport he covers and has a genuine desire to see that sport flourish, and that is a right and proper attitude of the media to sport. The media also have a duty to promote, foster and nourish. When this happens, all is well and the publicity and promotion are accepted. On the other hand, criticisms are not always palatable, nor the stories that uncover a drug scandal in sport, illegal payments to sportsmen or violent and barbaric behaviour.

Now, as long as the story is told in an honest and fair way, this is a genuine responsibility of the media to sport. Ten years ago, on this very subject, a distinguished Fleet Street journalist, Bill Hicks, said 'Surely, it is the duty of the media to report what happened, pleasant or unpleasant. Unpleasant news is very often the best guarantee that it will not happen again'. This can be illustrated by a recent example. In the England–Wales rugby international match at Twickenham in February 1980 certain players, on both teams, disgraced themselves in a game which had acts of violence that should not be tolerated in our society. Some distinguished rugby men suggested that an item should be produced on television to show the lunacy and stupidity of this sort of behaviour – to protect the millions of decent people who play for enjoyment; to offer the opinion that no game is worth recklessly risking life and limb; to say that winning at all costs is totally unacceptable. This was attempted but the reaction from certain quarters has been one of bitterness, anger and resentment. From Wales, came the accusation that the programme supported the England team and was biased against Wales, while English people thought the England players were being blamed for starting it all. For some, the point was totally lost. It was not about England and Wales but about an attitude in sport. In fact, the script actually read that 'some players of both teams were a disgrace'. Was there no such thing left as the 'spirit of the game'? This is fair and proper comment. However, in another television programme, before the game, certain players were pre-judged, as they also were by a few newspapers. This is not the role of the media, which should be to report, judge and assess the event and then comment forthrightly. A great British editor, C.P. Scott, once said 'It is well to be frank – even better to be fair'. May our aim be no less.

It is not easy these days for young sportsmen or women to cope with the pressures to which they are subjected. Forty years ago, when life was less complicated and the whole of this country was together in spirit, it was easy. There was one simple path to follow but today there are deep divisions in our society. Political exploitation and the ever increasing commercial exploitation are burdens that sports people should not have to carry. Consequently it is an obligation on the part of the media to show compassion and understanding and, even more important, to avoid sneering and hand-wringing. And, in return, the sportsmen and women and the administrators of sport have a responsibility to the media, and to the public, actually to give a little, as well as, in some cases, taking so much. Honesty and decency on both sides will produce a rich, satisfying and rewarding relationship, and the winner then must be sport.

Role of television

The BBC's Television Sports Department produces over 1200 hours of television sport each year – slightly more than 25% of the total output of the BBC television service. Sports coverage on television started many years ago and in those early days almost every sport was keen to co-operate and be seen on television. The genius and flair, the drive and enthusiasm of the early commentators all added up to a new wonderment. Suddenly, every big event was there in the living room, and for the first time sport came under the microscope; the miracle had come to the people at large. All the big events – Wimbledon, the Cup Final, the Olympic Games – were available at the flick of a switch. What had previously been words on the printed page was now a reality and alive and moving. Maybe there was a tentativeness surrounding the whole development. There certainly was, in some sports, a suspicion, a fear that the comfort of watching sport in an arm chair would stop people going to sporting events. But the overall pattern was set, and with sophistication in production and technological advances it has become an accepted part of everyday existence.

So what is the role of television in sport? It is certainly not to kill sport by saturation coverage with 'live' broadcasting. The restrictions imposed by the football and rugby union authorities, for instance, where only an agreed, acceptable number of matches are allowed to be shown 'live' are wholly justified. At the moment, the mixture seems to be about right. Who, for instance, would want to watch a match played in an empty stadium with no atmosphere and none of the emotional involvement of the crowds that makes sport so attractive and exciting? Television certainly does not want that.

The range of television coverage should be as wide as the public demand, facilities and finances allow. It is fair to say that television can rightly be accused of failing to offer extensive coverage of certain sports such as judo, squash, sailing and angling; but from time to time they all get a showing – though not nearly enough to satisfy the fans of these sports. Maybe when the whole structure of the British working week changes, and leisure becomes a thriving industry, new and different tastes and attitudes will have to be taken into account. On the other hand, snooker, bowls and darts have, in the past couple of years, become compulsive viewing and television's success has helped to promote these sports. That is the vital key, that both sides should benefit. That is a responsibility that is an important part of television's involvement in sport.

Sponsorship

The shortage of money, of course, is the popular topic and money has also come into sport through sponsorship, bringing its benefits to sport and a few, but not insurmountable, problems for the broadcaster.

There is a real problem for the BBC, which is a public corporation, financed out of licence money, and operating under a Royal Charter which lays down certain rules and public service requirements. The aim is to be uninfluenced by commercial or political pressure. The actual wording is: 'Shall not send or emit by means thereof any sponsored programme'. So the conflict arises through a charter which says sponsored programmes cannot be transmitted and, on the other hand, sport which relies so heavily on sponsorship. There therefore has to be flexibility, and the broadcasting organizations have become as co-operative as possible in using their prestige and their audiences to march, for the most part, in the vanguard of society where, without sponsorship, many sports would fade away. The electronic media are under an obligation to sport, which gives television such rich sustenance, to find a way of reflecting a sponsor's financial commitment to a sport without destroying it as a spectacle. In other words, making certain that any credits for a sponsor do not come between the action and the viewer and consistently spoil his enjoyment. For the most part, this is working happily and is a proper association between the electronic media and sport.

It is, however, difficult to ensure that all sponsors are treated equally. In general terms, for their investment, they receive a *Radio Times* credit, two verbal credits and two banners which bear the name of the company but not a brand name. There have been problems in specific instances but with good sense, good taste and integrity, sport and the media can co-operate with confidence, each contributing to the welfare and future development of sport. The reason for the strict controls on the reflecting of advertising on individual sportsmen is that, in this case, it is the individual who receives money in his own pocket. The sport itself, particularly at grass roots level, is not receiving the benefit. This restriction has the approval of the sports authorities. The other important reason for sport and television to avoid individual sponsorship is because if a major sponsor, investing say £100,000, finds that in the event he supports there are individuals sponsored at say £1000 each, the main sponsor will withdraw and then there will be no event for the individuals to take part in.

Sponsorship cannot be allowed to take over the administration of sport. Good sponsorship (which it is in this country) is totally acceptable; exploitation of sport on television is not. This very important question is constantly under review and at this moment a final draft of new guidelines is being prepared by the BBC. These are designed to allow producers and commentators to concentrate on reflecting the sport, at its very best, on the television screens.

Other factors

Another obligation is for television to employ directors and commentators who have a personal commitment to sport. They are encouraged to have an involvement in the sporting scene, to contribute as much as they possibly can, to converse at receptions, to speak at dinners, to present sports prizes at schools – not for financial reward but as a service. Theirs is not simply to plan, map, photograph and signpost but to rub shoulders with and generally savour the company of sportsmen and sportswomen.

Criticising sports commentators is a popular pastime but working in this area of instant journalism is not easy. All that can be expected of the broadcaster is what can reasonably be expected from the sportsman: that he should give of his best on the day. It is not the role of the electronic media in sport to exploit the advantage of hindsight by the use of slow-motion replays and making judgements on referees. Slow-motion inevitably proves that the referee was right but the best use of this facility is to make people better informed and educated on the many and varied aspects of sport.

In 1922 the BBC set out to educate, to inform and to entertain; information and entertainment have been mentioned but the role of education in the area of sports is very important. From Bristol, over the years, have come some instructional films for young people; from Wales, there has been a splendid rugby coaching series. A remarkable series with the Football Association has just been finished; this is a coaching series which will be a success all over the world. It has been a great pleasure to watch international soccer stars making these films for no reward, save the joy of putting something back into the game in return for the privilege and status the game of football has given to them.

To return to money for a moment. Five years ago, the late Sir Charles Curran, then Director General of the BBC and President of the EBU, felt that there were danger signs on the horizon; he believed that sporting bodies were becoming too greedy and making excessive financial demands for the rights to televise their events. He warned then that if acceding to these demands meant that the BBC could not fulfil its obligations to schools broadcasting, drama, news, current affairs, light entertainment, comedy and so on, then sport could disappear from the television screen. His warning is still as real today. Should this happen it would be a sad day for everyone. Already, in the United States, the rival network companies pay such astronomical sums for baseball and football that, for hours on end, nothing is screened but sport and the occasional quiz game. This is far from desirable.

Money is an inadequate test where moral and social questions are at issue. The electronic media's financial role in sport is, therefore, a fair price for the product. Neither sport nor the media should be debased by allowing triviality, or the obscenity of ludicrous prize money for staged gimmicks. It is admirable that outstanding games players can now make a good living in sport; cricketers, at last, have a substantial wage. If the players are stars they should be paid accordingly, but the responsibility of newspapers, television and radio is to avoid making too much of the sportsman in the publicity machine. This can lead to potential stars being ruined by providing too much too soon. That is not good for either the individual or the sport. Earning big money is one thing but a concern for the sport and a true sense of values must be maintained.

Ideally, sport should be played to win, but to win within the rules. The media should highlight, emphasize and encourage this. Newspapers, television and radio should serve the real needs of sport and the public – both are important. The opportunities should be grasped to the full to prove through mutual respect, and simple decency that the whole is truly the sum of the parts, and that we all are dedicated to a better life and a better society.

GENERAL DISCUSSION

The question was raised whether attendance at football matches was affected by television coverage and Mr Morgan explained that it was the wish of the Football Association that announcements about games to be televised should not be made in advance.

On the problem of violence associated with sporting events, the view was expressed that if violence interfered with the actual game it had to be shown on television but that undue emphasis should not be placed on violent events peripheral to the sporting occasion. Mr Dunning pointed out that a distinction needed to be drawn between simple high spirits and serious violence, although these were not always separated in statistics of football-related offences. Most of the violence in and around sport was probably of the former category but a small core of real violence existed, both in the context of sport itself and in a wider society, and it was this which was of significance.

The idea that a sports journalist had a duty to promote his particular sport was discussed. It was recognized that a knowledge and love of the sport were essential requirements for informed comment but that properly directed criticism could also, on occasions, be necessary and positively beneficial.

Biosocial Aspects of Sport

COMMENT

JAMES WALVIN

Department of History, University of York

I decided while listening to the last two speakers that I could not possibly summarize two such diverse contributions and certainly I find it very hard to follow the eloquence of the last speaker. I ought really to explain my own role which is that of an academic historian, interested in the history of sports and recreation and having written a number of times on this subject. You may feel, particularly from what Mr Morgan has just been saying, that that almost excludes me from this fraternity of activists. What I have to say is really rather tangential, though not quite as distant as it may seem because one should bear in mind the historical dimension to sport and society, not only in this country but internationally. By a 'historical dimension' I mean not merely the longer term, which Mr Dunning was talking about, but the more immediate context. The kind of history which a lot of people in this room will be familiar with in their own lifetime is, for many younger people, particularly teenagers, as distant as the dark ages. Events that happened just after the second world war are as distant to young poeple today as anything you would find in a traditional history textbook. It seems to me that, if one looks at the history of sports in this country particularly, you will find an explanation for many of the phenomena which we now think of as brand new; one would see recurring patterns – different in shape, in size, and in their movement, but phenomena which are remarkably familiar in a whole range of very different historical settings. Let me illustrate this anecdotally. Take the case of Lord Kinnaird – a High Commisioner of the Church of Scotland, the man who to this day holds the record number of appearances in FA Cup Finals, a man who when he scored a goal would stand on this head, and who was well known as a tough player. It is said that, on one occasion his mother complained at dinner to guests about this violent game of football which her son played: 'One day, I'm afraid Lord Kinnaird will come home with a broken leg'. 'Don't worry', said one of the guests, 'if he does, it won't be his own'. That was in the late 19th century, not the 1960s or 1970s.

I was struck while listening to the previous speakers that one of the elements in the discussion of sport and society is that it defies rationality at certain points. In a sense it was a point that Mr Morgan was trying to make at the end – a sheer excitement and love of things is often very elusive to analyse. I think particularly of the memorable anecdotal but factual instances of Bill Shankly in the 1960s with Liverpool being beaten 5-0 by Ajax and when the press poured in to Shankly for a comment he said 'We can't play against a defensive team'. Those who can remember instances like that will realize that there is a whole area of sporting endeavour which is simply irrational and which defies objective, academic explanation; yet that is the kind of task I have set myself. I want to do it, not because I think that sport is necessarily important in itself, but because I think that the history of sport is important as an interesting area of social history; I want to try to relate this to the role of history as it ought perhaps to be seen. If you think of history as our collective memory, try to imagine what would happen if we forgot it. Think of what happens when an individual loses his memory, with all the catastrophic events that follow from this. It does then seem that if we lose sight of our collective memory, that is our history, whether mythological or substantive history, it would alter dramatically the way in which we see the world around us. This is especially true of sporting activities. Despite everything that has been written and said about the world of classical sports, many of the sports that so many people here are interested in are, in terms of historical development, very recent phenomena. More particularly the great bulk of them came out of the reformed English public schools of the 19th century. Those of you who have enjoyed, endured or simply lived through the recent television series on Radley will have seen one institution that is an example of that peculiar 19th century phenomenon, the English public school. In those schools, in the last century, sports were used to create a new kind of Englishman. The virtues and values of the sporting ethos which people in the game of sport value today are, to a very large extent, the historical product of those English public schools. Think of the public school before Arnold; where boys at Eton threw all their books into the Thames in a pupil revolt. In 1797 the boys at Rugby had a rebellion which was put down by troops with fixed bayonets, who were on standby for a threatened French invasion. Those public schools were transformed by the followers of Dr Arnold and he used sports to introduce discipline, team playing, selflessness and physical toughness; putting the interest of the team over and above the individual self interest. All of this is a historical phenomenon. But what is interesting is the way those values were taken out into the wider world, not merely, for example in the case of soccer, into working class communities, in the late 19th century by ex-public school men who believed in those virtues of toughness, selflessness, and the value of physical recreation. When taking those virtues into working class communities, particularly into poorer areas, it was not immediately obvious to the medical officers of health in, let us say, Salford or Blackburn, that working class children suffering from rickets would benefit from playing rugby. There was a series of social factors which both encouraged and yet inhibited the spread of these formerly exclusively public school sports into the world outside. There is also another factor which has not been described or examined, namely the way this sporting ethos, which some of you are engaged in, was taken around the world and how these issues, these commitments became the passions of a global community. We often spend too much time looking at the problem of soccer, and yet soccer is very revealing for, by 1914, it was played right around the world. Yet in the 1880s it was played almost exclusively in the public schools, with one or two isolated plebeian games. How was it that this game, shaped and reformed in the public school, was taken around the world? It is to be explained in terms of the peculiar spread of Britons, not merely to parts of the world which became the colonies, but also in those parts of South America and Europe where British people settled, traded, invested and took their commercial expertise and economic well-being. They also took their games. The British prided themselves on being a sporting nation and they did their best to take their sports to the rest of the world. So, to understand how, not merely the British, but the world at large was converted to the commitment to sport and sporting endeavour you really have to take a wider historical view.

I will give one illustration of the way history happened and the way it has been distorted. If you read official Soviet accounts of the development of soccer in that country you will see that it was yet another dimension of the revolution of 1917. In fact what happened was that British workers and employers took the game to Russia in the late 19th century. For example two brothers from Lancashire set up a textile mill near Moscow taking with them British people able to work in the textile mills. Those people also took with them their sporting skills, notably football. In one such case, when the Russian revolution came along the factory was taken over by a local Soviet dominated by the electrical trade union. Their team was renamed Dynamo – hence the origin of Moscow Dynamo. This was a pure historical accident which had its roots in the British trading experience in a particular part of the world. These phenomena cannot be explained except in the wider historical context.

In many sports, turbulence and toughness have been there from very early days. While such toughness has clearly been transformed it remains true that if removed, it would destroy the essence of the game itself. To a certain extent it was the physical element in many of those games which people of diverse regions, races, and cultural and economic development found so attractive.

It must be emphasized, as I said at the beginning, that many of the phenomena in relation to sport today are not recent developments. Consider, for instance, the whole question of broadcasting – which we tend to think of, now, solely in terms of TV. One thing that was not mentioned by Mr Morgan was the impact of radio which, in fact, laid the groundwork for the wider public interest in sport among people who did not go to watch sport but simply sat at home and listened. Radio made an enormous impact on sporting activity in the years between the foundation of the BBC in the 1920s and the mass availability of television in the 1950s. Similarly commercialization goes back much further than you might imagine. For instance in the late 19th century it was the newspapers that created football as a 'star' game. The newspapers gave coverage to the games and made the stars. How could you become a star unless you received public coverage? It was through the printed word, through the media even in the years before 1914. In the inter-war years, the whole development of the star was enhanced by the cigarette cards. But there are whole areas of commercial and media involvement in sport which were extremely important in bringing sports to the mass audience which we think of as being created by radio or television but which in fact go back much further than that. How, for instance, on Saturday night in the late 19th century did you hear the results of matches? You went to the local press office where there was a telegraph terminal and where results were printed and put in the window. This was a precursor of the Saturday night football papers which are produced today. The point I wish to make here is that involvement of the media was instrumental in shaping the public's involvement in sporting activity from a very early date.

Finally, I would like to return to an earlier theme that often eludes analysis. This is the question of irrationality, the question of the emotions that are involved in sport. There is for instance the humour of sports. One can easily lose sight of the excitement and of the humour in many of the activities involved. I would, however, like to conclude with a plea for a wider historical understanding of the way particular sports and the sporting ethos itself evolved, because without it, the sporting community loses its collective and individual memory.

Biosocial Aspects of Sport

WOMEN AND SPORT – SOCIAL ASPECTS

MARGARET TALBOT

Trinity and All Saints College, Leeds

Summary. A wide ranging coverage is given of the issues involved in the interaction between women and sport. The pressures on girls and women to take part in or to refrain from various sports are considered. The question of the leisure time available to women in various situations, and the pressures on that leisure time, are discussed, and space is also given to the opportunities available at school level, the Equal Opportunities Commission's involvement in sport and the problems of sportswomen at the highest level.

Introduction

The focus in this paper will be on the interaction between women and sport, rather than merely women in sport. Knowledge of and insight into the problems shared by all women or by large groups of women provide understanding, in social terms, of many of the problems encountered, not only by international sportswomen, but by sportswomen at many levels of commitment and excellence.

Similarly, it would be folly to exclude from the discussion the interaction between men, women and sport. Fundamental to the structure of contemporary society is the complementary relationship between men and women, and this relationship pervades sport and sports participation, and changes in women's sport and leisure behaviour necessarily imply crucial changes in that complementary relationship.

An immediate difficulty in approaching a topic of this kind stems from the size of the population: women constitute rather more than half the population of Great Britain and cannot be regarded as a homogeneous group. *Vive la difference* could as easily apply to the differences between women, as to the differences between men and women, with regard to sports involvement. When one adds further parameters, such as social class and stage of life cycle, these differences between women become wider than the differences between men and women. Willis (1974) has identified the task:

> '... not to measure these differences precisely and explain them physically, but to ask *why* some differences, and not others, are taken as so important, become so exaggerated, are used to buttress social attitudes or prejudice.'

In order to fulfil this task, the interaction between women and sport needs to be placed firmly in the society in which it takes place. This social perspective, while not focusing directly on physical–physiological bases of behaviour, nevertheless encompasses the interaction between social expectations and the development of self-esteem through the process of coming to terms with one's own body.

The approaches and insights of the social sciences are used in the same way as they are used in the emerging field of leisure studies, rather than depending only on sports sociology, since it will be argued that women's sport participation and involvement can be seen more rationally as a function of their wider patterns of leisure behaviour, than as an essential value conflict between sport and femininity, as has been suggested by Critcher (1974). Sports sociology has also been criticised as androcentric by Hall (1978), and neglects almost totally the constraint of time, which, evidence suggests, is crucial to women's leisure behaviour. Finally, concentration will be on British sources wherever possible, since historically the development of women's sports participation, particularly with regard to physical education, has been very different in the United States from Great Britain.

Definitions

It may seem superfluous to define a term so commonly used as sex, but the synonymous use of the terms sex, gender, femininity and sex role by various writers means that some kind of definition is necessary. For the purposes of this discussion sex will be taken to mean the innate, biological bases of male/female status; gender the normative but not eternal conception of male/female status, constructed by society; femininity the stereotyped set of expected attributes and qualities associated with a particular society's idea of gender; and sex role will refer to the dynamic interaction between society's expectations of behaviour related to sex and gender and the individual's own perceptions of that status.

Problems

The student interested in women and sport or women and leisure is faced with a range of problems. Until recently, the most serious one was the 'invisibility' of women in academic research (Oakley, 1974; Tivers, 1978) and the failure of researchers to allow women to be subjects of research in their own right, rather than merely reflections of or inferences from their husbands' or fathers' responses (Talbot, 1979a). The tendency to regard women, sport and leisure as either 'residual' or trivial subjects for research, further restricted serious study.

The plethora of feminist writing and the development of degree courses in women's studies has to some extent redressed this balance, but not with regard to sport or leisure. British feminists have mainly concerned themselves with inequality of opportunity in work (paid and unpaid) and education and have not yet centred much attention on women's leisure. The 'Our Bodies, Ourselves' approach, too, has tended to focus on a rejection of the use of the female body as a sex object and on a woman's right to direct her own sexual and reproductive life, rather than on the body as an efficient, functional, expressive, integral part of self.

A further problem is that this area is pervaded by myths. These myths are supposedly based on scientific evidence of the possible effects of sports participation on women's reproductive functions (Kenealy, 1920) and are easy to discredit but still carry credence; they relate to 'inevitable' differences in physical performance and potential between men and women, which are constantly being challenged and disproved both in action and in concept (Ferris, 1978); myths regarding boys' innate tendency to higher levels of motor activity than girls, belied by observation at any discotheque. All these myths are rooted in ideologies, child rearing practices and socialization where it is almost impossible to separate the influences of nature and nurture (Belotti, 1975).

Much of the writing on women and sport has been in response to the definition of sportswomen as a problem.

> 'Indeed there is an important element in the popular response to the female athlete, of uncertainty before the deviant, distrust of the strange, dislike of the marginal. As the athlete becomes even more outstanding, she marks herself out even more as deviant.'
>
> (Willis, 1974)

It is perhaps ironic that in leisure studies in general, and in policy making, it has been the female non-participant who has been defined as the problem, rather than the participant. We need to know why subjects are defined as problems, and by whom, and whether those subjects see themselves or their behaviour as problematic.

The value positions of various agencies have engendered the view that participation in leisure activities is 'good', and therefore women who do not participate in these activities are described as 'disadvantaged' (Dept of Environment, 1977), or 'sports illiterate' (Boothby, 1979), or leading a 'stunted lifestyle' (Parry & Johnson, 1974). It has been argued elsewhere (Talbot, 1979a) that a value position need not invalidate research or analysis; but it is essential that any value position should be overt and understood.

Leisure studies

Leisure research has only recently begun to be sensitive enough to provide information about women's leisure behaviour: much of the earlier work either makes no sex distinction in data collection, or depends on inferences or gleanings from research focused on men's behaviour or on family studies. However, from the data available, one can make several generalizations about women's leisure behaviour (Sillitoe, 1969; North West Sports Council, 1972; Greater London Council, 1975; Veal, 1979; Central Statistical Office, 1979). Not only do fewer women than men participate in leisure activities but women also participate in a narrower range of activities and watch sport, both live and on television, less than men. The surveys also established that inter-sex differences are more marked when combined with other variables such as age, social class and marital status. It is even more interesting that there is greater difference in participation between women of different social classes, middle-class women showing significantly higher rates of participation than working class women, than between men and women from the same social stratum, or between men from different social strata. This intra-sex difference is particularly marked in regard to sport (Sillitoe, 1969; Emmett, 1971b).

Sport is essentially a facility based on outdoor activity. However, when data from surveys which include informal leisure activity are added to the knowledge gained from family and community studies, there emerges a picture of home-based, domestic leisure for women, especially for those from the lower socioeconomic groups (Young & Wilmott, 1973; Rapoport & Rapoport, 1975; Lopata, 1966). The fact that women less often have access to the family car (Hillman & Whalley, 1977) (where there is one) and the findings of the studies on isolated, housebound women (Gavron, 1966; Hobson, 1978; Parry & Johnson, 1974; Pearson, 1976; Berk & Berk, 1979) further emphasize the structural barriers to participation encountered by large numbers of the female population.

One constraint shared by nearly all women appears to be lack of time.

> 'The inordinately small amounts of free time at the disposal of employed women and the constraints put on the housewives' life are two factors that bear a heavy responsibility for women's reduced participation in civic life, in professional training, and education, etc. The implications for women's social advancement and professional career are quite obvious.'
>
> (Szalai, 1975)

Not only is the amount of free time limited, especially for employed women, but its occurrence is often not sufficiently predictable for planning to take place. The time budget research does not support the contention that married couples share household tasks equally: there is overwhelming evidence that it is the wives who suffer from overload.

Leisure has been described both as time 'free from' and 'free to'; that is, time which is so free from obligation that one may choose how to use it. However, even when women are free from domestic and other commitments, they may not be free to do what they wish, because their time is perceived as accountable to their husbands and families, and their presence in the home is often taken for granted. This accountability is expressed in an extreme, but common, form by those wives whose husbands allow them no 'right' to leisure (Hobson, 1978). A further difficulty is that conjugal free time is often prevented by differences in the perceived needs of husband and wife:

> '... husband and wife each want to do different things: he often prefers to be or go off by himself; she would rather spend her free time with him.'
>
> (DeGrazia, 1964)

Other researchers note a difference in desired locus of free time; wives who have been at home all day yearn to go out, whilst their husbands prefer to stay at home (Rubin, 1976). And even time itself can be perceived differently when the *status quo* is upset, leading to domestic conflict, for example, when unemployed husbands lose all sense of time and arrive late for meals prepared punctually by their wives, whose domestic routine remains the same (Jahoda, Lazarsfeld & Zeisel, 1933). Such examples show that the sexes' perceptions of leisure and free time can be very different, and this must have some effect on how they choose to use that time.

Leisure studies have depended heavily on the inter-relationships of work and leisure. Rapoport & Rapoport (1971, 1975) found 'sharp sex differences in the meaning of work outside the home in the lives of women as compared with men', these differences being marked particularly after the birth of children. The fact also that many more women than men are restricted to jobs (often part-time) rather than a career (Hunt, 1968) further influences any long term qualitative relationship between their work and their leisure. Indeed, many women go out to work primarily for the social contacts offered by the job – a case of work being recreational.

Following the recognition that domestic age or life cycle stage interacts dynamically with sex to influence leisure participation, several researchers, notably Rapoport &

Rapoport (1975), have used the life cycle approach, where characteristic predominant preoccupations are seen as sources for development of interests and activities. This approach provides insight into the central concerns of different age- and stage-groups. Leonard (1980), for example, focuses on the period of courtship and marriage of couples in South Wales: this is the period when many girls and young women drop out of active participation during leisure time. Leonard describes how, on achieving a steady boyfriend, the female peer group 'collapses' and the girl becomes increasingly dependent, socially, on her boyfriend and family: she tends to drop her own interests and adopt, or at least service, his, until 'she has virtually no leisure activities which are not courtship orientated', while the boy continues activities with his own peer group. Leonard also notes that this pattern continues into early marriage, until the children are born. The social barriers to young women going out alone, (Stanley, 1977), further emphasize the girl's dependence on her boyfriend or fiancé. The natural reluctance of parents to allow girls the same freedom and mobility enjoyed by their brothers begins even earlier than adolescence, and contributes towards their future home-based way of life. The interest recently shown by the former Minister for Sport and Recreation (Mr Dennis Howell) in pleasant provision for young people to 'do their courting' is, in part, a recognition of the gap between the facilities provided by youth organizations or the state and the commercial provision which, by law, excludes under-18s from licensed premises.

The importance, particularly for working class single women, of finding a husband, should not be underestimated. The traditional argument that recreation can provide an alternative to early courtship and marriage provides only a partial solution; the power of the boyfriend can be strong enough to militate against a girl's committed interests, as Leonard's work (1980) and Payne's work (1976) with female athletes shows. Rapoport & Rapoport (1975) highlight the failure of young women to 'maintain adequate bases for the resumption of meaningful interests'. For many girls, the only meaningful interests they develop before marriage are related directly to their object of finding a marriage partner and therefore are forbidden to them after marriage – dancing is a good example. This 'cut-off' in leisure activity by working class girls has been reported by several researchers (Hobson, 1978; Leonard, 1980), but there is an acute need for more research on the place of girls in youth culture, in spite of the difficulties described by McRobbie (1978):

> 'there is something about their culture which shuns outside interference of any sort, and this, I would argue, is gender specific. Unlike the boys at the youth-club who played football and table tennis with the male youth leaders, the girls guarded their free time and privacy jealously and consistently refused to join in 'official' club activities.'

It could be argued that this phase of the life cycle for women is a logical preparation for the 'captive wife' phase after the arrival of young children. It is during this stage and afterwards that women's use of time increasingly becomes a function of the needs of their families: the extent to which mothers and wives 'service' the leisure activities of the rest of the family would be a fascinating and enlightening piece of research. The complementary role relationships within the family would be seriously disrupted, were women to cease this particular set of functions, and it is equally certain that some essential bases of women's self-esteem would be removed, and possibly some men's privileges would be at risk.

The dependence of family members on mothers is illustrated by two recent articles on mothers' commitment to others' activities. Toynbee (1980) writes of women who transport their children to skating rinks for early morning and late night sessions:

> 'Lesser women might quail at the astonishing dedication of these skating mothers. They invest so much of their free time in their children that the rest of us could feel ashamed at not giving our children the same kind of undivided attention.'

It is possible, however, that Toynbee underestimates the more often taken-for-granted servicing of activities by mothers, described by Barker (1980), herself a physical education teacher:

> 'It is 11.30 p.m. and tears of tiredness run down my face as I hold out a rugby shirt to the fire in a desperate attempt to dry it before morning.
> ... I sometimes wonder whether *they* (p.e. teachers) realise the effort that is put in by parents. I wouldn't mind an extra slip in the report books with a "well done" for me.'

These extracts amply justify the title of this paper being 'women and sport', rather than 'women in sport'.

In summing up the contribution of leisure studies, then, there is evidence that leisure for women is different in quality and quantity from men's leisure, and that women operate under more and stronger constraints than do men. The physical constraints of time, place, skill and access, the social constraints related to concepts of sex role and femininity, particularly marked among working class women, and the structural constraints of the family, finance, power and the law, combine to work against active leisure participation by women outside the home. For women, the social filter to participation (Emmett, 1971a) seems finer than it is for men.

Women and sport

It is appropriate to apply this knowledge from leisure studies to the relationship between women and sport. It is in the sports context that the differences described in the leisure research become most marked. Willis (1974) has argued that 'sport reflects a crucial central feature of our culture – anxiety about sex roles', and the North American literature confirms this premise. Participation in sport (an essentially masculine preserve) by women is seen as threatening to conceptions of both masculine and feminine behaviour, and the stereotyped American conception of femininity is a severe constraint to women's participation in sport. Additionally, the real inequality of provision for physical education in American schools and colleges explains the efforts made in the United States by female physical educationists, sports sociologists and the feminist movement towards more egalitarian programmes of physical education and the equal right to facilities and funding. Lever (1978) cites the Syracuse (New York) School Board allocation of $90,000 for boys' extracurricular sports compared with $200 for girls' sports; the Fairfield area of rural Pennsylvania set its 1972–73 budget at a ratio of 40:1 in favour of male athletes. It is not surprising, therefore, that changes in the law under Title IX of the Education Amendment Acts of 1972 have been achieved in order to make more equitable provision for girls and women possible, through financial sanctions. Problems of implementation have arisen, particularly with regard to the allocation of gate receipts from men's inter-collegiate matches (traditionally a bone of contention in American physical education departments), but it is clear that women in the United States have received more of the 'sport dollar' as a direct result of Title IX (Kleinberg, 1978).

The situation in Britain is rather different. The development of physical education in state schools in this country was heavily dependent on female innovators and educators and provision for girls' physical education is officially comprehensive in schools. There is an obvious difference in provision, however, in extra-curricular school activities and in post-school provision and in colleges and universities. However, this difference in allocation of staffing and other resources is not, as Wetton (1980) recently implied, only a function of the male-dominated power structure in sport, but also reflects the heavy dependence by sport and recreation management on expressed demand as a criterion (often the only criterion) of programming of staff and facilities, rather than seeking a real awareness of women's (and other low-participating groups') needs and constraints.

Equal Opportunities Commission

It is relevant, having referred to changes in the law in the United States, to consider the effects of the Sex Discrimination Act and the institution of the Equal Opportunities Commission (EOC) on women's leisure opportunities. The terms of the Sex Discrimination Act mean that 'it is unlawful to discriminate on grounds of sex in employment, in sport, or in training facilities offered, or in the general sporting facilities available' (Howe, 1978). There are, however, two important qualifications to this: first, that it is lawful to hold one-sex competitions in events where physical strength, stamina or physique puts women at a disadvantage compared with men, and second, that private clubs and organizations are exempt from the terms of the Act.

The EOC is a quasi-governmental body which has responsibility for implementing the Equal Pay Act and the Sex Discrimination Act, and which is empowered to give informal or legal advice to women – and men – who feel they have a grievance stemming from sex discrimination. It is significant that of all the enquiries received by the EOC regarding goods, facilities and services, in 1978, 36% were related to leisure; this represents 5% of all the enquiries received by the EOC. In 1976, the EOC's first year, leisure enquiries represented 8.5% of total enquiries, or 700 separate problems, of which 440 related to clubs, 174 to sports and competitions and the rest to restaurants, cafes and public houses (Table 1).

The case of Theresa Bennett, whom the Football Association refused to register to play in an under-12 league, is possibly the most famous case sponsored by the EOC. Her case was won in the courts, but the decision was reversed by Lord Denning at Appeal, in favour of the Football Association, in spite of overwhelming evidence that the girl was pre-pubertal and therefore not at a physical disadvantage in comparison with boys. Indeed, her coach said of her:

> 'I regard her as something like a guided missile in football boots. She's a first-rate tackler and she distributes the ball properly. As far as her tackling is concerned, she's something like a cross between Tommy Smith of Liverpool and Norman Hunter who was of Leeds. She's absolutely first rate.'
>
> (EOC files)

In spite of this testimonial, and the evidence of eminent experts like Professor J.M. Tanner, Lord Denning at Appeal set the previous judgement aside, countering the argument that there is no significant difference in stamina, strength, etc. between boys and girls of 12 years by saying: 'We don't enquire about the ages of ladies'. He further refused appeal to the House of Lords on the grounds that the case was of no importance whatsoever.

Table 1. Enquiries relating to discrimination against women in leisure facilities, received by the Equal Opportunities Commission, 1976–79

Facility	1976	1977	1978	1979
Clubs	440	124	98	106
Public houses	74	43	29	15
Restaurants/cafes	12	8	11	2
Sports/competitions	174	53	61	34
Total	700	228	199	157
As % of all GFS* enquiries	47.1	42.07	35.85	32.9
As % of complaints to EOC	8.5	5.6	5.0	Not yet available

Figures provided by the EOC.
*Goods, facilities and services.

What makes the case even more intriguing is the fact that the EOC received several letters from irate women and women's organizations, criticizing the EOC for spending public money on such a trivial case, and expressing concern that Theresa Bennett's future normal development would be at risk. It is also worth noting that the Women's Football Association also forbids mixed matches at all ages. These responses further reflect the lack of consensus among women, and a general ambivalence in society towards women, sport and particular sports, which will be discussed later.

As well as attempting change through the law, the EOC has also successfully brought pressure to bear on some private clubs and other organizations which are exempt from the terms of the Act, for example, to allow access to clubrooms, annual dinners, and to allow women to compete in various sporting events from which they had been excluded (see Howe, 1978; EOC News, 1978). It is therefore encouraging that the EOC recognizes the importance of sport, in spite of the problems with regard to the terms of the Act. Howe (1978), former Deputy Chairman of the EOC has said:

'The arguments about equality of opportunity in sport are fundamentally similar to those about equality of opportunity anywhere else.'

Pressure groups

It has often been argued that pressure groups are predominantly middle class affairs. One current pressure group, relevant to this discussion, and providing an exception to this rule, is ERICCA (Equal Rights in Clubs Campaign for Action). The group aims to obtain full membership rights for women in working men's clubs, which they wish to designate 'workers' clubs, and the right of affiliation to the Club and Institute Union. The group arose out of a sudden ban on women playing snooker at a Wakefield working men's club: one woman, who had been playing snooker there with her husband for 3 years, organized a 50-strong picket of the club and a 2000 name petition to protest against the ban. This is a relatively rare but encouraging example of the power of a concerted group of women (and men), working to accomplish change in a traditionally male-dominated sphere.

Social expectations

Changes resulting from legal or informal pressures are possible only where there is a recognition of a clear-cut problem. The ambivalence towards women in sport often disallows action of this kind, since this ambivalence is shared by both men and women, in respect of the conflict which is seen between femininity and sports competition. The value conflict is seen as inevitable when the competition is at top-level, or where the sports event is not congruent with the 'female attributes' of passivity, nurturance, etc. Loverock (1978), a Canadian track athlete, recorded with annoyance her recognition of her own surprise when she overheard Rumanian, Czech and Soviet women 19-meter shot putters discussing intricate embroidery designs. Riordan (1980) has noted that in the Soviet Union positive attitudes towards women competitors in the 'heavy' field events are rooted in a concept of femininity which includes heavy body build and capacity for hard physical labour. The challenge to culturally determined stereotyped notions of femininity presented by female sports participation is further strengthened by recent questioning of the inevitability of men's superior performance in all sports (Ferris, 1978; Dyer, 1979; Besford, 1971; Jokl, 1971) and, in a wider context, by the current controversy over relative innate or cultural influences on sex-typing.

Nevertheless, social expectations still present an immediate challenge to women aspiring to participation in sport: Hall (1974) and Payne (1976) have examined the psychosocial constraints on female sports participation and Moir (1977) has compared characteristics of female participants and non-participants in a biographical context. The importance for future participation of success in school physical education for girls is emphasized by Emmett's work (1971b), and the contribution of parental and family support also appears to be crucial. Payne's list of deterrents to competition in athletics included lack of progress in training, competitive disappointments, injury, expense, poor facilities, lack of coaching and social disapproval, not dissimilar to the general difficulties experienced by all athletes, male and female. It would be useful to know the strength of these deterrents for boys and girls respectively. Payne further identified a need to find a subtle means of improving the image of the female athlete. Moir concluded, unsurprisingly, that females who are exceptionally keen on physical activities have an early dedication to them, and are normally good at physical activities; she notes also that many girls want to play football.

The recognition of sport as an essential component of boys' sex role socialization seems to exclude it from girls', except in a temporary form:

'A girl may refuse the constraints of femininity during the period of childhood which the psychoanalysts have called 'latency' – that is, between the ages of about 7 and 11. She may climb trees, play football, get into scrapes and generally emulate acceptable masculine behaviour, *but only on condition that she grows out of it.* No such tolerance is extended to the boy. He can never, even temporarily, abdicate from his role. The boy who goes around with girls, plays girls' games and rejects his male peers would very probably be referred to Child Guidance.'

(Comer, 1974)

The expected distinction between boys' and girls' sex roles is illustrated by a 10-year-old boy quoted by Comer:

'I would not like to be a girl because you have to do the washing up and clean the house and you couldn't play football or rugby ... Girls are soft and weak and they haven't got the brains to play football and rugby.'

The difference in the place of sport (and other leisure activities) in the socialization of boys and girls is an area for further research. Physical education (particularly games) is one of the few school subjects consistently segregated by sex. A report by the Department of Education and Science (1975) questions the necessity for sex segregation in all aspects of physical education, which often seems to be based on tradition, rather than on problems with resources as is so often claimed. The relationship of physical education to future participation in physical recreation seems to be more marked for girls, especially in terms of the activities pursued (Emmett, 1971b), which underlines the significance of the exclusion of sport from the concern of other agents of girls' socialization. The greater conflict between the values of girls' peer groups and the school physical education programme is recognized and the drop out rate of girls from physical education has been investigated (James & Webb, 1965): being 'no good' or 'bored' were the major reasons given for sitting out physical education lessons by girls. It has been argued elsewhere (Talbot, 1979b) that sports may have different sets of meanings for males and females and that it may be difficult for girls, in the absence of supporting socializing agents, to 'know' physical activities well enough ever to achieve intrinsic satisfaction from them.

The lack of female reference models in the media further weakens the place of sport relative to the peer group culture. Comer (1974) quotes some magazine advice: 'even if you can't participate in his sport you can be there to cheer him on'. Sharpe (1976) has noted the 'passive supporting characters' portrayed by women in the media, and the 1978 CCPR Conference on Women in Sport identified the need for all organizations concerned with women's sports to work towards media exposure reflecting women's sporting interests and achievement. Eppel & Eppel's (1966) work with teenagers found no sportswomen as role models by either boys or girls, although the boys consistently chose sportsmen as examples of 'glamorous occupations'.

The recognition by sports clothing manufacturers that sportswear can be designed for women and that women do form a profitable proportion of the market has led to developments like the Mary Peters range of sportswear which combines required sports specifications with attractive colours and fabrics and female shapes (Kay, 1980). Mary Peters has herself recognized the ambivalence towards sportswomen and that sportswomen themselves have attempted to resolve this by extra concentration on a feminine image:

> 'We've been very fortunate in the Commonwealth Games that all our girls who have won so far are very pretty because they'll get more coverage when they get home.'
>
> (Purdy, 1978)

Probably the most vehement criticism of the media has been in response to representation of women participating in sport as 'bizarre'. Glanville (1969) epitomizes the view that sport for women is acceptable as long as they do not involve themselves to excess:

> 'There is no reason why a woman should not indulge in any kind of sport she wishes ...
>
> A girl who goes out to run, swim or play tennis for the joy of it is still being a girl. But a girl who slogs away all winter in a gymnasium lifting weights so she can beat other girls in the summer is behaving like an imitation man.'

The whole notion of what is excess or acceptable for men and women is confused and confusing. If the idea of women doping is nauseating, why is it not equally so for men? Are not both sexes human? Gymnastics has been described as 'really designed' for girls (Howarth, 1978), yet the repeated and exaggerated hyperextension of the spine, which would be described as 'excessive' by many anatomists, has been accepted as an integral part of that form of movement.

The use of aesthetic criteria in judging sports seems also to determine a sport as 'feminine', with unfortunate results for boys who aspire to skate, dance or do gymnastics (Lightbown, 1979), while contact sports, classified as 'masculine', tend to discourage female participation. Douglas (1966) writes: 'It is not the act itself which has absolute value, but the social classification of it', and she suggests five solutions which society finds to the problem of anomaly, which are directly relevant to this discussion.

(1) Place it in a category and deny its other attributes.
(2) Remove the anomaly by physical control.
(3) Avoid the anomaly as abhorrent.
(4) See the anomaly as highly dangerous and not to be associated with.
(5) Use ambiguous symbols in poetry, mythology and ritual.

It is not difficult to find examples of society's resolution of the sportswoman anomaly for each of these solutions.

(1) 'Girls can't play football'.
(2) Women are not allowed in many sports pavilions, club houses and on golf courses at peak times.
(3) The claim that successful sportswomen are masculine, or even lesbian.
(4) 'It's not natural' (for girls to play football): statement by Ted Croker, Secretary of the Football Association (Howe, 1978).
(5) The recurrent theme of Amazons in literature; St. Trinian's image of hockey players.

There are, of course, many examples of sportswomen who have managed to resolve or ignore the anomaly between femininity and sports participation. But we know little about the extent to which this anomaly contributes towards the low rate of female participation, and whether this anomaly is challenged or reinforced by school physical education and the media's portrayals of women's and men's sport. We also need to know more about the ways in which some women overcome constraints which prevent other women from participating. There is evidence that the supportive networks offered by husbands and families actively contribute towards some women's involvement in sport. But there is also evidence that in some families, leisure interests can never be shared because husbands' and wives' enthusiasms can be so different: 69% of the people interviewed for the Institute for Family and Environmental Studies/Dartington Amenity Research Trust project in 1978 said they 'often' or 'sometimes' wished that they shared more interests with their spouse. Of those interests, sport accounted for 17%: when the detailed interviews are reported, we may gain valuable insight into these realms of life not shared by marriage partners.

Effect of body image

Very little is known about the influence of differences between the sexes in attitudes towards the body. Studies suggest that women are more critical of their bodies than men, experiencing their body boundaries more definitely than men (Fisher, 1964): how much this self-evaluation is a function of society's ideal body type for women, and to what extent this influences women's attitude to physical recreation, is impossible to measure without further research. Bardwick (1971) points out that women's self concept and self esteem are closely linked to the appearance and function of their bodies. Erikson (1964) has postulated that inner and outer body space are sex related, boys tending to think in terms of open, and girls in terms of closed, space. Pilot studies have indicated that, in spite of negative social pressures, women athletes show more positive self-attitudes than non-athletes in measures of psychological well-being and body image, although the question must be asked whether this is a cause or a function of sports participation (Snyder & Kivlin, 1975). Weiss (1969) believes that women have less strong a need than men to see what their bodies can do, because they are more established in their roles as social beings, wives and mothers, than men are in their work roles and as husbands and fathers. Arguably, 'established' in these roles could be more accurately described as 'conditioned' or 'restricted' and that by denying women the opportunities of non-reproductive physical fulfilment, society is depriving them of a human (not merely masculine) experience. The words of several talented sportswomen lend support to this view:

Debbie Brill:
'I high jump because it is an expression of me ... It gives me a great sense of my body and mind. When I clear the bar I have a great sense of control and accomplishment.'

(Loverock, 1978)

'Swimming was my passion and I gave it all. Letting loose with all of me. An effortless fish, finning forever to a rhythm of breathing and stroking across the pool, a healthy, powerful, well-disciplined body that could take me anywhere.

And on land, after, light-headed, giddy, at the peak of condition – on a natural high so few women have ever experienced – so few, I now realise.'

(Lamblin, 1977)

and finally, Suzy Chaffee:

'Tell it like it is
That women overpopulate for lack of other physical skills
That sex machines replace loving muscles
That the mind has lost the body in a neon maze
And the masses sell out for happiness in rainbow packages.'

(O'Connor, 1975)

References

BARDWICK, J. (1971) *Psychology of Women: a Study of Bio-cultural Conflicts.* Harper & Row, New York.
BARKER, P. (1980) Pity the poor parent. *Br. J. phys. Educ.* **11**, 16.
BELOTTI, E.G. (1975) *Little Girls.* Writers and Readers Publishing Cooperative, London.
BERK, R.A. & BERK, S.F. (1979) *Labor and Leisure at Home: Content and Organisation of the Household Day.* Sage, Beverley Hills.
BESFORD, P. (1971) Our vital statistics. *World Sports*, June, p. 8.
BOOTHBY, J. (1979) The sporting illiterate. *Sport & Recreation,* **20**, No. 4.
CENTRAL STATISTICAL OFFICE (1979) *Social Trends*, No. 9, p. 177. HM Stationery Office, London.
COMER, L. (1974) *Wedlocked Women.* Feminist Books, Leeds.
CRITCHER, C. (1974) Women in sport. *Cult. Stud.* **5**, 3.
DEGRAZIA, S. (1964) *Of Time, Work and Leisure.* Anchor Books, New York.
DEPARTMENT OF EDUCATION AND SCIENCE (1975) *Curricular Differences for Boys and Girls.* Education Survey 21. HM Stationery Office, London.
DEPARTMENT OF THE ENVIRONMENT (1977) *Recreation and Deprivation in Inner Urban Areas.* HM Stationery Office, London.
DOUGLAS, M. (1966) *Purity and Danger.* Routledge & Kegan Paul, London.
DYER, K. (1979) Women in athletics. *Medisport*, June, p. 25.
EMMETT, I. (1971a) *The Social Filter in the Leisure Field.* Recreation News Supplement No. 4. Countryside Commission, Cheltenham.
EMMETT, I. (1971b) *Youth and Leisure in an Urban Sprawl.* University of Manchester Press, Manchester.
EPPEL, E.M. & EPPEL, E. (1966) Teenage idols. In: *Youth in New Society.* Edited by T. Raison. Hart Davis, London.
ERIKSON, E. (1964) Inner and outer space: reflections on womanhood. *Daedalus*, **93**, 586.
FERRIS, E. (1978) Sportswomen and medicine. In: *Report of the 1st International Conference on Women in Sport.* Central Council of Physical Recreation, London.
FISHER, S. (1964) Sex differences in body perception. *Psychol. Monogr.* **78**, 1.
GAVRON, H. (1966) *The Captive Wife.* Penguin, Harmondsworth, Middlesex.
GLANVILLE, B. (1969) What is happening to girls in sport? *Sunday Times*, 31 August.
GREATER LONDON COUNCIL (1975) *Greater London Recreation Study: Part 1 — Demand Study.* Research Report 19. GLC, London.
HALL, M.A. (1974) *Women and Physical Recreation: a Causal Analysis.* PhD thesis, University of Birmingham.
HALL, M.A. (1978) *Sport and Gender: a Feminist Perspective on the Sociology of Sport.* Canadian Association for Health, Physical Education and Recreation, Ottawa.

HILLMAN, M. & WHALLEY, A. (1977) *Fair Play For All: a Study of Access to Sport and Informal Recreation.* Political and Economic Planning, London.
HOBSON, D. (1978) Housewives: isolation as oppression. In: *Women Take Issue.* Women's Studies Group, Centre for Contemporary Cultural Studies, University of Birmingham. Hutchinson, London.
HOWARTH, A.E.S. (1978) Daring sport designed for girls. *Times Educational Supplement,* 5 May.
HOWE, E. (1978) A little too strenuous for women? In: *Report of the 1st International Conference on Women in Sport.* Central Council of Physical Recreation, London.
HUNT, A. (1968) *A Survey of Women's Employment.* HM Stationery Office, London.
JAHODA, M., LAZARSFELD, P.H. & ZEISEL, H. (1933) *Marienthal.* Reprinted 1972, Tavistock, London.
JAMES, J.M. & WEBB, I.M. (1965) Why girls 'sit-out' during PE lessons: an investigation. *Phys. Educ.* **57**, 75.
JOKL, E. (1971) *Physiology of Exercise.* Thomas, Springfield, Illinois.
KAY, B. (1980) Fashion and Mary Peters. *Sport and Recreation,* **21**, 13.
KENEALY. A. (1920) *Feminism and Sex Extinction.* Fisher Unwin, London.
KLEINBERG, J. (1978) Women's sport in American life. In: *Report of the 1st International Conference on Women in Sport.* Central Council of Physical Recreation, London.
LAMBLIN, B. (1977) Reclaiming personal power. *Arena Newsletter,* Institute for Sport and Social Analysis, **11**, 21.
LEONARD, D. (1980) *Sex and Generation: a Study of Courtship and Weddings.* Tavistock, London.
LEVER, J. (1978) Sex differences in the complexity of children's play and games. *Am. sociol. Rev.* **43**, 471.
LIGHTBOWN, C. (1979) Boys in the gym – killing off the girlie image. *Sunday Times,* 9 December.
LOPATA, H.Z. (1966) The life cycle of the social role of the housewife. *Sociol. Social Res.* **51**, 5.
LOVEROCK, P. (1978) Pink bows and sweat. *Branching Out,* **5**, 32.
MCROBBIE, A. (1978) Working class girls and the culture of femininity. In: *Women Take Issue.* Tavistock, London.
MOIR, E. (1977) *Female Participation in Physical Activities: a Scottish Study.* Dunfermline College of Physical Education, Edinburgh.
NORTH WEST SPORTS COUNCIL (1972) *Leisure in the North West.* Deansgate Press, Salford.
OAKLEY, A. (1974) *Housewife.* Allen Lane, London.
O'CONNOR, U. (1975) Suzy – fighting the false oaths to grey ideals. *Sunday Times,* 17 August.
PARRY, N.C.A. & JOHNSON, D. (1974) *Leisure and Social Structure.* Social Science Research Council, London.
PAYNE, R. (1976) *An Investigation into Female Participation in Athletics.* MSc thesis, University of Birmingham.
PEARSON, L. (1976) *Working Class Non Work Time: a Case Study in Birmingham.* PhD thesis, University of Birmingham.
PURDY, K. (1978) Fair coverage. *Branching Out,* **5**, 8.
RAPOPORT, R. & RAPOPORT, R. (1971) *Dual Career Families.* Penguin, Harmondsworth, Middlesex.
RAPOPORT, R. & RAPOPORT, R. (1975) *Leisure and the Family Life Cycle.* Routledge & Kegan Paul, London.
RIORDAN, J. (1980) *Soviet Sport.* Blackwell, Oxford.
RUBIN, L.B. (1976) *Worlds of Pain.* Basic Books, New York.
SHARPE, S. (1976) *Just Like a Girl: How Girls Grow up to be Women.* Penguin, Harmondsworth, Middlesex.
SILLITOE, K.K. (1969) *Planning for Leisure.* HM Stationery Office, London.
SNYDER, E.E. & KIVLIN, J.E. (1975) Women athletes and aspects of psychological well-being and body image. *Res. Q.* **46**, 191.
STANLEY, E. (1977) Sex, gender and the sociology of leisure. In: *Leisure and the Urban Society.* Edited by M.A. Smith. Leisure Studies Association, London.
SZALAI, A. (1975) Women's time: women in the light of contemporary time budget research. *Futures,* **7**, 391.
TALBOT, M. (1979a) *Women and Leisure.* Sports Council/Social Science Research Council, London.

TALBOT, M. (1979b) Meaning in physical activity: a speculative discussion. *Momentum*, **4**, 28.
TIVERS, J. (1978) How the other half lives: the geographical study of women. *Area*, **10**, 302.
TOYNBEE, P. (1980) Guardian women. *Guardian*, 28 January.
VEAL, A.J. (1979) *Sport and Recreation in England and Wales: an Analysis of Adult Participation Patterns in 1977*. Research Memorandum 74. Centre for Urban and Regional Studies, University of Birmingham.
WEISS, P. (1969) *Sport: a Philosophic Inquiry*. Southern Illinois University Press, Illinois.
WETTON, P. (1980) It's a man's world as far as money goes. *Br. J. phys. Educ.* **11**, 39.
WILLIS, P. (1974) Performance and meaning – a socio-cultural view of women in sport, *Cult. Stud.* **5**.
YOUNG, M. & WILLMOTT, P. (1973) *The Symmetrical Family*. Routledge & Kegan Paul, London.

Biosocial Aspects of Sport

COMMENT

ROSEMARY PAYNE

School of Psychological Studies, Polytechnic of Birmingham

First, I would like to congratulate Margaret Talbot on her interesting paper in which such a range of issues was raised. At various times I remembered feeling exactly as she described and I believe she was touching on issues that are very important for sportswomen. So my personal and individual reactions were to agree about the time issue; that trying to be a wife and mother, to keep a career and training going and trying to keep an interest in sport causes tremendous conflicts and there is never enough time to go round. There is always the feeling that you are never achieving your optimum in any of the varied roles that you are trying to perform. This raises great problems for women about guilt and this in one of society's subtle devices. When a woman is training she feels she should be looking after her children or her husband; if she is marking her essays she ought to be doing her training and so on. So there is a great deal of conflict.

The other area that I felt was rightly expressed was the servicing role; I can remember my own mother many years ago always washing by brother's rugby strip and even at the age of 10, I was asked to clean his boots, which I resented, even if he was playing in the First XV. I remember the problems I experienced later when I first had to organize babysitters for my own children, and then, when the boys were big enough to be competing themselves, trying to organize how four people could go to different sports competitions at the same time in different directions. With the endless washing and cooking for a family the servicing role can become a problem, particularly if you are trying to keep involved with sport yourself.

I agree also about the feelings of ambivalence in regard to femininity. These anxieties about femininity are certainly not hysterical imaginings of young adolescents. I remember feeling very reassured after marriage and having children. I have been complaining about the work they brought, but on the other side they brought a great relief, because it was going to be difficult for anybody to accuse me of being unfeminine once I actually had children. I also had to face the sex tests, as so often young women have to do, and when it was obvious to the doctors that I had had children there clearly could be no uncertainty. But I thought about all those younger girls and the implications and anxieties being raised in their minds – that if they were that good, maybe they were men! The whole basis underlying the sex test is the suspicion about a woman who is above average in performance; really it is not a joke, even though one tries to joke about it, because of the pressure it puts on girls. I know that when I have been asked about problems of femininity for a thrower or any female athlete who does weight training and the suggestion has been made that she is becoming an 'imitation man', I have been tempted to say: 'What documentary evidence have you got to prove what sex you are? I have sex certificates in three languages telling me I'm female'.

I resolved my problems in certain ways but I am worried that young girls today are still being subjected to these pressures. Surely, after 20 years, we should not be exerting the same kind of pressures but unfortunately this is still the case, as I found when I did my research with the girls only 4 years ago and when I question and discuss things with the young athletes with whom I am now in contact. These threats, both psychological and social, are perceived as being very real.

Now one would hope that the aim of a healthy society would be to allow individuals of both sexes to make the best use of their talents and to provide avenues for recreation and for self-realization and for feelings of worth. Boys feel threatened too, often in adolescence, but the threats are usually not away from sport but towards it; that is the opposite kind of pressure. The boys gain self esteem through sports participation. I remember one girl saying to me that boys prove their masculinity by being good at sport whereas girls prove their femininity by being bad at it and I thought that this was a poor reflection on our society, or a young girl's perception of it. Now these feelings are certainly a consequence of social pressures – the sex-stereotyping which Margaret Talbot mentioned and these social constraints and expectations operate in all areas of our life besides sport, so it is going to be difficult for sport to change without bigger societal changes also taking place. There is a certain amount that can be legislated for, and I quote the American example of the recent dramatic adjustments that have been made in sports' budgets for men's and women's colleges. In one college the women got 0·75% of what the men got for their sports budget. Now that has been changed and legislation is doing away with this inequality. But perhaps we should be more interested in the very subtle attitudes and pressures that are difficult to legislate for but are extremely influential.

Society is perhaps becoming used to the changing role of women, and maybe even becoming a little tired of hearing and reading about it, and certainly different avenues are opening up for women, albeit at quite a cost to them. But it is assumed that if opportunities are opening up for women they must also be closing for men and a great deal of tolerance and understanding is required in both directions. I heard a man physical educationalist say 'If more and more girls keep doing more and more of the boys' things, like their sport and their games and so on, then there are going to be fewer and fewer boys' things left for boys to be'; and he saw this as a terrible problem, instead of realizing that all boys do not want to be, or can be, sports stars and would it not be preferable if we allowed and encouraged other opportunities for the boys to gain self esteem?

This anxiety about the different roles, as the football example showed, begins in the schools, although perhaps less in primary schools. One hopes that the more mature, which is not always related to age, could resolve the problems of women being better than men in certain things and men being better than women in others and come to accept that both sexes should have opportunities for success and failure.

The most vulnerable age is perhaps between about 10 and the early 20s, when the dangers of mixed sports and the dangers of comparison are very great. The peer group is ready to reject the boy if a girl beats him and to reject the girl for doing it, so they both lose socially. But let us not be destructive about mixed sports because I feel the main issue is how we should encourage positive and rewarding participation for girls and women.

Reasons for dropping out have been mentioned: these include bad facilities, injuries and so on and I wonder how the boys' list of reasons would compare. There would certainly be two very important things missing. The problem of boyfriends would not arise and this really is a very great problem for the girls. 'My boyfriend doesn't like it'; 'my fiancé doesn't like it'; 'my fiancé says that if I don't stop my training he's going to break off the engagement', etc; these are frequent explanations. The tendency, as Margaret Talbot said, is for the girls to start following the boys' interests instead of carrying on with their own. They go and watch his sport, or meet for tea at the cricket club or rugby club, becoming spectators of their boyfriends' activities. It requires a very strong willed girl to be able to fight against that kind of pressure.

The other thing that would not appear on the boys' list as a reason for giving up sport is that the girls are repeatedly being told that 'it's unladylike'. It is not only men that say that; women say it too. Mothers say to their daughters: 'I wish you wouldn't play these unladylike games' etc., and that is a very heavy burden for a teenager to bear. If they want to do weight training, 'You don't want to be like Mrs Universe, do you?' is the kind of thing which is said to them. So how then do we resist this stereotype? This is the important issue. Among the girls that I know, the capacity to resist was often the consequence of their childhood experience. Their parents tended to be supportive and both parents encouraged them. Where they were in a mixed family they felt they were not differentiated from their brothers; they both had chores to do in the house, they were both encouraged to play games and they were both applauded if they did well. They had to share the activities. They felt too that their parents shared the authority patterns.

The girls who were able to resist this stereotype had had this type of experience; they had received independence training and they were encouraged to be good at something. They were encouraged to be independent. They were encouraged to acquire some skills and control and gain some mastery. And if I can be forgiven for raising some psychological jargon, attribution theory seems to matter here; and by attribution theory I mean simply that what you perceive as the cause of your success or failure is extremely important. This is so whether you succeed by chance or because of somebody else, or whether you succeed or fail by your own efforts or your own ability; that is, whether your locus of control is external or internal. Am I master of my fate or not, can I make decisions or not, can I be responsible for my performance or not? In our society the tendency is to encourage boys to have this kind of independence. Boys do believe in themselves and their own abilities a lot more, whereas girls tend to feel themselves much more at the mercy of external circumstances. Boys attain self esteem through achievement but girls feel they gain self esteem through acceptance, through being approved of, through being a good girl which does not always mean being a good sportswoman. So I think this matters.

Now is this some kind of conspiracy theory? Are we saying that somebody is working against the female of the species? Who are these conspirators who are making it difficult for all the girls and women who are trying to do things? Well it is difficult to say who the conspirators are, and I am certainly not saying that they are always the men, but of course there is a strong residue of tradition, authority and power in most sporting areas, as well as in political life. My own feeling is that all of us are very responsible, and that in our own way, whether we are in education, the communications media, administration, as parents or as somebody's brother or sister, son or daughter, we are all significant others to somebody who might be trying to participate. We must therefore be very sensitive indeed in handling the sexist situation wherever it arises. We must avoid things like the girls from one school saying 'Every time it's raining the boys get in the gym and we have to tidy up the changing room. That's the rule for the girls'. I am sure that applies to physical education teachers who act with a very good will but that is what the girls felt. Or as in the media, that one teenage girl said, 'That reporter kept asking about vital statistics and it wasn't about how far and how fast I could run; he was only going to put my picture in if I was a blonde and had nice legs'. This is the kind of issue which raises great problems for the girls themselves.

So all of us must be very sensitive indeed to the situation; we must be very aware of what we are doing, what we are encouraging, and what we are saying, and try very hard to 'be fair'.

GENERAL DISCUSSION

From the Chair, Miss Newson commented that, in relation to women and sport, winning medals in high powered competition should not be the only consideration and suggested that many women were quite happy with the other roles assigned to them. The definition of sport as a pastime implied that it should be fun and a pleasurable activity, and this could be achieved by different people in different ways.

The propriety of men and women participating together in the martial arts was questioned. This raised the response that the martial arts, particularly boxing, were perhaps inappropriate activities even for men and that the role of ritual violence in society as a whole needed to be re-examined.

In the wider context of society generally, it was suggested that the concept of equal opportunities for men and women had to be considered in relation to the whole family and, although not all the problems could be solved by legislation, a policy of development of integrated sports clubs where all members of the family could enjoy a variety of activities might help to remove some of the difficulties which tended to prevent women from participating fully. Mrs Talbot did not entirely agree with this suggestion and drew attention to the successful results obtained by the Equal Opportunities Commission, not only in sport but also in other areas of informal leisure. However, she agreed that legislation would be unlikely to change social attitudes and she pointed out that 9% of families in Britain were now one-parent families, mainly dependent on the mothers whose opportunities for leisure activities were extremely limited by their circumstances.

Another speaker asked how girls could become top class sportswomen without being considered deviant and, from personal experience, the encouragement of parents and determination to the point of selfishness, coupled perhaps with an unawareness of conscious deviancy, emerged as being of prime importance.

The role of the schools was questioned and the attitudes of PE teachers towards sport for boys and girls and it was suggested that much more help could be given in this area. Officially, PE was compulsory in both primary and secondary schools but current practice was for it to become optional at some stage in the secondary school. In primary schools there was less differentiation between boys' and girls' activities but, nevertheless, specialist PE help tended to be directed mainly towards the boys' games, especially football. Further research was needed into the attitudes, often acquired at training college, of PE teachers towards sport, and to other aspects of leisure education, for which they were very often given responsibility.

II

SPORT AND HEALTH

Chairman: Christopher Brasher

Biosocial Aspects of Sport

SPORT AND PERSONALITY

J. E. KANE

*West London Institute of Higher Education,
Borough Road, Isleworth, Middlesex*

Summary. In a wide-ranging survey, ways are examined in which human personalities can be categorized and the relevance of these categories to sporting performance is examined. The profiles produced by studies of the Eysenck and Cattell type, the significance of the 'trait' and the 'interactional' approaches and the correlation of personalities with physical performance are considered. The importance of such factors as achievement motivation, causal attribution, self-efficacy, mental rehearsal and concentration is examined. Consideration is given to the role of sport in the fulfilment of the personality.

Introduction

Explanatory analyses of sports performance and sports involvement have until recently depended almost entirely on the researchers in the fields of applied biology, biomechanics and medicine. Major advances in, for example, the biochemistry and biomechanics of athletic performance have in the last few years greatly advanced scientific interpretations with respect to the selection, guidance and training of athletes, and have contributed to some of the current and dramatic improvements in performance. Only very recently, however, have researchers begun to unravel some of the psychological and psychosocial aspects which account for variation in athletic and sporting performance, especially in stressful situations. The huge increase in published research literature, in new journals, books, and proceedings of national and international societies, is a testimony to the developing interest in the psychological parameters of athletic behaviour which, in the last analysis, may be the crucial discriminators between success and failure in competitive sport. Although in this area issues concerning the acquisition of skills have long been debated in courses for physical education teachers and coaches, the emphasis has tended to be on pragmatic procedures which, at best, have relied on the application of knowledge collated speculatively from various areas of general psychology. In recent years, thanks largely to the stimulation and support of such scholars as Professor Alan Welford during his tenure at the Department of Experimental Psychology at Cambridge University, a much more specific programme of research into sports-based psychology has been discernible in this country, and similar academic and research programmes have developed throughout the world. A milestone for co-ordinated international enterprise was the establishment in 1966 of the International Society of Sports Psychology, the first proceedings of which ran to over 1200 pages, giving a most comprehensive perspective to this new disciplinary area. Since then, succeeding cohorts of teachers, researchers and writers have added substantially to our understanding of a wide range of psychological topics related to sports performance; in general terms, these encompass the interacting psychomotor processes categorized as cognitive, perceptual affective and motor (cf. Singer, 1975).

Notwithstanding the growth of knowledge and understanding about aptitude, abilities and skills, the explanation of performance differences is acknowledged as depending to a crucial extent on the individual's unique personal and behavioural dispositions. Such dispositions as an individual brings to a performance, while clearly important with respect to the outcome, are not yet well understood, neither as to their nature and source, their quantification nor their predictive value. This is not surprising, since this area of psychology – essentially personality psychology – is complex and currently imprecise, embracing such issues as, for example, the relative permanence/impermanence of personality states, the effects of cognitive and perceptual styles, the nature of intrinsic motivation, the person's modes of construing and the effects of learning and experience. Nevertheless the study of the person in the context of behaving and performing is not without a sound pedigree in psychology, and there are current signs of a new and healthy increase of interest in this area which promises to establish a stronger theoretical basis for experimental work. No group of professional workers will be more sensitive to new explanations and findings which make operational sense than those involved in teaching and advising in physical education and sport, where it has long been held that performance, especially in competition, ultimately rests on the psychological dispositions which the individual brings to the event, and that in turn the nature of the event may affect subsequent dispositions. The bases for these assumptions are not hard to find. The physical education literature is, for example, heavy with implied and stated links between personality development and involvement in appropriately conducted programmes of planned physical activities, games, dance and sport. Most recently and interestingly the argument for the existence of these links has focused attention on the possible effects of physical activity on body image and self concept (Kane, 1972). Additionally, some recent literature of a psychological nature has tended to strengthen the hopes and expectations of coaches and advisers that the selection, training and performance of talented athletes could benefit from psychological insights (e.g. Cofer & Johnson, 1960); Ogilvie & Tutko, 1966; Vanek & Cratty, 1970; Rushall & Siedentrop, 1975; Ponsonby & Yaffé, 1976) and psychological education and training is becoming an acknowledged prerequisite of an athlete's total preparation.

Since about 1960, considerable research has been undertaken (mostly by physical educationists) to investigate the validity of these assumptions but, on the whole, it has not produced coherent and unequivocal findings on which to rely for predictive purposes. It has, however, produced a great deal of useful descriptive information about the nature and extent of the relationship between personality and physical (athletics) ability and performance on which more sophisticated research may be based. The main criticisms of much of this research have focused attention on methodological inadequacies (e.g. Cooper, 1969; Rushall, 1973), and on the virtual absence of any sound theoretical reference base (e.g. Kroll, 1970; Kane, 1976).

In the last few years, however, a new urgent awakening in the field of personality psychology is apparent, focusing to a great extent on the search for alternatives or extensions of trait 'theory'. Trait theory is under attack not so much because it is an unsound theory but because *ipso facto* personality traits emphasize the personal dispositions in explaining behaviour and minimize the role of situational factors. The result is that a number of alternative models and approaches have been proposed in an effort to explain a more vital and dynamic concept of personality sensitive to situational factors in behaviour. In these recent developments there appear to be the kinds of explanations, theories and models that may be particularly attractive and apposite for research in physical education and sport. In particular the current efforts to develop an interactional model of behaviour emphasize the cognitive interpretations of the person (his perceptions and constructs) in a given situation and it is to these issues in particular that this paper is directed.

A brief and, admittedly, personalized account of the state of knowledge to which the so-called trait approach has brought us in the personality/sports behaviour area will first be given. The possibilities of an interaction approach involving personal dispositions and cognitive styles will then be developed.

The trait approach

Personality traits have been described as the relatively stable and enduring elements explaining behaviour, though Cattell, in whose current and monumental researches the word trait most often appears, distinguishes 'source traits' (i.e. relatively enduring dimensions of personality) from 'surface traits' (i.e. dimensions susceptible to change). Nevertheless 'trait' and 'type' approaches tend to emphasize the developed and established personality 'equipment' of the individual which gives rise to a certain expectation of his routine behaviour.

A number of useful reviews are available (e.g. Hendry, 1970; Harris, 1972; Hardman, 1973; Kane, 1976) which, while not totally in agreement, give a useful indication of the present understanding of the link between personality and physical abilities and also point to many of the possibilities for clarifying the nature of this link. The studies included in these reviews tend to fall into two categories; those attempting a relatively simple personality (via Cattell or Eysenck) description and/or comparison of selected groups of athletes and a few correlational studies demonstrating the relationship between personality and physical ability variables. While reviewers have found difficulty in coming to unequivocal or generalized conclusions, there is a tendency for the male athlete to be described in terms of extraverted and stable dispositions (such as high dominance, social aggression, leadership, tough-mindedness and emotional control) and for women athletes to be shown as relatively anxious extraverts. However, if, for example, we were to find that certain personality variables are related to outstanding goalkeeping ability in soccer, it would be surprising to find that all the same variables are linked with high level performance in javelin throwing, cross-country running or rifle shooting. A few illustrations and examples will summarize the kinds of analyses that have been undertaken.

Descriptive profiles and comparisons

Figure 1 typifies the profile description. This early and classic account by Heusner

(1952) describes champion athletes as stable (C, L, O traits) and extraverted (A, E, F, traits). However, subsequent studies have never demonstrated such a definite description of champion athletes. Although this kind of profile analysis has been used mainly to establish fundamental descriptive data of a variety of athletes and activity groups a number of researchers have found that when the activity and level of participation are held constant interesting similarities of personality type have been recorded for groups of, for example, racing drivers (Ogilvie, 1968), wrestlers (Kroll, 1967), soccer players and (Fig. 2) women athletes (Kane, 1966).

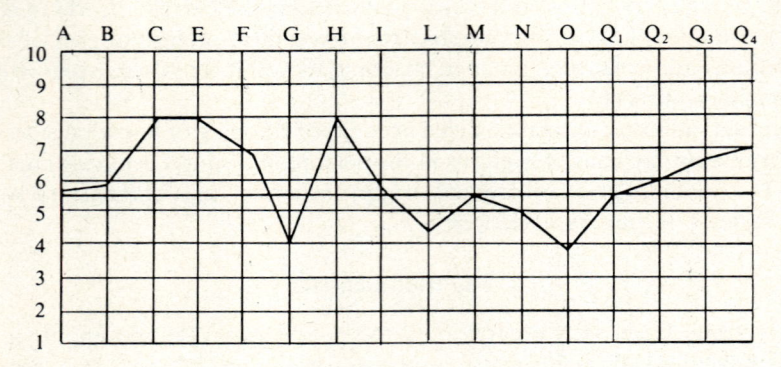

Fig. 1. Profile analysis of champion athletes (Heusner, 1952): A, sociability; B, general ability; C, ego strength; E, dominance; F, surgency; G, conscientiousness; H, adventurousness; I, sensitiveness; L, protension; M, Bohemianism; N, shrewdness; O, insecurity; Q_1, radicalism; Q_2, self-sufficiency; Q_3, will-power; Q_4, tenseness.

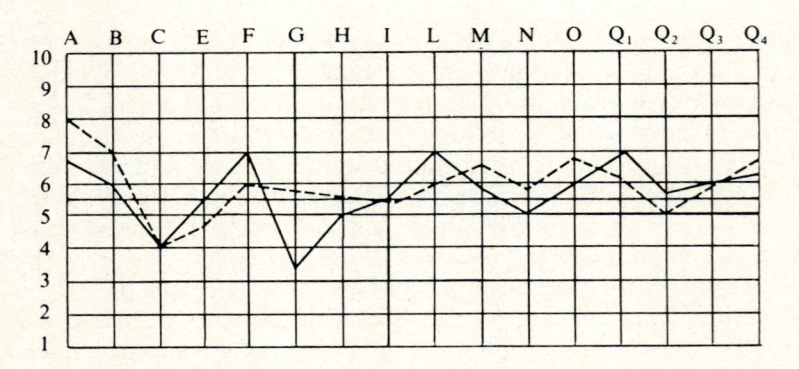

Fig. 2. Profile analysis of women swimmers and track athletes (Kane, 1966): symbols as for Fig. 1.

Comparison of profile data has often been reduced to focus on similarities and differences based on the two major Eysenckian dimensions of extraversion and neuroticism. In most of these studies, even when significant differences (from the population norms or from other criterion groups) have been established, the problem has been to interpret the real meaning of such group differences. Moreover, group means hide individual differences and the operational implications, for an individual or group, of being, for example, more or less extraverted, tough-minded or emotionally stable have seldom been touched on.

This may well have resulted from researchers being more concerned with the personality tests and their popular descriptive meaning than with the theoretical framework which underpins the whole personality assessment procedure being used. Eysenck (1972) has constantly referred to this point and, in particular, to the way in which careful attention to the niceties of both personality theory and parameter values is needed in order to interpret experimental findings. As an illustration he refers to the proposed link between extraversion and conditionability and explains the contradictory findings of research in this area as being a direct reflection of the parameter values used; e.g. weak, unconditioned stimulus values favouring quick conditioning of introverts relative to extraverts, while strong unconditioned stimulus values have the opposite effect. It seems that, in the kind of investigations so far described which attempt to relate personality to performance, little account has been taken of such theoretical subtleties, so that results have tended to be poorly interpreted. Lack of reference to a sound theoretical framework has, moreover, caused confusion in trying to explain apparent inconsistencies in findings by different investigators. Nevertheless the better descriptive studies, based on the measurement of traits, have been useful in opening up the possibilities for further advanced study. Practically none of them pretended to offer a predictive platform for sports performance.

Correlational analyses

Surprisingly few correlational studies, attempting to tease out the nature of the personality/physical performance relationship, have been reported. Where a relationship exists appropriate correlational procedures could best demonstrate the circumstances under which it is maximized and this, in turn, could give rise to a better understanding of the nature of the relationship. Some attempts to consider the values of correlational strategies have been reported (Kane, 1970; 1972; 1976) and these have included intercorrelation to factor analysis, higher order factoring, multiple regression and canonical analysis. In these correlational studies the two domains – personality and gross physical (athletic) performance – were each assessed by a battery of tests among specialist men and women physical educationists.

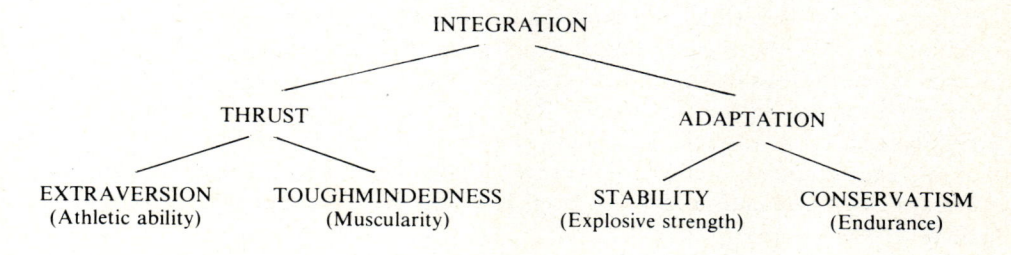

```
                        INTEGRATION
                       /           \
                THRUST              ADAPTATION
                /    \                /      \
        EXTRAVERSION  TOUGHMINDEDNESS  STABILITY  CONSERVATISM
      (Athletic ability) (Muscularity) (Explosive strength) (Endurance)
```

Fig. 3. Personality–athletic ability–hierarchical factor structure.

Figure 3 summarizes the higher order general factor structure and emphasizes that the largest second order factor links extraversion with general athletic ability (i.e. speed, strength and power). A series of multivariate analyses demonstrated, as expected, the increasing value of the correlation coefficients from simple bivariate techniques (i.e. one personality variable with one physical performance variable), through multiple correlation, to canonical correlation. A number of these analyses with multivariate vectors have produced significant coefficients averaging about 0·7, permitting in many cases a clear interpretation of tough-minded, stable extraversion accompanying general athletic ability. Notwithstanding the known instability of factor and vector structure, these correlational studies have clearly taken the study of the personality–physical performance relationship to a serious and useful level. Here again, however, the purpose of the studies using trait measures was not to seek predictive indices of sports performance but rather to search for an understanding of the relationship between the two domains.

Theoretical considerations

Descriptive and correlational studies of the kind so far described are highly valuable if designed and interpreted within the context of a sound theoretical framework and if well standardized measures (with or without trait theory implications) and reasonably sophisticated analyses are used. Few studies so far reported seem to satisfy these criteria but, as a contribution to seeking an appropriate framework, three observations are offered to indicate the general value to the teacher or coach of relatively simple information.

If, for simplicity, consideration of personality is limited to the two major dimensions extraversion and anxiety (neuroticism), in order to investigate the performance via the arousal paradigm, the Eysenckian version of the causative neurological substrates of behaviour summated in the excitatory–inhibitory balance might be considered. Such a theoretical approach has the advantage of allowing reasoned comparisons with mainstream Russian psychologists whose applied work, though more clinically based, is nevertheless centrally concerned with excitatory–inhibitory processes following the lead of Pavlov and, more recently, Teplov (1972).

Again following Eysenckian theory and empirical evidence and restricting consideration to extraversion and anxiety (neuroticism) there are some interesting guidelines for the teacher or coach with respect to performance and training. It has been strongly argued (e.g. Langer, 1966) that, in sport, anxiety is the most important factor in performance. Anxiety, which is a composite of a relatively stable trait and a situationally-specific state, may be regarded as a strong drive to autonomic and perhaps cortical arousal. The net arousal level under conditions of stress will depend on the athlete's trait level and his ability to control anxiety. The teacher's or coach's problem therefore is to manipulate, as far as possible, the athlete's anxiety-based arousal with a view to bringing him into the competition at a level which will give rise to optimal performance. Some success in such a daunting task has been reported by some sports psychologists (e.g. Ogilvie, 1968).

If anxiety (or neuroticism) appears to be the most important constituent of athletic performance, then it might appear that the other major personality dimensions, introversion/extraversion may be of greater significance for athletic training. The essentially physical training that athletes undergo is intended to increase performance potential by regular and systematic submission to strenuous programmes aimed at physiological adaptation and contextual skill development. The extent to which an athlete submits and perseveres with these demanding, repetitive and often dull programmes, and therefore the benefit he gains in performance potential, is likely to be associated with his standing on the introversion/extraversion continuum. It seems not unreasonable to expect, for instance, that, compared with the more introverted, the more extraverted athletes would persevere longer where pain is involved, would react more positively to incentives, would need more variation in training stimuli, would condition more slowly to risky and dangerous situations, would react more positively to public criticism, would train better in group situations, would more quickly develop reactive inhibition especially in massed practice circumstances, and would be less consistent in training effort and results. Additionally, Eysenck and his colleagues have demonstrated the way in which extraverts and introverts systematically differ in the learning and performance of a number of fine and gross skills and in activities where perceptual processes (e.g. vigilance, selective attention, kinesthetic awareness and recall) are important. Such a catalogue of the behaviour patterns of introverts and extraverts must constitute a very useful basis on which coaches may plan schedules to maximize the training effect on their athletes.

The interactional approach

For the past 10 years a fascinating debate has been developing which goes to the roots of personality psychology, and reverberations have been felt in sports research. As a result a number of alternative models and approaches have been proposed in an effort to explain a more vital and dynamic concept of personality, and the one most favoured at the moment is the interactional model which centres on the cognitive perceptions and interpretations of the person in a given situation.

An interactionist model of behaviour appears to be a matter of re-emphasis rather than incorporating a new mode of thinking. Indeed, the layman might be forgiven for assuming that to consider both the person and the situation in attempting to explain behaviour was commonsense. Moreover, interactionist explanations of behaviour go back quite a way in the psychology literature. Lewin (1935) suggested the formula $B = f(P,S)$ where B refers to the behaviour resulting from a choice of possibilities or a performance measurement on a scale; P refers to structural dimensions (physiological and psychological) represented in personality measures; S refers to variable aspects of the situation and f refers to the functional relationship (or interaction between P and S in explaining B).

Since 1935, there has been a consistent flow of research following Lewin's general interaction theory of behaviour and emphasizing different aspects of it. Present day interactionists (e.g. Mischel, 1976; Endler & Magnusson, 1976) apparently wish to attribute overriding importance in behaviour to the $P \times S$ interaction and support their case in two ways – by theoretical postulates concerning the way a person construes a situation and by demonstrating the relatively large size of the $P \times S$ variance in selected studies (Bowers, 1973; Argyle, 1976).

The interactionist approach is of undoubted interest to sports psychologists, who have always recognized the variable effects on performance of different sport situations, particularly where competitiveness and stress are high. The attractiveness of interactionist explanations of behaviour seems therefore reasonably assured if only to complement trait descriptions. Some attempts to follow this line of thinking in sports research are becoming increasingly evident, though Langer (1966) had earlier planned a model design for investigating behaviour and performance in different situations of sporting stress. The study monitored anxiety, as measured by the IPAT scale, of university footballers during the off-season (no stress), during the pre-game period (high stress) and immediately after the games (reduced stress) throughout a season and in concluding that anxiety level was a most important determinant of football performance Langer demonstrated the sensitivity of the IPAT anxiety scale for recording changes linked with levels of sporting stress and performance.

More recently the increased use in sports behaviour research of various adaptations of Speilberger's (1972) State/Trait Anxiety Inventory is a strong indication of the need to distinguish between the individual's chronic anxiety level (his anxiety trait score) and the additional anxiety attributable to the anticipation of or the involvement in a sports competition (his anxiety state score). In general this state–trait approach, especially when refined specifically for the sports situation as in Martens' (1976) Sports Competition Anxiety Test, has tended to support the person–situation model of anxiety: those with higher A-trait scores manifest greater A-state changes (increases) in the face of ego-threatening competitive situations. There are, of course, ways in which a coach or the athlete himself may seek to reduce state anxiety and thereby enhance performance, but a discussion of these procedures is beyond the scope of this paper.

Personal dispositions and cognitive styles

The central importance given to cognition, in an interactional approach to behaviour, calls for an appreciation of the very personal and idiosyncratic ways in which a person views, perceives, construes and interprets a situation. A number of such personal dispositions and cognitive styles have been proposed in the psychological literature over the past 20 years and some appear to be particularly relevant to the context of sports involvement and performance (e.g. Harris, 1978; Kane, 1978). The final part of this paper gives a brief commentary on some that seem to be interrelated.

Achievement motivation

Achievement motivation is the most widely studied personal disposition. McClelland (1961) indicated that those with a high need to achieve (nach) showed a major concern with doing something well and tended to be independent and persistent. Subsequent research indicates that achievement motivation is learned at an early age and becomes a relatively stable aspect of behaviour and that those with a high need for achievement perform better on tasks requiring individual initiative, take responsibility for outcomes, go for moderate risk-taking options and are, in general, motivated by a 'wish to succeed' rather than a desire to 'avoid failure'. The theoretical formulation of the achievement motivation approach to explaining behaviour is summarized in Fig. 4 as an approach versus avoidance model. It includes two decision making components, subjective probability (P) and incentive value (I) which are placed in direct inverse relationship to each other, and two kinds of construct – a motive to achieve success (Ms) and a motive to avoid failure (Mf).

The attractiveness of the achievement motivation disposition to researchers in physical education and sport has not been as high as one might expect, though a number of studies have satisfactorily demonstrated that achievement motivation is linked with the degree and nature of sports involvement (Weinberg, 1975; Dunleavy, 1979) and with sports related risk-taking and intrinsic motivation (Lefebvre, 1979).

$$T_s = M_s \times P_s \times I_s$$

The tendency to approach success = Motive to achieve success × Probability of success × Incentive value of success

$$T_{af} = M_{af} \times P_f \times I_f$$

The tendency to avoid failure = Motive to avoid failure × Probability of failure × Incentive value of failure

Fig. 4. Approach–avoidance model of behaviour.

Causal attribution

It seems likely that the development and subsequent shifts of achievement motivation will be affected by the way in which individuals attribute causes to their successes and failures. Rotter (1966) suggested that high achievers attribute the causes of success or failure internally, that is to their own ability and effort, whereas low achievers tend to consider outcomes to be largely externally determined, by the task difficulty and luck. According to attribution theory the perceived causes of success or failure have both emotional and behavioural consequences and affect the degree and nature of further involvement and the aspiration, expectations and self-esteem brought to it. Weiner *et al.* (1971) have proposed a summary model of attribution theory which includes four causal elements: luck, ability, effort and task. These elements are located along two independent dimensions (Table 1): locus of control (internal versus external) and stability (stable versus unstable). Ability and task difficulty are understood to be relatively unchanged over time, whereas effort and luck vary. Weiner *et al.* suggest that the locus of control

Table 1. Dimensions of causal attributions

Stability	Locus of control	
	Internal	External
Stable	Ability	Task difficulty
Unstable	Effort	Luck

dimension determines the emotional reactions to winning or losing and the stability dimension predicates the expectancies for future performance. More particularly, success associated with effort and ability (internal) increases the feeling of pride, but concerning expectation in future performance the attribution of each of the four elements gives rise to different interpretations – success associated with ability and task performance (stable) leads to the expectation of a similar performance but not if associated with effort or luck (unstable).

The causal attribution model has obvious value for interpreting competitive sports behaviour and a few studies have indicated interesting possibilities. Lefebvre (1979), for example, has studied aspects of the attributions ascribed by coaches and athletes for winning and losing and his findings support Weiner *et al.*'s general contentions in that effort and ability (internal) were considered by both men and women subjects as the primary causes for successful achievement, while lack of effort and bad luck were the elements regularly attributed as causes of failure. Roberts (1977) undertook a detailed analysis of the effects of winning and losing on the causal attributions of Little League athletes. He found that, in line with general attribution theory, teams with a history of winning were (a) more confident about the next game, (b) attributed their winning to ability and effort and (c) when they occasionally lost attributed this to other elements. Teams with a history of losing were understandably less confident, saw themselves as lower in ability and attributed occasional winning to effort.

The tendency is therefore for consistent winning or losing to be attributed to the internal dimensions, and to ability in particular. While high achievement oriented individuals attribute failure to lack of effort, others do not. The low achievement oriented youngsters, even in Roberts' study of young athletes, linked their lack of success with perceptions of inadequacy in their ability and effort; that is, they felt they had no control over the outcome. Such perceptions will surely turn both the young and the not-so-young away from achievement-oriented sports involvement. While the curriculum of physical and sports education will properly introduce children to success/failure experiences, one speculates on the effect of an overweaning emphasis on competition, with the attendant winners and losers. Is it possible that children who regularly experience failure will begin to avoid involvement, feeling that they have little or no control over the outcome?

Self-efficacy

Bandura (1977) recently outlined a theory of self-efficacy, the central theme being that the strength of an individual's convictions of his effectiveness determines the amount of effort and persistence he will apply to a task. Assuming that the individual is capable (has sufficient skill) and is motivated, the actual performance is likely to be predicted by the person's belief in his own competence relative to the particular task. In one of the few studies relating the theory to sports, Mahoney & Avener (1977) report a generally high self-efficacy expectation level for the USA men's gymnastic team, and moderately high correlation between pre-meeting self-confidence scores and actual performance. Many coaches are aware of the apparent appropriateness of this self-efficacy theory in reverse in explaining athletes' 'sticking points'. Athletes often perceive difficulty in going beyond a certain performance level, and only by some deception can they be enticed and convinced of their ability to perform at a higher level. In a similar way, placebo studies in the areas of sports nutrition and drugs point to a gap between ability and performance that may well be explained by self-efficacy theory. The issue is clearly one that merits the careful collaborative investigation of the coaches and the behavioural scientists.

Imagery

Mental practice and mental rehearsal are well reviewed in the physical education and sports literature. Corbin (1972) makes a cautious interpretation:–

'There seems to be little doubt that mental practice can positively affect skilled motor performance, especially when practice conditions are "optional". It is equally clear however that mental practice is not always an aid to performance'.

Apparently, familiarity with the task and the timing of the mental practice are the two major factors which may affect the influence of this procedure. Mahoney & Avener (1977) have also suggested that there may be two kinds of athletes when it comes to utilizing imagery techniques – the ones who use 'internal' (phenomenological) imagery, and the others who use 'external' (third person) imagery. These authors have reported tentatively on a positive relationship between internal imagery and success in gymnastics, and they have also suggested the wider use in skill-learning situations of the 'coping/mastery' models that are regularly used in cognitive-behavioural research.

Attentional styles

The importance of selective attention has only recently been emphasized in the process of skills acquisition but the generalized importance of 'paying attention' or 'concentrating' throughout an athletic performance has long been recommended by coaches. Genov (1970) found that, Zhabotinski, the outstanding weight lifter, increased his preparatory concentration time with each attempt at a heavier weight and gave more concentration time to the more complex lifts. Nideffer (1976) has investigated the attentional processes that regulate human behaviour and has suggested applications for sports performance. He writes:– 'It is hard to imagine a variable more central to performance than the ability to direct and control one's attention'. His Test of Attentional and Interpersonal Style (TAIS) incorporates dimensions which distinguish between internal and external attention styles and between styles described as either broad or narrow. The TAIS scale measuring funnelled attention was found by the author to discriminate between consistency of performance among athletes.

From other studies (e.g. Fenz, 1969) it seems likely that a strategy for shifting attention (especially from internal to external styles) may be particularly helpful in some stressful performances, and may even reduce arousal from high to optimal levels.

Intrinsic motivation

The literature of psychology is heavy with theories and speculations about motivation. Earlier reviews have attempted to unravel this confused area of psychology (e.g. Kane, 1972; Alderman, 1974). The purpose here is to direct attention to the attractiveness of intrinsic motivation as one developing interpretation of motivation which seems particularly suited to athletic experience and involvement. Although the terms intrinsic and extrinsic have been commonplace in discussions of motivation for some time, the notion of intrinsic motivation has been elaborated in recent years to take account of a wave of interest in personality psychology that focuses on personal satisfaction, meaning, fulfilment levels of consciousness, self-actualization and joy. For those scientists, coaches and athletes who recognize that involvement in sports is not solely about successful performance but about inner feelings, experiences and satisfaction, this psychological approach deserves their careful attention. Its roots are in existential psychology and phenomenology and in such notions as, for example, 'personal knowledge' (Polanyi, 1958) and 'needs of the mind' (Maddi, 1970), which lay emphasis on the unique knowledge derived by the individual from his perceptions in the course of satisfying his need to understand himself. Maslow (1970) most nearly sets out a comprehensive, if speculative, theory to encompass the main elements of this psychological thrust which has been referred to as third-force psychology. Maslow categorized human needs into five sets which are placed in a hierarchical arrangement of importance and development, ranging from the lower level of physiological needs through those of security, safety, belonging and respect, to the final monarchical need for 'self-actualization'. The self-actualizing person, according to Maslow, would have clear perceptions, be self-accepting, spontaneous, autonomous and natural, appreciate the basic qualities of life, have a deep affection and sympathy for all humans, enjoy peak experiences (i.e. mystical or transpersonal experiences) and know himself in order to maximize his potentialities. For Maslow, self-actualization is regarded as the highest and most fulfilled state of human existence.

In more conventional psychological terms Deci (1975) touches on the processes involved in self-actualizing behaviour in his treatise on intrinsic motivation. Deci develops the model of intrinsically motivated behaviours as ones chosen by the person in the pursuit of 'feeling competent' and 'self determining' in relation to his environment. He assumes that in these pursuits the person has access to his own internal states (understanding, orientations, attitudes, etc.) in a way which others cannot, and effectively argues the importance of cognitions and experiences in changing the individual's internal states. Czikszentmihalyi (1975), investigating the inner experiences concerned with joy and pleasure in play games and life styles, described a common form of experience enjoyed by the intrinsically motivated. He called this experience 'flow' which incorporated feelings of exhilaration, creative accomplishment and heightened functioning. He writes, 'they concentrate their attention on a limited stimulus field, forget personal problems, lose their sense of time and of themselves, feel competent and in control, and have a sense of harmony and union with their surroundings. To the extent that these elements of experience are present, a person enjoys what he or she is doing and ceases to worry about whether the activity will be productive or whether it will be rewarded'.

One of the most common approaches today towards re-establishing the body as a sensitive vehicle for the recognition and enjoyment of feelings is running or jogging. The experiences of runners of all kinds are being increasingly recorded and analysed, and accounts ranging from mystical and ecstatic interpretations to physiologically sensuous occurrences are to be found. As part of a general revolution which has 'rediscovered' the body as the source of awareness and vital sensation, running seems to be successfully competing with more elaborate practices involving biofeedback mechanisms, various body therapies and even the martial arts, as a means of generating and controlling inner states.

The dimensions of intrinsic states of being such as joy, delight and ecstacy are indeed hard to record, but their existence is undoubted. For those involved in sports activities at any level the intrinsic rewards and satisfactions are clear and are unmistakably the product of a sensitized body.

References

ALDERMAN, R. (1974) *Psychological Behaviour in Sport.* Saunders, Philadelphia.
ARGYLE, M. (1976) Personality and social behaviour. In: *Personality.* Edited by R. Harré. Blackwell, Oxford.
BANDURA, A. (1977) Toward a unifying theory of behavioural change. *Psychol. Rev.* **84**, 46.
BOWERS, K. (1973) Situationism in psychology: an analysis and critique. *Psychol. Rev.* **30**, 53.
COFER, C. & JOHNSON, W. (1960) Personality dynamics in relation to exercise and sport. In: *Science and Medicine of Exercise and Sport.* Edited by W. Johnson. Harper, New York.
COOPER, L. (1969) Athletics, activity and personality: a review of the literature. *Res. Q.* **40**, 42.
CORBIN, C. (1972) Mental practice. In: *Ergogenic Aids and Muscular Performance.* Edited by Morgan. Academic Press, New York.
CZIKSZENTMIHALYI, M. (1975) *Beyond Boredom and Anxiety.* Jossey-Bass, San Francisco.
DECI, E.L. (1975) *Intrinsic Motivation.* Plenum, New York.
DUNLEAVY, A.O. (1979) The effect of achievement motivation and sports exposure upon the sports involvement of American college males. *Int. J. Sport Psychol.* **10**, 17.
ENDLER, N.S. & MAGNUSSON, D. (1976) Personality and person by situation interactions. In: *Interactional Psychology and Personality.* Edited by N.S. Endler & D. Magnusson. Wiley, Washington.
EYSENCK, H.J. (1972) Human typology, higher nervous activity and factor analysis. In: *Biological Bases of Individual Behaviour.* Edited by V.D. Nebylitsyn & J.A. Gray. Academic Press, London.
FENZ, W.D. (1969) Stress in the air. *Psychology Today*, **27**, 22.
GENOV, F. (1970) The nature of mobilization readiness of the sportsman and the influence of different factors upon its formation. In: *Contemporary Psychology of Sport.* Edited by Kenyon. Athletic Institute, Chicago.
HARDMAN, K. (1973) A dual approach to the study of personality and performance in sport. In: *Personality and Performance in Physical Education and Sport.* Edited by Whiting. Kimpton, London.
HARRIS, D.V. (1972) *Involvement in Sport.* Lea & Febinger, Philadelphia.
HARRIS, D.V. (1978) Assessment of motivation in sport and physical education. In: *Sport Psychology.* Edited by W. Straub. Mouvement Publications, New York.
HENDRY, L. (1970) Some notions on personality and sporting ability: certain comparisons with scholastic achievement. *Quest,* **13**, 89.
HEUSNER, W. (1952) *Personality Traits of Champion and Former Champion Athletes.* MA thesis, University of Illinois, Champaign.
KANE, J.E. (1966) Personality description of soccer ability. *Res. in phys. Educ.* **1**, 5.
KANE, J.E. (1970) Personality and physical abilities. In: *Contemporary Psychology of Sport.* Edited by Kenyon. Athletic Institute, Chicago.
KANE, J.E. (1972) *Psychological Aspects of Physical Education and Sport.* Routledge & Kegan Paul, London.
KANE, J.E. (1976) Personality and performance in sport. In: *Sports Medicine.* Edited by J. Williams & P. Sperryn. Arnold, London.
KANE, J.E. (1978) Personality research: the current controversy and implications for sports studies. In: *Sport Psychology.* Edited by W. Straub. Mouvement Publications, New York.
KROLL, W. (1967) Sixteen personality factor profiles of collegiate wrestlers. *Res. Q.* **38**, 43.
KROLL, W. (1970) Current strategies and problems in personality assessment of athletes. In: *Proceedings of the Symposium on Motor Learning.* Edited by L. Smith. Athletic Institute, Chicago.
LANGER, P. (1966) Varsity football performance. *Perceptual and Motor Skills,* **23**, 53.
LEFEBVRE, L. (1979) Achievement motivation and causal attribution in male and female athletes. *Int. J. Sport Psychol.* **10**, 19.
LEWIN, K. (1935) *A Dynamic Theory of Personality.* McGraw-Hill, New York.

MADDI, S.R. (1970) The search for meaning. *Nebraska Symposium on Motivation,* **18**, 14.
MAHONEY, M.J. & AVENER, M. (1977) Psychology of the elite athlete. *Cognitive Therapy and Research,* **1**, 14.
MARTENS, R. (1976) *The Sport Competition Anxiety Test.* Human Kinetic Publications, Champaign, Illinois.
MASLOW, A.H. (1970) *Motivation and Personality.* Harper & Row, New York.
MCCLELLAND, D. (1961) *The Achieving Society.* Van Nostrand, New York.
MISCHEL, W. (1976) *Introduction to Personality.* Holt, Rinehart, New York.
NIDEFFER, R.M. (1976) *The Inner Athlete.* Thomas Crowell, New York.
OGILVIE, B. (1968) Psychological consistencies within the personalities of high level competitors. *J. Am. Med. Ass.* **28**, 14.
OGILVIE, B. & TUTKO, T. (1966) *Problem Athletes and How to Handle Them.* Pelham, London.
POLANYI, M. (1958) *Personal Knowledge.* University of Chicago Press, Chicago.
PONSONBY, D. & YAFFE, M. (1976) Psychology takes the soccer field. *FIFA News,* July.
ROBERTS, G.C. (1977) Children in competition: assignment of responsibility for winning and losing. In: *Proceedings NCPEAM/NAPEW.* Athletic Institute, Chicago.
ROTTER, J.P. (1966) Generalised expectancies for internal v external control of reinforcement. *Psychol. Monogr.* **81**, 15.
RUSHALL, B. (1973) The status of personality research and application in sports and physical education. *J. Sports Med. phys. Fitness,* **13**, 23.
RUSHALL, B. & SIEDENTROP, D. (1975) *The Development and Control of Behaviour in Sport and Physical Education.* Lea & Febiger, Philadelphia.
SINGER, R.N. (1975) *Motor Learning and Human Performance.* Macmillan, New York.
SPEILBERGER, C. (1972) Anxiety as an emotional state. In: *Current Trends in Theory and Research,* Vol. 1. Edited by C. Speilberger. Academic Press, New York.
TEPLOV, B.M. (1972) The problem of types of human higher nervous activity and methods of determining them. In: *Biological Bases of Individual Behaviour.* Edited by V.D. Nebylitsyn & J.A. Gray. Academic Press, London.
VANEK, M. & CRATTY, B.J. (1970) *Psychology and the Superior Athlete.* Macmillan, London.
WEINBERG, W. (1975) *Perceived Instrumentality as a Determinant of Achievement-related Performance for Groups of Athletes and Non-athletes.* PhD thesis, University of Maryland.
WEINER, B., FRIEZE, S., KUKIA, H., REED, L., REST, S. & ROSENBAUM, R.M. (1971) *Perceiving the Causes of Success and Failure.* General Learning Press, New York.

Biosocial Aspects of Sport

COMMENT

BRUCE TULLOH

Marlborough College, Wiltshire

There is not enough time to talk as much as I would like on John Kane's lecture but having had the opportunity to read the full paper I recommend the rest of you to spend time reading and digesting that because there are so many useful things one could get from it.

Being a biologist and teacher I look at things from a slightly different angle and I think that sporting activity has six distinct roles in the life of man. We start with child's play – trial and error learning – and that becomes adolescent character development, forming those traits of behaviour and the establishment of trait patterns which have already begun during the child's play era; then you go into what I call the 'simulated battle' phase, which is a test of the physical and mental ability of the individual, in a ritualized way. I was quite horrified yesterday to hear one of the speakers express surprise that anyone should want to fight. The very basis of sport is this relentless drive which forces a competitor into these extreme situations, the drive which produces a burst over the last few hundred metres of a race. It is the same basic drive which makes a 'hell's angel' get on his motor bicycle and 'bomb' down the high street; the understanding and the channelling of this drive is one of our most important roles as educators and coaches. Related to that, in our civilized society, is the development of confidence and ability, so simulated or ritualized battle is helping us to understand our limitations; as the battle becomes more and more real we are putting ourselves into a success or failure situation which we must learn to handle. Some will turn right away from it and others will learn to cope, and so it gives us a model of life. Only in sports can we go through all the phases of life in such a short space of time and the lesson which everybody learns is that 'you can't win them all'. Once we learn to accept failure as well as success we have gone a long way.

The next role of sport in life is as a profession and a way of earning a living, perhaps as an entertainer, professional sports instructor or an administrator; or it also plays its role as a leisure pursuit, as a means of forming a harmonious life. I found Maslow's concept of the self-actualizing man to be a very good one, close to the Confucian ideal of the complete man: it is good that we now recognize that physical performance and physical condition are significant in forming the complete person and that sporting activity has to be related to the person's life. It interacts too with his business life and his social life, but not always positively. The final role of sporting activity comes in old age, as a means of giving significance to your activities and thus prolonging life. We must consider all these when thinking about how sport affects personality and life.

We do not, in this or any country, get the sports we deserve or even the sports we want. A country tends to get the sports it can afford at any stage of development, as exemplified by, for example, the decline in archery since the 14th century or the rise of Grand Prix racing. We can relate sporting success in a country to its curve of affluence and say: 'at this point in the growth of a country it will produce good athletes.'

We must consider next what effect the actual sports being done are having on the people living there and whether changes would be desirable. The part of public schools in setting trends in sport has been mentioned. Sport was then supposed to be character forming, but now we realize that sport does not really mould character but gives an opportunity for certain traits to develop. John Kane has shown that certain aspects of the character will alter through involvement in sport and all of us involved in coaching can think of examples of this. Anecdotal evidence shows that character does change with involvement in sport but the same sport can affect different personalities in different ways. We all know the type of schoolboy sportsman, very gifted physically, who always wins, despite the fact that he does no training and smokes heavily. Sport does nothing much for him as a person and the coach has an entirely different job trying to give him the right sort of incentives than he has when he is handling the more timid and less able person. If there is a current trend in public school sport it is this one of giving the opportunity for the right activity being available to the right person, so as to achieve wisdom, self-knowledge and self-satisfaction. It is in this sense that we have to approach sport, bearing in mind that the development of a personality does not stop when a person reaches physical maturity but goes on into his adult working life and even beyond that.

Biosocial Aspects of Sport

SPORT AND PHYSICAL HEALTH

E. JOAN BASSEY AND P.H. FENTEM

*Department of Physiology and Pharmacology, Medical School,
Queens Medical Centre, Nottingham*

Summary. The role of sport is considered in the light of the health and physical capabilities of the average members of the population. It is shown how the different aspects of physical capacity can be extended, not only in the average sedentary person, but also in the elderly and the physically incapacitated. The efficacy of sport in the prevention of disease is also discussed.

Introduction

In recent years the hope that exercise might favourably influence coronary heart disease has led to renewed interest in exercise in general. There are now government sponsored campaigns in North America, West Germany, Scandinavia and Australia, promoting sport and exercise for the sake of the health of the population. So far governmental interest in Britain has been slight and the attitude of the medical profession less than enthusiastic. It is no wonder the man in the street either agrees that exercise is a good thing but does nothing about it, or dismisses the benefits altogether.

What are the benefits, and is there evidence that they are real? Some years ago the Sports Council asked us to find out by making a search of the available scientific literature. We have looked for answers under two headings. Does exercise improve the health of those who are already well? Can it ameliorate, prevent or cure disease?

The reply to the first question is a resounding 'yes'. Evidence which has appeared during the last ten years has focused attention on the working muscle and shown that it is here that remarkable improvements can occur. It is these changes which underly the improvements in health and well-being which exercise can produce.

The reply to the second question comes in two parts: exercise can ameliorate the effects of many chronic diseases, for the same reason that it is of benefit to those who are well, and it can also, in a few specific instances, contribute to the control and cure of disease.

If evidence is to be presented then the word 'sport' in the title needs to be interpreted rather liberally as 'exercise'. This is for two reasons. Most of the studies on which the evidence depends have inevitably been of exercise rather than sport because of the need to control and measure things if they are to be properly studied. Also, because we want to talk about people of moderate physical ability, not about athletes. The athlete often has a special genetic endowment and his levels of activity may be well above those which are necessary for the maintenance of adequate physical health. The proposition is that the health of the man who is suffering from an inability to run for the bus without getting breathless and exhausted could be greatly improved by a moderate increase in physical activity.

The problem of defining health is difficult. It is much easier to define illness. Epidemiologists have two categories, well or ill, when investigating the incidence of disease. A middle category might be inserted between the two in which people suffer from minor ailments which they treat with aspirins and liver pills without consulting the doctor. It would be of great interest to know whether exercise can shift people across this borderline from indifferent health into positive well-being but no good evidence has been found so far. A third approach is to think of a continuous line stretching from severe illness at the negative end to exuberant well-being at the positive end. This is particularly useful for considering improvements in positive health in people who are already well. Many factors add together to determine the exact position of a person on this line, and the evidence suggests that exercise can be particularly important.

Enhancement of health in normal people

Let us take the image of positive good health, for example, an exuberant youngster who enjoys vigorous exercise, indulges in it frequently, and clearly has a high capacity for it. Then think of older people and how they talk of the importance of retaining their health and strength. They mean something more than freedom from disease. So it seems reasonable to equate positive health with the strength to cope with the physical demands of life. If this definition is accepted and it is agreed that physical strength, meaning capacity for work, is one important element in physical health, then we have a basis for measurement and discussion.

The capacity for physical work rests on three distinct physiological bases which are determined by three different components of muscle cells. There is muscle strength, capacity for rapid short-term energy release (sprinting ability) and capacity for prolonged energy release in more moderate activities (stamina). All three are needed for satisfactory living. The elderly need enough strength in the legs to raise their body weight from the chair and a young woman needs strength to pick up her 30-lb youngster. It is helpful to be able to sprint for the bus and essential to be able to catch up with the youngster as he speeds towards the dangers of the main road.

For the man in the street, stamina is likely to be the most important of the three, so concentrating on this, let us see what the Sports Council recommends as a suitable level to which the non-athlete should aspire if he is to enjoy good physical health. They have suggested 'standards' for a self-imposed performance test. Men aged between 35 and 45 years should be able to complete a mile in 10 minutes (older people and women are given some latitude). In order to cover a mile in 10 minutes you have to run at 6 mph, assuming a steady pace. The allowances made for age and sex leave the 65-year-old woman merely walking at less than 4 mph.

This choice of a 10-min mile was probably determined by considering the physical demands of the activities which make up a full and varied life. According to Astrand & Rodahl (1977), to run at 6 mph costs about 35 ml/kg/min in oxygen uptake (ie. 2·45 l/min for a 70-kg man). If we can manage that for 10 min without getting exhausted, then, by implication we have a maximum oxygen uptake well above 35 ml/kg/min (Fig. 1). This means we can do more strenuous things costing more than that for short periods, such as climbing the stairs with a 30-lb child, and can take in our stride a whole variety of activities costing less, like bicycling, dancing or tennis.

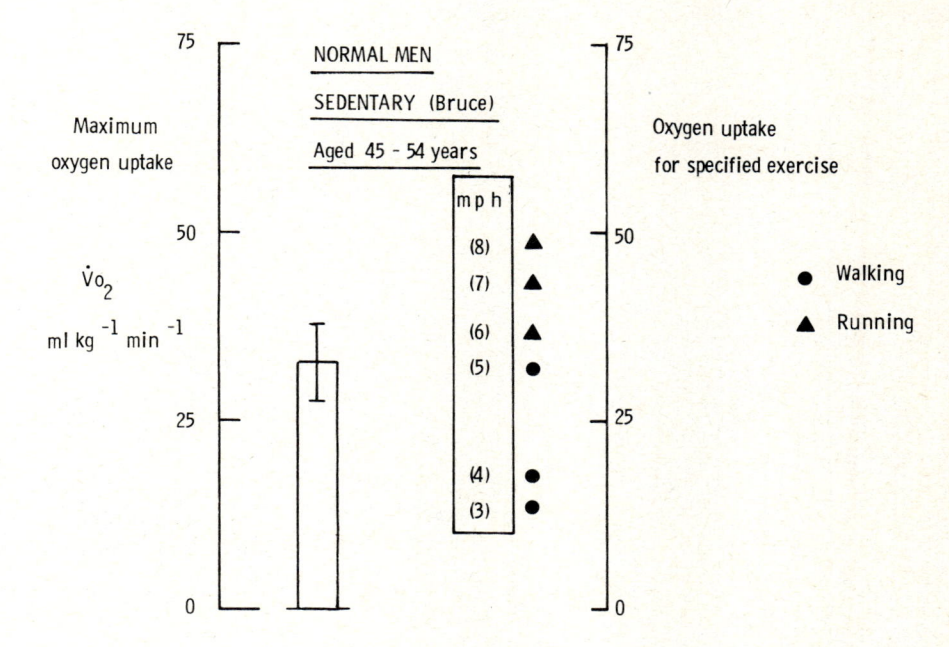

Fig. 1. Maximum oxygen uptake related to the oxygen cost of walking and running. The Sports Council recommended 10-min mile requires an ability to run at 6 mph if completed at a steady speed. Modified from Fentem, 1979.

The ability of muscle to respond to training by increasing its capacity for taking up and using oxygen is remarkable. Cardiac patients starting with a maximum capacity of only 25 ml/kg/min have been known to improve so much that they can run a marathon (Kavanagh, Shephard & Kennedy, 1977). This requires not only a maximum oxygen uptake of about 50 ml/kg/min but also the ability to tax about 80% of it for long periods. This is doubling the capacity to exercise. They now enjoy a level of positive good health which was probably beyond their wildest dreams before they had their heart attack. To their shame there are normal people, free from disease, with an exercise capacity as low as the cardiac patients. There is no reason why they should not improve to the same extent.

Fortunately muscle retains its capacity for improvement throughout life, however long it is left dormant. The unfortunate part is that it only stays improved with continued effort, and most people deteriorate slowly and insidiously as the years go by. The change will only be noticed if it happens quickly.

Professor Kozlowski brought us a story from Poland about a group of manual workers who were moved because of a factory closure from a factory where the work was very strenuous to another factory where it was not quite so hard. After a couple of weeks many of these men appeared in their doctors' surgeries complaining of vague ill-health. They said they felt tired and did not feel like gardening in the evenings any more. It transpired that they were suffering from the effects of a reduction in their levels of customary physical work. Because it had happened suddenly they noticed the change and interpreted it as a decline in physical health.

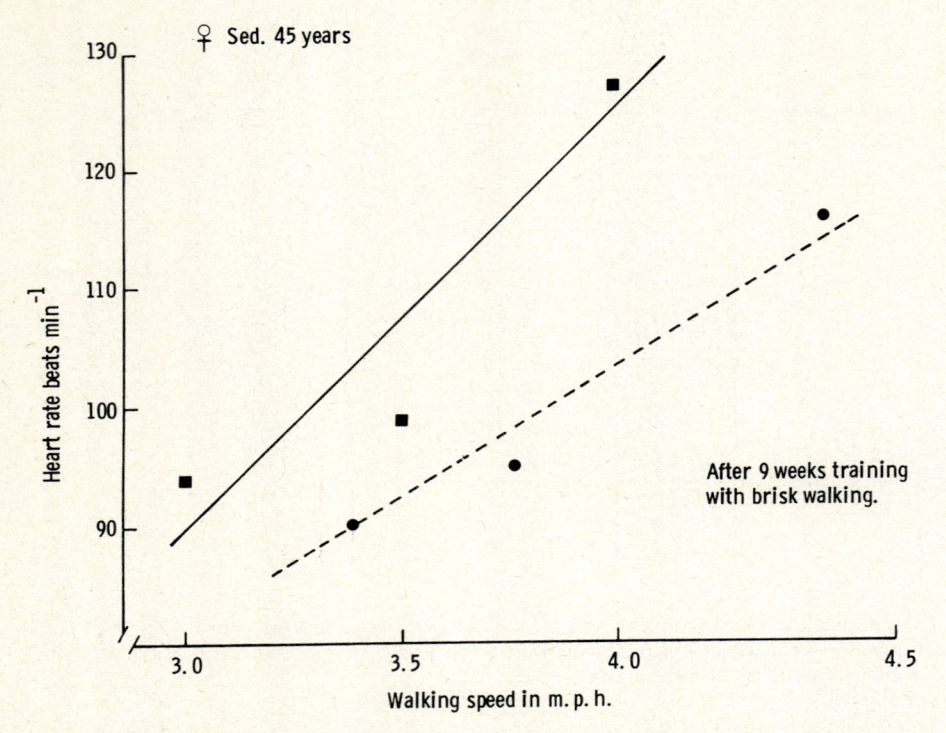

Fig. 2. The effects of moderate training on heart rate during a walking test (Bassey et al., 1976). Square symbols = before training, round symbols = after training.

Maximum oxygen uptake reflects the capacity of muscles to use it although they require the heart and lungs to deliver it to them and in a sedentary person the improvements produced in maximum oxygen uptake by training are largely in the muscles. In a normal person, free from disease, the respiratory system does not limit exercise despite acute awareness of breathlessness.

Neither is the cardiovascular system limiting in an untrained person although it may be in an endurance athlete. Voluntary overbreathing can achieve higher ventilation rates than are called upon during maximal exercise (Cotes, 1965), and even at maximal rates of work the blood leaving the lungs is almost fully loaded with oxygen. Oxygen is being delivered, there is even some left in the blood leaving the working muscle tissue, but the untrained muscle cannot extract it. The maximum performance of the heart can improve (Saltin et al., 1968) but even without that there is oxygen to spare for the muscles to take up. For normal people working at submaximal levels the emphasis must remain firmly on the muscles when training is considered.

For years we have all been side-tracked into thinking that it is only the cardiovascular system which changes with training because it is so much easier to measure heart rates than muscle oxygen uptake. At any given exercise intensity the trained individuals will have the lowest heart rates and those who are unused to exercise the highest. With training the heart rate comes down. Surprisingly, exercise as modest as brisk walking (20 min, three times a week) can produce a reduction in heart rate of some 10 beats/min at a standard walking speed of 3 mph (4·8 km/hr). This is in an individual who is not used to exercise (Fig. 2). What has caused the change? Neither the oxygen cost of the walking, nor the cardiac output changes; and those two facts are supported by many studies.

What has happened is that the same cardiac output is being achieved by a lower heart rate with a bigger stroke volume (cardiac output = heart rate × stroke volume). It is tempting to assume that the heart has grown bigger but there is no evidence for this happening to any great extent in moderate training. The heart chambers may be a little bigger to achieve the greater stroke volume but there is little if any increase in the mass of heart muscle. On the other hand the skeletal muscles have changed dramatically. This can be shown by testing the response to exercising the arms and legs after an exercise programme designed to train just the arms. The training effects on cardiovascular function are only apparent when the arms do the work (Clausen, Trap-Jensen & Lassen, 1970).

It is understood how some cardiovascular control mechanisms work but how the linear relation between heart rate and oxygen uptake is achieved remains a mystery. Even less is known about why this relation can change dramatically with training. One theory is that the muscles are making less demand on the central supplies of oxygenated blood flow because their capacity for taking up and using oxygen has improved. Heart rate and the distribution of blood flow away from organs other than muscle is centrally controlled, but there is also a reflex influence from the working muscles themselves (Fig. 3). It seems likely that the improvement in muscle function reduces that part of the drive to increase the heart rate which originates in the working muscles. A lower heart rate means there is a longer filling time between each beat and so the stroke volume rises. There is also a longer time for coronary blood flow which can only take place when the heart is relaxed. Almost the same effect can be achieved by blocking the effects of adrenaline on the heart with drugs. If the heart rate drops then the heart is doing less work for the same cardiac output. It is more economical to carry water in a few large buckets than in a lot of small cups.

Evidence which supports this view comes from studies of muscle (Clausen, 1971) and splanchnic (gut) blood flow (Rowell, 1969) before and after training. These studies are technically difficult and so they are few but they show clearly that there is a reduction in muscle blood flow and an increase in splanchnic blood flow at a given submaximal exercise intensity. The cardiac output (which does not change) is being distributed more equally.

This, as well as the improvements in the muscle cells, may be responsible for the reduced perception of effort after training (Borg, Edgren & Noble, 1975). Physical tasks seem less of a burden. This change may originate entirely in the muscles which now complain less, or it may be that the sparing of blood flow for the gut and the skin (for dissipation of heat) is perceived as a reduced strain in various ways. Whatever the precise

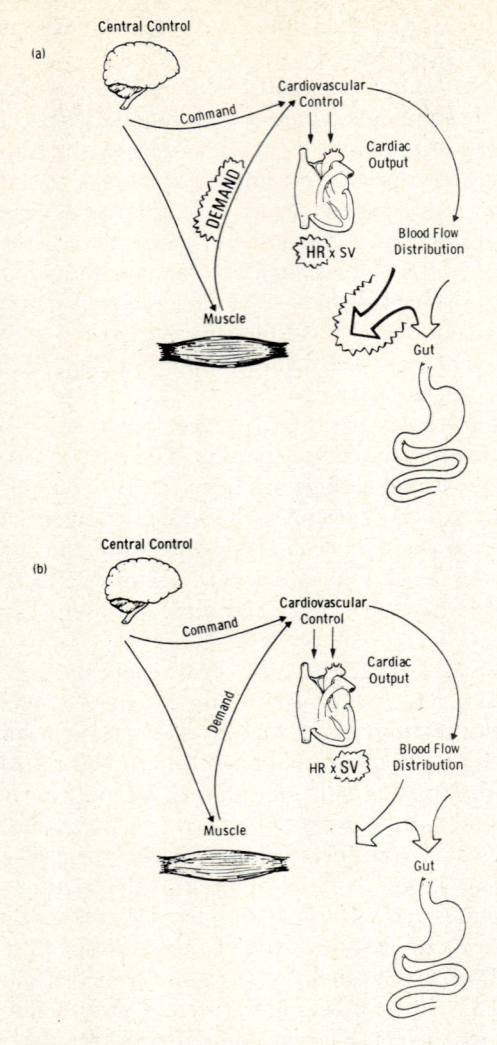

Fig. 3. Diagrammatic representation of the possible link between skeletal muscle and cardiovascular control. HR = heart rate, SV = stroke volume; a = before training, b = after training.

origin of the enhanced sense of well-being there is undoubtedly an improvement in the ease with which tasks can be achieved because the muscles have a greater capacity for work. This may lead to a more varied life style and be the basis for the suggested psychological benefits of exercise.

What then is it that changes within the muscle cell that has such remarkable consequences for other body systems? The technique of muscle biopsy developed in recent years has made it possible to look at the structure within muscle cells and to analyse their contents for enzyme concentrations.

Stamina depends upon having plenty of mitochondria in the muscle cells. These have been called the power houses of the cell which use oxygen to release energy from fuel supplies of various kinds. Improvements in stamina with training result in an increase in the number of mitochondria, their size and the concentration of enzymes within them (Gollnick, Armstrong & Saltin, 1973). There are also increases in the capillary network in the muscle. The end result is a muscle cell far better equipped than before to take up and use oxygen (Fig. 4).

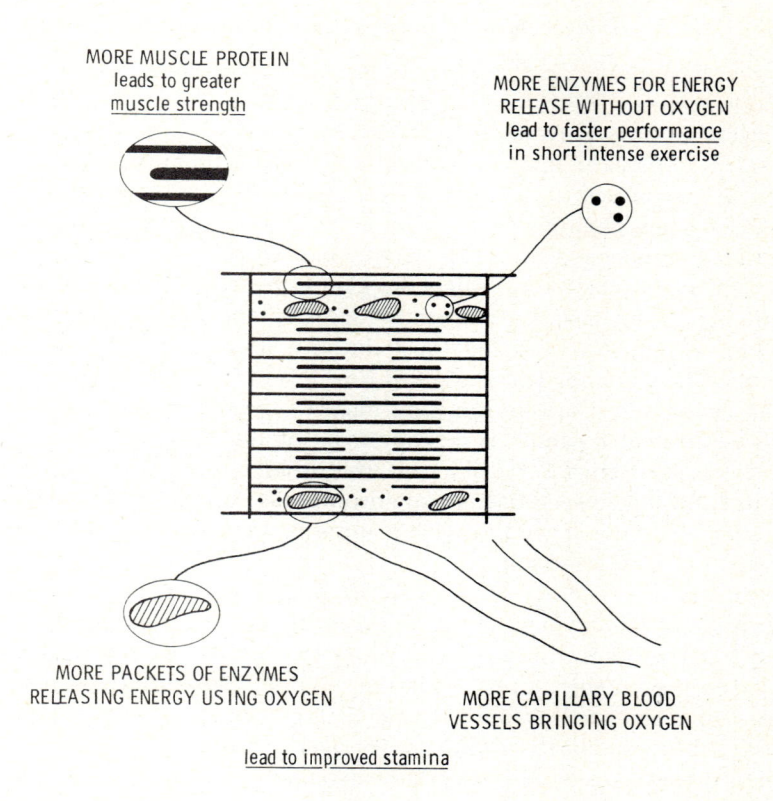

Fig. 4. Diagrammatic representation of changes in a skeletal muscle cell after training.

Where will our 10-min mile leave us as far as these things are concerned? If we had worked up to it gradually, always maintaining a steady pace, then our stamina and mitochondria would have increased. If on the other hand we had covered the mile in short bursts of fast running interspersed with walking then we would have increased our sprint capacity which does not depend on mitochondria because there is no time in a sprint to mobilize the oxygen supplies. Unfortunately we have done nothing for other major muscle groups like arm muscles. Training is specific to the muscle groups used and also to the kind of activity.

Therefore what we need for the maintenance of optimum physical health is a stimulating mixture of activities which train all the major muscles in all three ways. This is where sport is important because often it provides exercise for the whole body, at varying paces.

So far I have had in mind the middle-aged chair-bound adult who is in need of more activity in order to improve his health, but what about the older age groups? Are they too old to benefit?

Enhancement of normal health in the elderly

Many studies have shown that, as with younger groups, they can improve their stamina with suitable activities (Suominen, Heikkinen & Parkatti, 1977). They often start with a very low exercise capacity (which is probably due to excessive inactivity rather than age, Bassey, 1978), so they can improve markedly (De Vries, 1971). When activity levels are very low it is not difficult to increase them considerably and reap the benefits.

At the lowest level of aspiration the elderly need to maintain enough physical capacity to continue to live independently. They need enough strength in the arm to pick up a kettle full of boiling water. They need a safety margin for the times when little used muscles are called into action, for instance to maintain balance when the pavement is broken and uneven. They also need to know that the decline produced by a few days in bed with a cold is reversible. There is a tendency to put it down to old age and never struggle back to digging the allotment. Capacity for high intensity exercise of short duration is of less importance in the elderly and may deteriorate inevitably, but in addition to strength and stamina flexibility is crucial. Flexibility is easily maintained by moving the joint gently through its full range once a day. Young people and those in early middle age have no need to worry about this. Their flexibility is almost always adequate, and there is no virtue in being able to overextend joints.

Physical health in old age requires freedom from severe disease and in addition a robust attitude of mind which refuses to accept the gradual slowing down which their friends and relations expect. There is a need for everyone to revise their expectations of the elderly and to keep higher normal values in mind. At present our vision of the normal elderly person is too much coloured by the high proportion who do, sadly, suffer from bronchitis, arthritis and heart conditions. The average values are too low because they are weighted by disease. We should think of the outstanding elderly people we know who are still playing hockey at 60, and going hang-gliding at 79.

Sport and the elderly do not mix easily in the imagination, but many sports or activities are suitable. The old should not be restricted to bowls or golf. Swimming is a splendid activity for anyone of any age. The whole body can be used and sudden stresses and strains are buffered by the water. Keep fit classes for the over-sixties and old-time dancing clubs are expanding rapidly. There are veteran bicycle clubs where men in their seventies clock-up as good a time in trials as they did in their fifties. Stamina is something that may even improve with age; the best marathon runners are not young.

A study in Russia has demonstrated that exercise could improve and then maintain the physical capacities of a group of elderly people for 10 years (Gore, 1972). The group were aged 51–74 years at the beginning of the study (Fig. 5) and the activities which were arranged for them included walking, skiing and rambling. Although this study was small it showed that a group of elderly people could improve and then hold their own over an age span when most people in our society deteriorate. They were surely in better physical health as a result of their exercise, and showed that the deterioration with age may not be inevitable. Anecdotal evidence from many parts of the world suggests that the old can continue to work usefully despite grey hairs and wrinkled skin. Their legendary ages are unsubstantiated but their excellent working capacity is obvious.

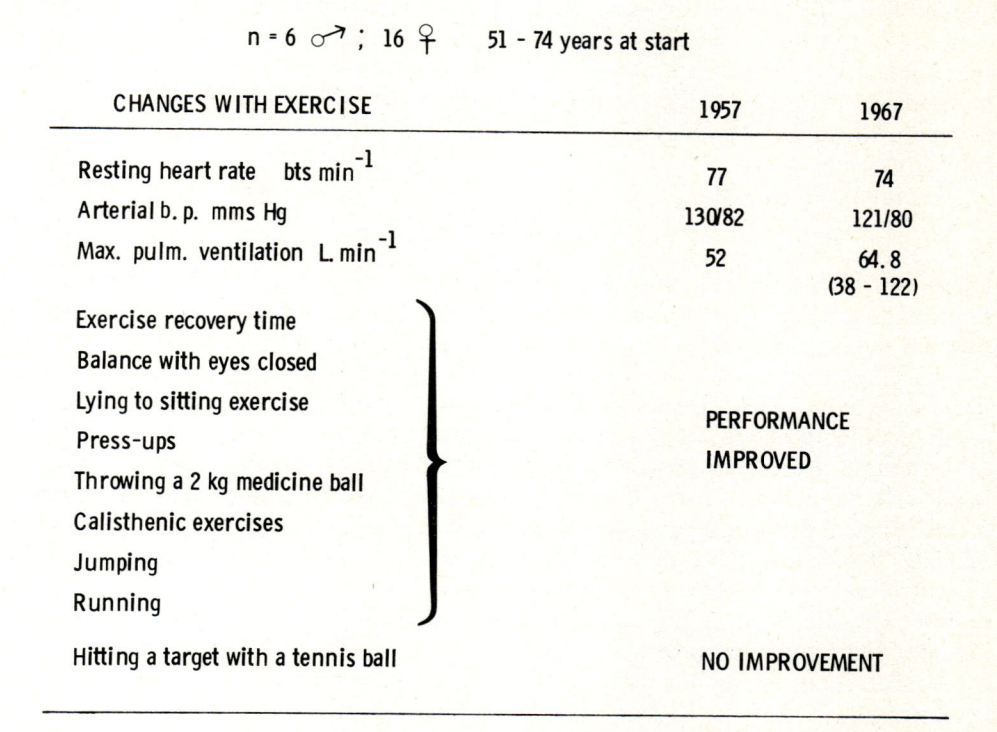

n = 6 ♂ ; 16 ♀   51 - 74 years at start

CHANGES WITH EXERCISE	1957	1967
Resting heart rate bts min^{-1}	77	74
Arterial b. p. mms Hg	130/82	121/80
Max. pulm. ventilation L. min^{-1}	52	64.8 (38 - 122)
Exercise recovery time		
Balance with eyes closed		
Lying to sitting exercise		
Press-ups		PERFORMANCE IMPROVED
Throwing a 2 kg medicine ball		
Calisthenic exercises		
Jumping		
Running		
Hitting a target with a tennis ball		NO IMPROVEMENT

Fig. 5. Improvements or maintenance in factors relevant to physical working capacity in the elderly over 10 years; from a study by Deshin reported in Gore (1972).

Amelioration of ill-health

The benefits of exercise to physical health which have been described should be exploited to the full by the chronically ill. Their need is greater than any one else's. The physically handicapped should be encouraged to make the most of the muscle power which remains to them (Vignos & Watkins, 1966). Bronchitics (Sinclair & Ingram, 1980) and asthmatics (Fitch, Morton & Blanksby, 1976) should take exercise, in order to keep their skeletal muscles in good condition so that they spare the labouring lungs and heart. They may need the help of bronchodilators and supervision from their doctor to achieve this safely, but the benefits are real. They feel better and can do more. The bronchitis and their lung function will be just as bad, but their physical health will be better and the quality of their life will improve.

The same argument applies to those with heart disease and symptoms of angina or those who have had a heart attack and are trying to rehabilitate themselves. No-one has found evidence that the exercise will stimulate the growth of new coronary blood vessels or widen existing ones, but the improvements in skeletal muscle function will reduce the burden on the diseased heart and there may be an improvement in the power which the remaining cardiac muscle can generate. After training, a cardiac patient can work harder (Sim & Neill, 1974) before he gets angina (the chest pain which signals that the heart is short of oxygen and which therefore limits his exercise). This is because, as already mentioned, the reduced heart rate allows the heart to deliver its cardiac output at a lower energy cost to the heart, and so it can achieve more without pain. There is often a reduction in cardiac output for a given oxygen uptake and a drop in heart size when cardiac patients train.

Prevention of disease

Up to now we have been considering how exercise can move people up towards positive physical health but can it also prevent them from developing diseases and dropping down towards the negative end?

If you consider obesity a disease then exercise provides a way of preventing it from developing and of curing it once it has developed (Gwinup, 1975). There may be forms of severe obesity which are not amenable to such treatment but the widespread milder form of the disease certainly responds to exercise. The drawback is that the treatment is slow. A brisk walk for half an hour will burn up only 17g of fat, but combined with moderate dietary control the long term benefits are obvious. It is a fallacy that exercise stimulates appetite. People may think they need more food after an hour's gardening, but that is a matter of social conditioning not physiology. Excess body fat is in itself a burden which makes physical activity harder but it also leads to other more serious diseases like diabetes and high blood pressure.

Apart from its interaction with obesity, diabetes can be ameliorated by exercise. There is increasing evidence that exercise specifically increases insulin sensitivity, and it is now being used along with diet to control milder forms of the disease (Kemmer *et al.*, 1979).

Finally, what influence does exercise have on heart disease? This question has been left until the last because the subject has already received more attention than the evidence warrants. The rising incidence of ischaemic heart disease among young middle-aged men has given rise to alarm, and the hope that lack of exercise had caused it has led to wishful thinking. We should be glad that this has focused everyone's attention on sport and activity, but the real benefits of exercise lie elsewhere.

First the 'epidemic' is not as alarming as many suppose because some of the increase in deaths due to ischaemic heart disease is due to changing diagnostic patterns among doctors (Clayton, Taylor & Shaper, 1977). The labels are changing and there has been a considerable drop in the incidence of 'myocardial degeneration'. When this is taken into account, there is no marked rise of ischaemic heart disease in women but its incidence has doubled in the last 25 years in middle-aged men.

What about the role of exercise? Many studies show that the most active groups suffer less from heart disease. The problem with this kind of evidence is that it may be the healthier people who take on the most active jobs in the first place. The only study that carries conviction is that by Morris and co-workers on thousands of civil servants (Chave *et al.*, 1978). The subjects were classified by questionnaire into two groups, those who took vigorous exercise and those who did not, and then followed for 8 years. The incidence of ischaemic heart disease was significantly lower in the exercise group than would be predicted from the known incidence of other diseases in that group. This study takes account, at least to some extent, of the argument that the subjects in the exercise group are more active because they are healthier rather than the other way round.

It suggests that exercise may reduce the incidence of the disease, but it is certainly not protective in the sense that a waterproof protects you from getting wet in the rain. Many people who take a great deal of vigorous exercise still die of heart attacks. Many other factors influence the disease, including genetic inheritance, smoking and diet. Moreover there is, as yet, no satisfactory explanation of how exercise might influence heart disease and so the association cannot be considered causal. Overstating this case merely gives it a bad press in the long run. Its effects will be small compared to other factors even if they are fully proven. There are much better reasons for taking exercise, positive rather than negative ones. A population running for fun is much healthier than one which runs because it is afraid.

I would like to leave you with a new version of an old slogan: 'Whatever the pleasure, good physical condition completes it'.

References

ASTRAND, P.O. & RODAHL, K. (1977) *Textbook of Work Physiology.* McGraw Hill, New York.

BASSEY, E.J. (1978) Age, inactivity and some physiological responses to exercise. *Gerontology,* **24**, 66.

BASSEY, E.J., FENTEM, P.H., MACDONALD, I.C. & SCRIVEN, P.M. (1976) Self-paced walking as a method for exercise testing in elderly and young men. *Clin. Sci. mol. Med.* **51**, 609.

BORG, G., EDGREN, B. & NOBLE, B. (1975) Effects of physical conditioning on perceived exertion and working capacity. *Reps Inst. Appl. Psychol. Univ. Stockholm,* No. **63**.

CHAVE, S.P.W., MORRIS, J.N., MOSS, S. & SEMMENCE, A.M. (1978) Vigorous exercise in leisure time and the death rate: a study of male civil servants. *J. Epid. & Community Health,* **32**, 239.

CLAUSEN, J.P. (1971) Muscle blood flow during exercise and its significance for maximal performance. In: *Limiting Factors of Physical Performance,* Part IV. Edited by J. Keul. George Thieme, Stuttgart.

CLAUSEN, J.P., TRAP-JENSEN, J. & LASSEN, N.A. (1970) The effects of training on the heart rate during arm and leg exercise. *Scand. J. clin. lab. Invest.* **26**, 295.

CLAYTON, D.G., TAYLOR, D. & SHAPER, A.G. (1977) Trends in heart disease in England and Wales, 1950-1973. *Health Trends,* **9**, 1.

COTES, J.E. (1965) *Lung Function.* Blackwell Scientific Publications, Oxford.

DE VRIES, H.A. (1971) Exercise intensity threshold for improvement of cardiovascular–respiratory function in older men. *Geriatrics,* **26**, 94.

FENTEM, P.H. (1979) Exercise: a prescription for health? *Br. J. Sports Med.* **12**, 223.

FITCH, K.D., MORTON, A.R. & BLANKSBY, B.A. (1976) Effects of swimming training on children with asthma. *Archs Dis. Childh.* **51**, 190.

GOLLNICK, P.D., ARMSTRONG, R.B. & SALTIN, B. (1973) Effect of training on enzyme activity and fiber composition of human skeletal muscle. *J. appl. Physiol.* **34**, 107.

GORE, I.Y. (1972) Physical activity and ageing – a survey of Soviet literature III. The character of physical activity; training and longitudinal results. *Geront. Clin.* **14**, 78.

GWINUP, G. (1975) Effect of exercise alone on the weight of obese women. *Archs intern. Med.* **135**, 676.

KAVANAGH, T., SHEPHARD, R.J. & KENNEDY, J. (1977) Characteristics of post-coronary marathon runners. *Ann. N.Y. Acad. Sci.* **301**, 455.

KEMMER, F.W., BERCHTOLD, P., BERGER, M., STARKE, A., CUPPERS, H.J., GRIES, F.A. & ZIMMERMAN, H. (1979) Exercise-induced fall of blood glucose in insulin-treated diabetics unrelated to alteration of insulin mobilization. *Diabetes,* **28**, 1131.

ROWELL, L. (1969) Circulation. *Med. Sci. in Sports,* **1**, 15.

SALTIN, B., BLOMQUIST, B., MITCHELL, J.H., JOHNSON, R.L.Jr, WILDENTHAL, K. & CHAPMAN, C.B. (1968) Response to exercise after bed-rest and after training. *Circulation,* **38**, 1.

SIM, D.N. & NEILL, W.A. (1974) Investigation of the physiological basis for increased exercise threshold for angina pectoris after physical conditioning. *J. clin. Invest.* **54**, 763.

SINCLAIR, D.J.M. & INGRAM, C.G. (1980) Controlled trial of improvised exercise training in chronic bronchitis. *Br. med. J.* **1**, 519.

SUOMINEN, H., HEIKKINEN, E. & PARKATTI, T. (1977) Effect of eight weeks' physical training on muscle and connective tissue of the M Vastus Lateralis in 69 year old men and women. *J. Gerontol.* **32**, 33.

VIGNOS, P.J. & WATKINS, M.P. (1966) The effect of exercise in muscular dystrophy. *J. Am. med. Ass.* **197**, 843.

Biosocial Aspects of Sport

SPORT AND MENTAL HEALTH

MAURICE YAFFÉ

Guy's Hospital, London

Bodily exercise profiteth little.
1 Timothy 4:8

Those who think they have not time for
bodily exercise will sooner or later
have to find time for illness.
Edward Stanley, Earl of Derby (1826-1893)

Cease, reverend Fathers! from those
    youthful Sports
Retire, before unfinish'd Feats betray
Your slacken'd Nerves.
The Economy of Love John Armstrong (1709-1779)

Summary. The contribution of mental health to sports performance in sports populations is discussed. Athletes' psychological needs and problems, and the various ways in which these may be resolved, are considered.

The benefits of physical activity in the treatment of psychiatric populations and the elderly are reviewed.

Recent emphasis on sports participation for its intrinsic rewards and the psychological benefits derived are also considered, and attention is drawn to the particular needs of children.

Introduction

It is fitting that a meeting on sport should be held under the aegis of the Galton Foundation. Sir Francis Galton was one of the first to recognize that people differ profoundly in their mental abilities; he claimed that these differences were correlated with their achievements in sport as well as in the mental field. Galton himself however was not one to pursue sport in his leisure time – his recreations are listed in the *Who's Who* of the time as 'sunshine, quiet, and good wholesome food'; in spite or perhaps because of this he lived to the ripe old age of 89.

A great deal has happened to sport over the past few years, especially in the United States, but for centuries man has had strong views about the importance of exercise and sport in the maintenance of physical and mental health – best illustrated by Homer's *'mens sana in corpore sano'*. However, there has been little systematic study as to whether or not there is a relationship between sport and mental health and, if a positive one exists, what specific factors are necessary for sport to be effective in the maintenance and restoration of health.

Definitions

According to Moore (1966) 'sport is the play of older children and adults', but of course those involved in physical education need something more specific; Loy's definition (Loy, McPherson & Kenyon, 1978) is more exacting:

> 'It is a formally organised, institutional game where outcome is determined by physical skills, strategy or chance, and has distinct characteristics such as rules, sanctions, roles, positions and the division of labour.'

This definition is somewhat narrow; it is useful, however, to make a distinction between those who play sport to get fit and those who get fit to play sport. For the former, sport represents a vehicle mainly to achieve or maintain physical fitness, whereas it is an end-in-itself for the second type of person where winning is often of paramount importance.

Mental health, of course, is more difficult to define, and for those involved in mental health – or rather, its converse, mental illness – there are disadvantages: the average person often has a lot to say about psychological problems (and other specialist topics) and usually speaks on the subject with confidence whereas the clinician has to qualify everything he says. Mental health is not simply the absence of mental disease; there are basically three ways of looking at and defining mental health according to Jahoda (1958):

> 1. 'A relatively constant and enduring function of personality'; although a person may have ups and downs, his general mental health is relatively stable, predictable and a characteristic of his personality.
> 2. 'A momentary function of personality and of situation'; in this sense, mental health varies, depending on external and internal circumstances, is relatively unstable and unpredictable over the long-term and is a characteristic of current actions and feelings, regardless of personality.
> 3. 'A group or cultural characteristic'; regardless of the status of individual members, the group ethos or behaviour is measured in relation to some ideal standard for mental health.

These three definitions are not incompatible, but they are independent and probably unrelated. Assessment of mental health also requires evaluation of an individual's attitude towards his own self; his growth, development or self-actualization; what he does with himself; his perception of reality; his mastery over his environment; and his autonomy and independence from social influences.

Discussion of the relationship between sport and mental health will be restricted to sports participants compared with spectators; for those interested in the psychological aspects of sports spectating a body of literature has started to appear, e.g. Proctor & Eckerd (1976). Two issues provide the principal focus of this paper: (1) the contribution of mental health to sports performance in sports populations, and (2) the effects of sports participation on mental health in psychiatric populations.

The contribution of mental health to sports performance

It is surprising that clinical psychologists have not become involved in top-level sport until relatively recently, especially as competition, by definition, is stressful and the environment is one in which individuals are constantly testing their limits. How many of us in the course of our daily life are testing our limits? By contrast, for sportsmen and women the pressure on winning, the emphasis on realizing potential when it matters, has become increasingly severe; that is why individuals like clinical psychologists have become involved in sport.

The psychological needs and problems of athletes

Yaffé (1979) conducted a study on the psychological factors that competitors at the Edmonton Commonwealth Games thought were necessary to do well at their sport, that is, on the psychological determinants of success (*Psychological Report on the Commonwealth Games, Edmonton 1978*, British Olympic Association, unpublished). A random sample of individuals (coaches and competitors) was interviewed and the total population was asked to complete a questionnaire prepared for this evaluation. Seventy-two per cent of the England team competitors filled in the questionnaire and participated in the survey. Attempts were made to encourage the rest, but it is seldom possible to get 100% return in investigations of this kind. Unfortunately, the ones who did not respond were probably the very ones that would have merited further attention. The questionnaire asked about the factors considered necessary, but not in themselves sufficient, for success in their sport. The result was that 31% of the male competitors and 25% of the female competitors said that concentration, while 33% of the male competitors and 36% of the females said that self-confidence was the most important factor for doing well in competition. As to the problem that people said they had in relation to the factors they felt were the most important, 18% of the men and 24% of the women said that concentration was a problem for them; 40% of men and 39% of women said that they had difficulty in relaxing; 29% of male competitors and nearly 50% of females said that they had problems with their self-confidence – they had doubts about their capabilities.

The coaches consistently overestimated the presence of problems, and this suggests their threshold for problem detection is more sensitive, or perhaps due to mis-labelling of psychological states.

There are specific categories of participants in each sport who present with psychological problems. Ogilvie & Tutko (1966) in California defined six different categories:

1. *The deliberate transgressor of the rules*: it is difficult to know whether cheating can be considered a component of mental health, and to what extent it is sanctioned by various organizations. One of the best known examples is Onyshenko, the Soviet pentathlete who deliberately short-circuited his epee in the fencing event at the Montreal Olympics, but there are likely to be others, including those taking illicit drugs in order to potentiate performance, who are never discovered.

2. *The hyper-anxious individual*, is the one who appears most frequently in the problem category: the person who peaks too early, who peaks too late, or perhaps does not peak at all, and whose arousal levels are beyond the optimal level. Hyper-anxious athletes not uncommonly do significantly better in training compared with competition, for this reason.

3. *The coaching-resistor*, usually a senior member of a squad, is another interesting individual who presents himself in training. In professional soccer there are prima donnas who will not be coached; and they often intimidate some younger members of the team, annoy others, and provide a poor model for identification. These are especially problematical in team sports, where the age range of competitors is broad.

4. *The success-phobic* is a specific kind of individual, described in detail by Ogilvie and his colleagues. These are individuals who have all the physical capabilities of doing well, but when it really matters they fail. This occurs for a multiplicity of reasons of which I will mention just two: there is the individual who deliberately does not compete and uses this as a weapon to get back at someone to whom he is hostile, perhaps an aggressive parent who pushed him into sport, wanting him to do all the things that the parent never did himself. Second, there is the individual who in a body-contact sport is reluctant to establish the full body contact necessary for doing well at the top level of such competitions.

By contrast the counter-phobic individual is fearful, but his fear is countered by aggressiveness.

5. *Injury-prone people*: these individuals present repeatedly with some kind of physical complaint, often when an organic basis cannot be found; but sometimes an individual like the counter-phobic gets injured in order to avoid worse injury – the kind of individual who in soccer uses his head where other people would perhaps hesitate to use even their feet.

6. *The depression-prone person*. Some people are very sensitive to failure, or to the possibility of failure and quite often the depression is subclinical; but when it presents clinically medication is sometimes indicated. These are individuals who never seem to do as well as everyone thinks that they ought to.

This group includes sports people with long-term injuries who feel that they should have fully recovered long ago and also sports addicts who develop a 'deprivation crisis' (Little, 1969; 1979) as a result of being kept out of sport by some minor physical illness.

Investigations and treatment of athletes

Over the past 10 years much attention in sports psychology has been directed towards groups rather than individuals (e.g. Straub, 1978); the emphasis has been on the assessment and prediction of group motivation, leadership style and team cohesion in particular. However, in dealing with someone who has a specific problem a combination of techniques to suit the individual has to be worked out using a standardized behavioural analysis procedure.

Techniques must be fitted to individuals, rather than the other way round. The latest developments in psychology, general as well as clinical, are in the cognitive sphere. In sport what seems to be important is to help people to become non-judgemental, or to reduce the judgemental statements they make, to prevent people from talking themselves into doing badly or making excuses. Cognitive behavioural interventions were originally applied with success clinically to treat neurotic or reactive stress and pain (e.g. Meichenbaum, 1977) and depression; the approach has great validity and usefulness in sport; it facilitates access to thoughts and feelings and provides the possibility of the modification of these where they are considered inappropriate.

Behaviour must be measured in order to obtain a base-line before any kind of intervention is attempted; there are basically six different approaches which are not necessarily exclusive:

The behavioural interview involves a face-to-face discussion of relevant issues with the psychologist in order to establish the onset and determinants of the problem behaviour; it may or may not be structured.

Self-report schedules and inventories (where available) are used to build up a picture of antecedents and consequences of the stressor (Table 1) and to compare the subjects' response profiles with an appropriate reference group (e.g. Martens, 1977).

Self-monitoring procedures involve documenting the frequency of particular behaviours, thoughts or feelings.

Analogue measures involve controlled experiments to see to what extent the problem behaviour can be replicated in a simulated or representative situation.

Direct observational procedures are usually readily available in sport as arenas are generally designed with this purpose in mind.

Psycho-physiological procedures concern the measurement of physiological parameters such as galvanic skin (sweating) response, pulse and respiration rate.

There are three different kinds of channels of response to consider. Taking anxiety as the example:

(1) Cognitive: refers to what people say to themselves or others about their state, e.g. 'I feel worried', 'I feel anxious' or 'I'm not going to succeed today'.
(2) Physiological: is there an increased sweating response, or pulse rate?
(3) Behavioural: does the person look tense? Does he run away from competition, literally or in some other way?

Sometimes there is a combination of all these three, sometimes two are present and sometimes only one; it is important therefore to measure each of these parameters as fully as possible.

Clinical psychology has developed, on the behavioural front at least, a very strong battery of techniques, based on learning theory principles, which are very effective in resolving these simple interference factors that prevent people from doing, under the stressful environment of competition, what is within their physical capabilities. Seven main techniques are available for individuals training for competition:

1. Autogenic training – literally 'self-generating' training originated in Berlin at the turn of the century, since developed by Schultz & Luthe (1969). It is a combination of relaxation and suggestion exercises, and is used very commonly by the East Germans. The Soviet technique of psychic self-regulation is slightly different, but all these techniques overlap to a greater or lesser extent.

2. Hypnosis is something about which we know less. There are no controlled studies in the literature on sport but several case studies are reported, e.g. Naruse (1965).

Table 1. A-B-C of pinpointing stress and anxiety (after Carr-Kaffashan et al., 1978)

Antecedent = stress = external event	Behaviour = thoughts and actions	Consequences = bodily sensations = emotional reactions
When (1) Date, (2) Time, (3) Location What (4) What was I engaged in? (5) Who was there with me?	Thoughts (6) What was I expecting to happen? (7) What image or memories were called up? (8) What worries, concerns, or doubts was I reminded of? (9) What was I saying to myself (self-statements)? (10) What core beliefs or assumptions are relevant? Action (11) What was I talking about? (12) What did I do in reaction to this situation?	Labels (13) What sensations, labels, or words best describe what I am feeling? Rate (14) How severe are the feelings I am experiencing? 1 2 3 4 5 slight some moderate severe very severe
Fictional example in sport (1) 21 July 1978 (2) 2.30 pm (3) Swimming pool (4) Preparing for final of breast stroke competition (Commonwealth Games) (5) Other competitors including current world champions	(6) To win by large margin; maybe break a world record (7) My last encounter with the champion when he just beat me (8) I never seem to do as well in big competitions compared to smaller ones or in training (9) Go off very hard, and keep your rhythm (10) My value as a person depends on how I do in competition (11) I was silent (12) Started to shake, heartbeat raised significantly	(13) Nervous, light-headed (14) No. 4

3. *Relaxation training* is the simplest way to learn to relax, usually using the Jacobson progressive muscle training exercises (Bernstein & Borkovec, 1975).

4. *Systematic de-sensitization* is a technique aimed specifically at the alleviation of maladaptive anxiety. It involves the pairing of relaxation with imagined scenes depicting situations that the subject has indicated cause him or her to feel anxious. It is generally found that experiencing relaxation rather than anxiety while imagining such scenes leads to much less discomfort when the real-life situations are confronted.

5. *Bio-feedback* is a procedure developed 10 years ago, which is very useful for teaching people to modify their bodily responses. It was not appreciated until relatively recently that heart rate can be made to go up and down while sitting in one place (Suinn, 1978, unpublished paper presented at the Congress of Canadian Society for Psychomotor Learning and Sport Psychology, Toronto); sweating response and several other parameters can be affected, even peripheral blood supply can be changed. It has been found that using autogenic training – a combination of suggestion and relaxation – body surface temperature can be changed by up to 3° C, which is quite considerable. In bio-feedback the mode of feedback can be auditory or visual; most individuals learn very quickly to change skin conductance or other parameter by monitoring their signals on devices that are often portable and so enable homework to be carried out in the person's home environment.

Spectators and even hardened coaches, sometimes show marked physiological changes in response to the ups and downs of their teams during competition. Two examples cited in the literature are: the pulse rate of a swimming coach rose from 122 to 160 while watching his swimmers and that of a baseball coach in the US varied between 90 and 150 during a game in which his team was involved.

6. *Assertiveness training.* There are many individuals who find it difficult to assert themselves and this can be a considerable handicap in sport, e.g. forwards in soccer who are easily knocked off the ball, and techniques developed in clinical practice have been shown to be very effective in getting people to externalize their feelings and to be aggressive, rather than violent (Alberti & Emmons, 1978). Aggressiveness and assertiveness do not have the negative connotations of violence which is more extreme and inappropriate in sport.

7. *Mental rehearsal.* People can learn how to develop appropriate movements and body responses in their sport using mental rehearsal, in the same way that individuals learn languages. If sequences and moves, or whatever skills need to be learned in the particular sport, are rehearsed in a systematic way, generally speaking, performance on the particular task can be improved. Such techniques are very useful indeed if combined with cognitive strategies (Suinn, 1978, unpublished). Mental practice can thus be used in many ways to improve skills, to reduce stressful situations and to think up coping images – when you are a striker and 3-1 down at half-time, you have to think about when you scored a superb goal in the past.

The contribution of sport to mental health

Observations of the addictive potential of running suggested a few years ago that exercise might change psychological characteristics in normal and psychologically-disturbed individuals both positively (Glasser, 1976) and negatively (Morgan, 1979). So it is no surprise to learn that 2 years ago there appeared a paper on running as a treatment for depression (Greist *et al.*, 1979). Only a few studies have been carried out (e.g. Blue, 1979) and they have not been very adequately controlled, but they are extremely valuable in suggesting ways in which sport can be used to help individuals who have destructive lifestyles.

Sport in depressive states

The typical study in this area is that reported by (Greist *et al.*, 1978) at the University of Wisconsin, Madison. They did a pilot study into the question of whether running has beneficial effects for patients seeking treatment for neurotic or reactive depression. They treated twelve male and fifteen female reactive depressive, but not psychotically-depressed, individuals, between the ages of 18 and 30, and assigned them randomly to one of three groups: (1) a running group; (2) an individual psychotherapy group for ten sessions; (3) an individual psychotherapy group for unlimited time. They assessed all the individuals physically and also did a maximal stress exercise treadmill test. The running group involved emphasis on running either with a leader or by the individuals themselves. The study lasted 10 weeks. The authors emphasized to the runners the importance of pain and fatigue, and stressed the need for walking if they wanted to – they were not pressured to run. The focus, though, was on the running itself – they were instructed to think about the foot strike, the stride, the arm carry and about the appropriate running equipment. There was no focus on depression, or discussion of it in the running group throughout the entire programme. There were two drop-outs in the running group, one in the time-limited psychotherapy group and two in the unlimited psychotherapy group. Only two out of eight in the running group showed little improvement, one because she had an extremely poor level of fitness initially, and another because she said that running could not be treatment and so would not participate. The conclusion of the study was that running was as effective as psychotherapy in alleviating depressive symptoms, as assessed by a check-list.

A second study was done over a period of 12 weeks, with raised criteria for getting into the group. There was a similar outcome, showing that graded skill training, in terms of running, had a positive effect in reducing depression. This result is very encouraging.

There are advantages in treating people this way: it is cost effective, there are no negative side-effects compared to drugs, and it is useful as a prophylactic prevention of future depressive episodes.

Sport in other mental states

Sport has not only been used for depressives. In the US it has been employed as a treatment adjunct for hard-driving people who have had coronaries and are worried about whether they will ever be men again, sexually and with respect to fitness; getting them to run seems to improve their self-esteem considerably (Hackett & Cassem, 1978; Froelicher, Battler & McKirnan, 1980). It has also been used in a wide variety of psychiatric, psychosomatic and somatic symptoms including aggression, obsessionality and hypochondriasis (Solomon & Bumpus, 1978; Lion, 1978; MacKinnon, 1980; Folkins, 1976). There are, in addition, references in the literature on treating phobic anxiety states by running (Greist *et al.*, 1979; Orwin, 1974) including agoraphobia – the fear of crowded and public situations (Orwin, 1973). Moreover, Clark *et al.* (1975) hypothesizing that restricted physical activity – seen as a decrement in sensory stimulation – could be a factor contributing to the boredom and deterioration commonly found in an ageing population, conducted a 12-week physical activity programme with 23 geriatric patients from a mental institution. They found that their general activity level and self-care standards were increased during the daily routine, though not to a significant level compared with a social group who underwent conventional recreational therapy, which consisted of activities such as games and conversation.

Turner & Dyer (1969) developed an aquatics programme for neuropsychiatric patients whose symptoms included restlessness, hyperactivity, aggressiveness, apathy, inactivity and withdrawal, and discovered major improvements in socialization, a more positive outlook towards recovery and increased tolerance to discomfort. Stubbert *et al.* (1975) developed a physical exertion programme for a 17-year old obese patient who had been a suicide attempter and destructive to property; this included swimming, calisthenics, stretching and tennis, and after 6 weeks she was behaving in a sociably acceptable manner and after 9 months had lost 60 lbs in weight. Simpson & Meaney (1979) demonstrated significant improvement in self-concept of mentally retarded boys and girls (IQ range 40–60; age 14–20 years) which was related to the success achieved in a 5-week learning to ski course.

Sport and enjoyment

For the past 5 or so years a 'new wave' has made its presence felt in sport; this evolved out of the humanistic approach to psychology whose philosophy centres on the search for inner-directed growth of human potential as opposed to one provided by advanced technology and material wealth (Rowan, 1976; Sugarman & Tarter, 1978; Maslow, 1968). In sport the principal proponents of this development which emanated from California are Nideffer (1976), Sheehan (1978) and Leonard (1975); similar views have been expounded in a number of texts including Spino (1976, 1977) and Andrews (1979) on running, by far the most common activity described. The essential focus of this approach is on participation for its own sake rather than on a philosophy of win at all costs. This does not mean that winning is less likely to occur, but that the preoccupation many sportsmen have about 'getting it right' is essential for neither enjoyment nor success; what seems to be important is the meaning exercise and sport have for individuals.

One way to examine experiential states of mind is to study individuals who are deeply involved in activities which require great expenditure of time, effort and skill for which there seem to be little or no extrinsic (e.g. financial or status) rewards. Csikszentmihalyi (1975) did just that with, amongst others, dancers and basketball players. He found that 'enjoyment of the experience and the use of skills' and 'the activity itself: the pattern, the action, the world it provides' were the most important, though the sportsmen appeared to be motivated more than the dancers by competition and by the chance to develop their physical skill; the dancers, on the other hand, responded more strongly to the feedback from kinaesthetic sensations. On the basis of interview and questionnaire data, Csikszentmihalyi showed that: 'People who enjoy what they are doing enter a state of "flow": they concentrate their attention on a limited stimulus field, forget personal problems, lose their sense of time and of themselves, feel competent and in control, and have a sense of harmony and union with their surroundings'. A flow activity, he says, 'provides opportunities for actions which match a person's skill, limits the perceptual field, exclude irrelevant stimuli, contains clear goals and adequate means for reaching them, and gives clear and consistent feedback to the participant'. The central element of the flow state is a feeling of control over the environment, but internal skills one brings to the situation must be balanced against external challenges before a flow state can be experienced. (Fig. 1). The estimations of skills and challenges depend on cultural convention and are open to interpretation and change by the individual. Csikszentmihalyi provides methods by which to assess the flow potential of activities and persons. He documents that the extent to which one can control one's environment by limiting one's

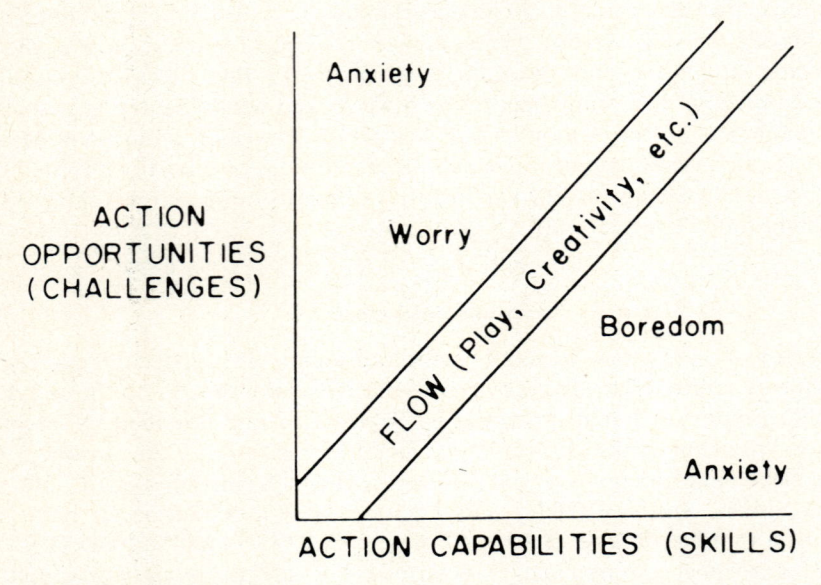

Fig. 1. Achievement of flow state by balancing internal skills against external challenges.

stimulus field, establishing clear goals and norms, and developing suitable skills, will determine the extent to which one can experience flow. Importantly, at the peak of involvement with their activity, whether indulging in dance or sport, individuals report that they lose a sense of themselves as separate entities, and feel harmony and even a merging of identity with the environment.

These phenomena are similar to those Maslow (1968) lists as components of the 'peak experience', namely: temporary transcendence of self, total engrossment, narrow focus of attention, everything is perfect, total control, total loss of fear, and effortless movement; and Murphy & White (1978) have fully documented links between such experiences described by athletes and Eastern mystics. In sport several practices are considered to facilitate the heightening of the level of consciousness, as well as improving the stream of flow; these include: breathing exercises, meditation, guided fantasy, and centering (balancing of energy) according to Spino (1976).

In 1974 a US tennis coach published a book called *The Inner Game of Tennis* which changed a nation's view of sport and their involvement with it (Gallwey, 1974). He has since written another volume on skiing (Gallwey & Kriegel, 1979) and the third on golf is in preparation. Inner game concepts include: teaching people how to develop the ability to concentrate in a relaxed way, to become non-judgemental, to focus on the here-and-now, and to 'let' things happen, and are closely related to the kinds of therapeutic interventions made by psychologists in clinical practice. They have been introduced as a way of helping to modify behaviour patterns in persons who, for example, overwork and are highly vulnerable to coronary heart disease, the so-called Type-A behaviour pattern (Rhoads, 1977; Friedman *et al.*, 1968).

Clearly psychology has a great deal to offer the sports person, and involvement in sport is now accepted as having psychological benefits for both the mentally healthy and those suffering from mental illness. But as Ogilvie (1979) points out, our attention needs to be drawn to issues of prevention of problems rather than on treatment, and he rightly questions the structure and social aims of children's participation in sport: 'Is the sports experience really child centred or are we imposing a model for participation derived from our observation of professional sports?' He suggests that if the sports activity is to be child centred, we must remind parents, coaches, and fans that the rewards for the child must be determined on the basis of their intrinsic needs. Parents and coaches need to be prepared to be more objective in their determination of the child's readiness to compete in highly demanding athletic programmes. This must be a focus for future concern if fun and enjoyment from sport are valued as part of the experience of participation.

The next breakthrough, however, might well be biochemical as recent research (Stein & Belluzzi, 1979) suggests that endogenous morphine-like chemicals (endorphins) in the brain, conceived as natural analgesic substances for regulation of the response to pain (Belluzzi *et al.*, 1976), may well mediate feelings of pleasure and reward. Endorphins might be released more readily during physical exercise than during more sedentary activities.

But the final word must go to Sir Francis Galton who in 1869 had this to say about oarsmen of the time:

> 'The successful rowers are mostly single men, and some of the best have no children. One well-known (Newcastle) man, who has trained for an enormous number of races, and during the time of each training was most abstemious and in amazing health; then, after each trial was over, he commonly gave way, and without committing any great excess, remained for weeks in a state of fuddle. This is too often the history of these men'.

Times have not changed very much over the past 111 years.

References

ALBERTI, R.E. & EMMONS, M.L. (1978) *Your Perfect Right: A Guide to Assertive Behaviour*, 3rd edn. Impact, San Luis Obispo, California.
ANDREWS, V. (1979) *The Psychic Power Of Running*. Thorsons, Wellingborough, Northants.
BELLUZZI, J.D., GRANT, N., GARSKY, U., SARANTARIS, D., WISE, C.D. & STEIN, C. (1976) Analgesia induced in vivo by central administration of encephalin in rat. *Nature, Lond.* **260**, 625.

BERNSTEIN, D.A. & BORKOVEC, T.D. (1975) *Progressive Relaxation Training: A Manual for the Helping Professions.* Research Press, Champaign, Illinois.

BLUE, F.R. (1979) Aerobic running as a treatment for moderate depression. *Percept. Mot. Skills,* **48**, 228.

CARR-KAFFASHAN, L., ETTIN, M., GALANO, J., LEHRER, P. & ROTHBERG, M. (1978) *Handbook of Techniques for Dealing with Stress.* Community Mental Health Centre, Rutgers Medical School, NJ.

CLARK, B.A., WADE, M.G., MASSEY, B.H. & VAN DYKE, R. (1975) Response of institutionalised geriatric mental patients to a twelve-week programme of regular physical activity. *J. Geront.* **30**, 565.

CSIKSZENTMIHALYI, M. (1975) *Beyond Boredom and Anxiety.* Jossey Bass, San Francisco.

FOLKINS, C.H. (1976) Effects of physical training on mood. *J. clin. Psychol.* **32**, 385.

FRIEDMAN, M., ROSENMAN, R.H., STRAUS, R. *et al.* (1968) The relationship of behaviour pattern A to the state of coronary vasculature. *Am. J. Med.* **44**, 525.

FROELICHER, V., BATTLER, A. & MCKIRNAN, M.D. (1980) Physical activity and coronary heart disease. *Cardiology,* **65**, 153.

GALLWEY, W.T. (1974) *The Inner Game of Tennis.* Cape, London.

GALLWEY, T. & KRIEGEL, B. (1979) *Inner Skiing.* Bantam, New York.

GALTON, F. (1869) *Hereditary Genius.* 1979 edn, p. 308. Friedman, London.

GLASSER, W. (1976) *Positive Addiction.* Harper & Row, Hagerstown, Md.

GREIST, J.H., KLEIN, M.H., EISCHENS, R.R., FARIS, J., GURMAN, A.S. & MORGAN, W.P. (1978) Running through your mind. *J. psychosom. Res.* **22**, 259.

GREIST, J.H., KLEIN, M.H., EISCHENS, R.R., FARIS, J., GURMAN, A.S. & MORGAN, W.P. (1979) Running as treatment for depression. *Compreh. Psychiat.* **20**, 41.

HACKETT, T.P. & CASSEM, N.H. (1978) Psychological factors related to exercise. *Cardiovasc. Clinics,* **9**, 223.

JAHODA, M. (1958) *Current Concepts of Positive Mental Health.* Basic, New York.

LEONARD, G. (1975) *The Ultimate Athlete: Re-visioning Sports, Physical Education and the Body.* Viking, New York.

LION, L.S. (1978) Psychological effects of jogging: a preliminary study. *Percept. Mot Skills,* **47**, 1215.

LITTLE, J.C. (1969) The athletes neurosis – a deprivation crisis. *Acta psychiat. scand.* **45**, 187.

LITTLE, J.C. (1979) Neurotic illness in fitness fanatics. *Psychiat. Ann.* **9**. 148.

LOY, J., MCPHERSON, B. & KENYON, G. (1978) *Sport and Social Systems.* Addison-Wesley, Don Mills, Ontario.

MACKINNON, B.L. (1980) The psychiatric aspects of sports and fitness. *J. Maine Med. Ass.* **71**, 101.

MARTENS, R. (1977) *Sport Competition Anxiety Test.* Human Kinetics, Champaign, Illinois.

MASLOW, A. (1968) *Towards A Psychology of Being,* 2nd edn. Van Nostrand, Princeton, NJ.

MEICHENBAUM, D.H. (1977) *Cognitive-Behaviour Modification.* Plenum, New York.

MOORE, R.A. (1966) *Sports and Mental Health.* Thomas, Springfield, Illinois.

MORGAN, W.P. (1979) Negative addiction in runners. *Physician & Sports Med.* **7**, 57.

MURPHY, M. & WHITE, R. (1978) *The Psychic Side of Sports.* Addison-Wesley, Reading, Mass.

NARUSE, G. (1965) The hypnotic treatment of stage fright in champion athletes. *Int. J. clin. exp. Hypnosis,* **13**, 63.

NIDEFFER, R.M. (1976) *The Inner Athlete: Mind Plus Muscle for Winning.* Crowell, New York.

OGILVIE, B. (1979) The child athlete: psychological implications of participation in sport. *Ann. Am. Acad. polit. soc. Sci.* **445**, 47.

OGILVIE, B.C. & TUTKO, T.S. (1966) *Problem Athletes and How to Handle Them.* Pelham, London.

ORWIN, A. (1973) The running treatment: a preliminary communication on a new use for an old therapy (physical activity) in the agoraphobic syndrome. *Br. J. Psychiat.* **122**, 175.

ORWIN, A. (1974) Treatment of a situational phobia – a case for running. *Br. J. Psychiat.* **125**, 95.

PROCTOR, R.C. & ECKERD, W.M. (1976) 'Toot-toot' or spectator sports: psychological and therapeutic implications. *Am. J. Sports Med.* **4**, 78.

RHOADS, J.M. (1977) Overwork. *J. Am. Med. Ass.* **257**, 2615.

ROWAN, J. (1976) *Ordinary Ecstasy: Humanistic Psychology in Action.* Routledge and Kegan Paul, London.

SCHULTZ, J. & LUTHE, W. (1969) *Autogenic Methods*, Vol 1. Grune and Stratton, New York.
SHEEHAN, G. (1978) *Running and Being: The Total Experience.* Simon and Schuster, New York.
SIMPSON, H.M. & MEANEY, C. (1979) Effects of learning to ski on the self-concept of mentally retarded children. *Am. J. ment. Defic.* **84**, 25.
SOLOMON, E.G. & BUMPUS, A.R. (1978) The running meditation response: an adjunct to psychotherapy. *Am. J. Psychother.* **32**, 583.
SPINO, M. (1976) *Beyond Jogging: The Innerspaces of Running.* Celestial Arts, Millbrae, California.
SPINO, M. (1977) *Running Home.* Celestial Arts, Millbrae, California.
STEIN, L. & BELLUZZI, J.D. (1979) Brain endorphins: possible mediators of pleasurable states. In: *Endorphins in Mental Health Research.* Edited by E. Usdin, W.E. Bunney & N.S. Kline. Oxford University Press, Oxford.
STRAUB, W.F. (Ed.) (1978) *Sport Psychology: An Analysis of Athlete Behaviour.* Mouvement, Ithaca, New York.
STUBBERT, J., CARUSO, M., BRECKENRIDGE, K. & NIES, R. (1975) Physical fitness: a key to emotional health. *RN*, August, 30.
SUGARMAN, A.A. & TARTER, R.E. (Eds) (1978) *Expanding Dimensions of Consciousness.* Springer, New York.
TURNER, D.J. & DYER, G.W. (1969) An evening aquatics programme for neuropsychiatric patients. *Am. Correct. Ther. J.* **23**. 104.

Biosocial Aspects of Sport

COMMENT

DAVID RYDE

56 Anerley Park, London

The sports medicine scene has changed greatly in the past 30 years, but are athletes victors or victims in this change? About 1950, Sir Adolph Abrahams, reporting on the longevity of oarsmen, introduced the question of the effects of health on training, or training on health. Concurrently, the sports press then reported that a Scandinavian athlete had died when competing too soon after an episode of tonsillitis and that a world class miler, after his performance had deteriorated, was found to have a haemoglobin level of 70%. In 1953, as a hospital houseman, I developed mononucleosis, losing 2 stones in weight in the process, being off work for 2 months and feeling depressed and debilitated for a year. During this time I was advised by a distinguished physician to give up sport but, slowly and fearfully, I resumed training until now, almost 30 years later, I can give many lads half my age a good run for their money.

As a founder member of the British Association of Sports Medicine, in 1952, I have noticed sports medicine changing from an adventure to a speciality, and as a general practitioner I find much of its modern literature difficult to relate to the physical and medical needs of sports people. So I often question whether the rank and file athletes, and that is the majority, are any better for this progress. An orthopaedic consultant writing in the March 1980 issue of *World Medicine* asks if sports medicine is a pseudo-speciality and what good does it do for sports people? Has this speciality become a form of occupational therapy for its practitioners? Has not the speciality of sports medicine arrived at a time for self-audit, to assess the mental and physical benefits, if any, gained by sportsmen and women and the virtues and advantages of the many journals and conferences?

I have seen a large number of good performers whose complaints have been misunderstood and consequently misdiagnosed. Training for competitions used to be fun; there were not too many worries about national prestige and even fewer worries at club and college level where most people compete. But the top of the pyramid, or the professional level of sport, is now big business, where ethics might be considered of secondary importance to winning and where the level of performance and the quick return to top performance after mental or physical illness or injury is considered essential. If this is so then how well do we assess the psychological overlay of the physical symptoms, or relate the physical symptoms to sport's medical problems? Is it then not time to reduce training, or is it paramount to devise new ways to keep players active?

The two previous speakers concentrated on the medical aspects of sport in which stress operates at an increasing level. Stress is necessary but how much can be tolerated? How much is self-induced and can it be initiated and intensified by coaches, doctors or families? The doctors' and coaches' role is not only to look at the participants' bodies but to understand their attitude towards competition, training and injury and towards life itself. It remains the doctors' responsibility to eliminate danger and to protect participants; but to remove every type of stress imposed upon athletes would destroy the concept of the competitiveness of sport. The ultimate opponent in sport is oneself; the destiny of players lies in their ability to compete with and to overcome their own doubts and deficiencies.

The moral behind Dr Bassey's talk is that, like life, sports medicine is a mixture of good and bad: you are never too old to train, but once you have started you had better not stop. Is exercise dangerous as a cause of coronary thrombosis? Does marathon running increase coronary vasculature? About 20 years ago the American marathon runner Clarence de Mar, who had run all his life, died from the secondary effects of a carcinoma and at post-mortem his coronary arteries were found to be 2½ times the average diameter; is that why he became a good marathon runner or did marathon running give him his unusual coronary circulation?

Dr Bassey also said that one can lose only 17g in weight for a ½-hr walk; in recent years of general practice it has become apparent to me that those who want to lose weight successfully should lose it slowly. It is no good trying to lose weight rapidly because this turns it into a contest in which eventually the loser has to be oneself, so, any person who goes on to a crash diet almost invariably loses the fight. Now 17g a day is equivalent to 4oz a week, or 1 stone in a year; I find that getting people to lose weight slowly is far more successful, and when they start moaning 'Oh, I don't want to lose only 3 stones in 3 years', I say 'Well, in 20 years of trying so far you have lost nothing!'.

Dr Bassey also stimulated me when she spoke about a definition of health: could you say that health is a reserve of body function or that illness is the manifestation of altered or reduced function?

Finally having heard Dr Yaffé, who gave the definition of sport, perhaps I could suggest that sport is the social equivalent of combat and it fulfils a biological need, so it may be therapeutic. The primitive form of competition is combat, perhaps mortal combat. It was suggested that coming here to speak was a test of oneself but I think it is really a test for the audience; we should be modifying their attitudes and making them ask questions.

GENERAL DISCUSSION

The discussion opened with a reference to the Inner Game, mentioned by Dr Yaffé, and there was some scepticism of it being an effective approach to the top levels of sport, although the importance of mental rehearsal, to improve concentration for example, was recognized.

It was suggested that meditative methods, leading to loss of fear, could also lead to lack of motivation but the positive benefits of these methods were thought to arise from the resulting ability to act spontaneously and uninhibitedly.

Reference was made to an American community study which showed, for a cohort moving from youth into adulthood, that there was no change in fitness, as measured by maximum oxygen uptake, irrespective of whether the individuals exercised or not. Dr Bassey pointed out that criteria varied between different studies and that many other results did show higher maximum oxygen uptake with real changes in exercise.

Discussion

A question was asked about the recent research on brown adipose tissue and its implications for diet, exercise and weight control in general. Dr Bassey explained that brown adipose tissue was a special form of fat tissue found in relative abundance in babies where its function seems to be to protect them from cold by becoming metabolically active and producing heat in response to circulating adrenalin. Because this process uses up calories it has become of interest in connection with obesity and there is a theory that thin people who never put on weight, however much they eat, have a lot of brown adipose tissue which is capable of using up extra calories which do not therefore give rise to fat. There is not yet evidence to prove this but, if true, it means that it is easy for thin people to stay thin while people who tend to put on weight have to resort to increased exercise and dietary control to remain thin. A further group of people who get very fat seem to have pathological problems and do not respond to exercise, but they are very unusual.

Attention was drawn to the different healthy and hazardous elements of sport, as opposed to physical exercise. Increasing evidence showed that exercise was good for physical and physiological health, but did not necessarily improve mental health; sport, however, could do a great deal to improve psychological health but because of the physical hazards involved, some doctors regarded it as more unhealthy than healthy. Dr Bassey agreed with this point and commented that, for ordinary people, not sportsmen who were already active enough to maintain optimum levels of physical health, the problem was that exercise itself was boring and to build it into everyday life it needed to be fun. A balance was therefore required whereby people could reap the benefits of exercise in the form of enjoyable sport, without excessive involvement leading to sports injuries. Dr Yaffé suggested that the psychological well-being associated with sport could be due to biochemical factors but it was difficult to separate these from the environmental and other considerations.

This led to a discussion of moderation, autoaddiction and obsessionality, especially among joggers and long distance runners. It was suggested that obsessionality could threaten the benefits which people could derive from participation in sport. Dr Yaffé said that the addictive potential was determined by the individual's personality but it did appear to have a definite physical aspect and deprivation could lead to withdrawal symptoms such as increased tension, anxiety and lack of sleep.

Finally, it was stressed that people participating in sport, especially long distance running, should not assume that they were immune to heart disease or that exercise would provide absolute protection. The importance of regular medical checks and the danger of ignoring warning signs and symptoms were emphasized.

III

FACTORS IN PERFORMANCE

Chairman: Ray Williams

Biosocial Aspects of Sport

THE BIOLOGICAL BASIS OF APTITUDE: THE ENDURANCE RUNNER

CLYDE WILLIAMS

Department of Physical Education and Sports Science, Loughborough University of Technology

Summary. Aptitude for a particular sport is governed by many factors, not least of which are obvious environmental influences. There are, however, individuals who, through genetic endowment, have the necessary biological characteristics which identify them as potentially elite athletes. These characteristics have been described more fully for endurance athletes because prolonged, almost steady-state running, lends itself more readily to investigation by biologists, than do the more complex sports.

These studies show that the potentially elite endurance athlete is an individual endowed with an above average cardio-respiratory system, capable of a high rate of oxygen transport and carbon dioxide elimination. Not only does the elite endurance athlete have a greater rate of oxygen transport than the average sportsman or sportswoman, but the muscles receiving the oxygen are composed mainly of type I, i.e. low-twitch oxidative fibres, which are designed for endurance exercise. Furthermore, the elite endurance athlete also appears to be pre-programmed genetically to lay down less fat, in the form of sub-cutaneous adipose tissue, than the average sportsman or sportswoman of the same age and sex.

Although genetic endowment dictates the potential ability of an individual for sustained high speed running, only appropriate training will allow the realization of this potential and so enable the individual to join the fraternity of the world's elite endurance athletes.

Introduction

Aptitude for a particular sport is commonly equated with success in that sport. Success in sport is measured in terms of the number of competitions won or world records established. Thus there is considerable interest in 'what makes a champion', whether it be at county, national or international levels of competition. Interest in 'championship material' is not only generated within a sport by those who hope to emulate the current champion(s) but also by the scientists who recognize in these sportsmen and sportswomen, the opportunity to extend the available knowledge of human performance and human adaptability.

One of the obvious realizations which comes from a consideration of aptitude for certain sports is that the successful sportsman or sportswoman could have been successful at sports other than those chosen. For example, the basketball player would probably have a good chance of success at high-jumping; the oarsman could have been a successful rugby player; the cyclo-cross champion could have been equally successful as an endurance athlete or cross-country skier. Environmental influences, such as, available facilities, expense, exposure to and prestige of the particular sport, all contribute to the selection of a sport by any individual. Thus the aptitude for a particular sport cannot be entirely explained in terms of the biology of the successful sportsman or sportswoman. Nevertheless there do appear to be biological similarities among those individuals who are successful at endurance sports as there are among individuals who are successful at sprint-type sport.

The biological characteristics of successful athletes who participate in long distance running events have received considerable attention from biologists. The reason for this popular choice is that running, even though complex from a biological point of view, offers a simpler model for study than many other sports which combine running and additional complex neuro-muscular skills. Thus the purpose of this paper is to describe the biological characteristics of those individuals who are successful at endurance running in an attempt to understand more fully their aptitudes for these particular activities. An additional aim is to try and explore what proportion nature (genetic endowment) and nurture (training) contribute to success in these activities.

Physique and physiology of the endurance athlete

The stature of the endurance athlete is obviously different from that of the sprinter. Whereas the sprinter is broad shouldered and muscular both in the legs and in the upper body, the endurance athlete is narrow shouldered, lean and without obvious muscular hypertrophy either in the legs or in the upper body. These differences have been documented more precisely by Tanner (1964) who studied 137 competitors at the 1960 Olympic Games at Rome. The body fat content of the male distance runner amounts to only 5-10% of his body weight (Costill, Bowers & Kammer, 1970), whereas in apparently lean looking active young men, fat accounts for approximately 12% of their body weight (Williams, Reid & Coutts, 1973; Costill *et al.*, 1970). Elite female distance runners also have a lower percentage of body fat than active, though untrained, females of the same age (Wilmore & Brown, 1974). The differences in physique of female sprinters and distance runners are of the same kind as reported by Tanner (1964) for men (Malina *et al.*, 1971). In distance running, as opposed to distance swimming, a large proportion of subcutaneous fat is a disadvantage, not simply because of the burden of transporting the additional load but because it makes temperature regulation less effective. The endurance swimmer benefits from the insulating quality of a large amount of subcutaneous adipose tissue which appears to help delay the onset of hypothermia (Pugh & Edholm, 1955). Exercise-induced hyperthermia is the constant threat of the long distance runner and so the minimum of heat conservation is necessary (Pugh, Corbet & Johnson, 1967).

Prolonged exercise is supported by aerobic energy metabolism of fat and carbohydrate. The better the supply of oxygen, by the athlete's cardio-respiratory system, from the external environment to the internal environment of the muscle cells, the greater the potential for successful endurance performance. The maximum rate of oxygen transport and consumption for an individual is dictated by the size of the respiratory and cardiovascular system, as well as the size of the oxygen-demanding muscle mass used during exercise. Endurance athletes have a characteristically large maximum oxygen uptake capacity (VO_2 max). Typical VO_2 max values for endurance athletes range

Table 1. Maximum respiratory response to treadmill exercise in male and female physical education students (mean ±SD)

	n	VE (l/min)	VCO_2 (l/min)	VO_2 (l/min)	VO_2 (ml/kg/min)	HR (b/min)
Males	18	129.4 ±15.8	5.3 ±0.9	4.3 ±0.5	54.3 ±0.9	194 ±10
Females	16	79.9 +11.5	3.0 ±0.5	2.5 ±0.4	41.6 ±4.8	193 ±10

between 70 and 85 ml/kg/min and owe more to genetic endowment of large respiratory and cardiovascular systems, per unit body weight, than to the adaptations from training (Åstrand & Rodahl, 1977). For example, the maximum respiratory values for a group of final year Loughborough University Physical Education students (Table 1) are unlikely to increase by more than 10–20% as a result of further training. Training produces only a modest improvement in the VO_2 max values of active individuals (Ekblom, 1969; Davies & Sargeant, 1975), though considerably larger changes can be produced in sedentary or previously immobile individuals (Saltin *et al.*, 1968; Pollock, 1973). The limitation to large improvements in the VO_2 max values of active or trained individuals, appears to be the inability of the cardiovascular system to deliver sufficient oxygen to the working muscles at the required rate (Davies & Sargeant, 1975). Increasing the amount of oxygen-carrying red blood cells in an athlete, blood-doping as it has unfortunately been called, is a useful experimental illustration of how skeletal muscles will increase their maximum oxygen uptake, during exercise, when offered more oxygen (Ekblom, Goldbarg & Gullbring, 1972).

Table 2. Blood lactate concentrations before and after 10 × 20-m shuttle runs, for male and female physical education students (mean ±SD)

	n	Time (sec)	Speed (m/sec)	Blood lactate (mM) Pre-	Post-	Difference
Males	11	40.86 ±1.31	4.90 ±0.16	2.46 ±0.45	12.99 ±1.61	10.53 ±1.34
Females	14	46.80 +1.95	4.28 ±0.18	2.55 ±0.66	12.44 ±1.81	9.88 ±1.96

One of the characteristics of successful sprinters may be their ability to produce energy more rapidly by the glycogen to lactate process and also to tolerate high concentrations of lactic acid to a greater degree than less successful athletes. The changes in blood lactate concentrations as a result of ten consecutive 20-metre shuttle runs are shown for male and female physical education students in Table 2. In this multiple sprint type of activity the demands for energy, by the working muscles, cannot be met rapidly enough by aerobic energy metabolism, hence the reliance on what is commonly called anaerobic metabolism. It is, then, not surprising that sprinters need not necessarily have high VO_2 max values as a prerequisite for success at sprint-type sports or events.

The distance runner needs a large VO_2 max value because the oxygen cost of running increases almost linearly with the running speed (Costill & Fox, 1969; Davies & Thompson, 1979). Furthermore the successful distance runners have the ability to utilize large fractions of their oxygen transport capacities, for prolonged periods of time (Costill & Fox, 1969; Costill, Thomason & Roberts, 1973; Davies & Thompson, 1979). For example, during a marathon race, a successful runner may utilize 75–85% of his maximum oxygen uptake (Costill & Fox, 1969; Davies & Thompson, 1979) whereas during a 10-mile road race, the demands may be as high as 90% VO_2 max (Costill et al., 1973). The cardiovascular, thermoregulatory and metabolic responses of a runner occur in proportion to the relative exercise intensity i.e. the oxygen cost of the activity in relationship to the individual's maximum oxygen uptake (%VO_2 max) (Saltin, 1973; Rowell, 1974). Thus the athlete with a large VO_2 max value can sustain higher running speeds with less discomfort than athletes with lower VO_2 max values. It has been suggested that the energy cost of running at different speeds is more or less the same for each runner, irrespective of his or her experience (Åstrand & Rodahl, 1977; Davies & Thompson, 1979). Thus success at distance running may be attributed simply to the genetic endowment of a large VO_2 max and the appropriate training, so that the athlete is able to utilize a large fraction of his/her VO_2 max for the duration of a race (Davies & Thompson, 1979). This generalization would not, however, explain the success of the world record holder for the marathon, whose VO_2 max value was a modest 69·7 ml/kg/min. It has been suggested that he was able to compensate for his low VO_2 max by developing an efficient running style (Costill et al., 1971). The estimated rate of oxygen utilization for the completion of the 42·2-km distance in 2hr 10min (i.e. approx. 12 mph) is suggested as 62 ml/kg/min (Pugh et al., 1967) or even 70 ml/kg/min (Davies & Thompson, 1979). Thus Clayton, the record holder, would have had to have utilized either 89% VO_2 max if the former estimate is taken or 100% VO_2 max if the latter estimate of oxygen cost of the speed is used. Both estimates of the oxygen cost of running at 12 mph, would lead to the suggestion that the world record holder was using too large a fraction of his maximum oxygen uptake to be sustainable for over 2 hours. The question of whether or not an endurance athlete can improve the economy with which he runs, so as to compensate for a modest VO_2 max value, remains to be answered. Some preliminary results from our own research laboratory suggest that there may be some significant variation in the oxygen costs of different running speeds between individuals. For example, Table 3 contains the values for three successful middle-distance runners and shows that, at a speed of 12 mph, the oxygen cost is different for each of these athletes. The athlete MD, with the highest VO_2 max value, also uses more oxygen at each of the higher speeds. Nevertheless he would probably be more capable of running at a pace of

5 min/mile (12 mph) for a prolonged period of time, than would the other two athletes, because he would utilize a smaller proportion of his VO_2 max (85%) than would athletes PL (93%) and KO (91%).

Table 3. Oxygen costs of running at different treadmill speeds for three middle-distance runners (MD, PL and KO)

Speed		VO_2(ml/kg/min)		
mph	m/min	MD	PL	KO
8·0	213·4	41·0	40·0	28·0
9·0	240·1	48·0	46·0	34·0
10·0	266·7	56·0	52·0	38·0
11·0	293·4	64·0	57·0	44·0
12·0	320·0	71·0	63·0	50·0
VO_2 max ml/kg/min		84·0	68·0	55·0

Muscle morphology

The muscle mass of the endurance athlete tends to be considerably less than the athlete involved in sprints. The distribution is also different in that the endurance athlete obviously has most of his muscle mass in his legs with a lean upper body, whereas the sprinter has an obviously larger muscle mass in both the lower and upper body. The endurance athlete uses his arms for balance whereas the sprinter's arms are used in a positive driving action. Recently it has become possible to look more closely at the fibre composition of skeletal muscles of athletes by using an atraumatic needle biopsy technique. The tissue obtained by this technique can be treated by various histochemical procedures to reveal the morphological features of the muscle fibres. The speed with which a muscle contracts is related to the rate at which a series of biochemical reactions occur and release energy for the contractile process. Central to the whole process, is the splitting of the high energy phosphate compound, adenosinetriphosphate (ATP) by an enzyme called myosin ATPase. The higher the activity of this enzyme, the more rapid the contractile speed of the muscle (Barany, 1967). The presence of the enzyme myosin ATPase can be located in muscle fibres by using histochemical techniques. Thus muscle fibres which are either fast contracting or slow contracting can be readily identified using simple histochemical and light microscopy techniques. In addition, these techniques allow a qualitative assessment of the oxidative and glycolytic capacities of the fast contracting (fast-twitch) and slow contracting (slow-twitch) muscle fibres. The oxidative capacity of muscle is reflected by the activity of an enzyme called nicotinamide adenine dinucleotine tetrazolium reductase (NADH-TR), and the glycolytic capacity (i.e. anaerobic energy releasing system) by the activity of alpha-glycerophosphate dehydrogenase (AGPDH). Thus using a combination of these histochemical methods of identifying the reference enzymes in muscle fibres, a more complete description of the fibre composition of a muscle can be established.

The contrast between the histochemical staining intensity for myosin ATPase in fast-twitch and slow-twitch fibres of human muscle can be increased by using alkaline conditions (pH 10·4) and acid conditions (pH 4·6). Several sections from the same muscle allow each type of fibre to be characterized, not only in terms of its relative speed of contraction i.e. fast-twitch or slow-twitch, but also in terms of its predominant metabolic means of producing energy e.g. oxidative or anaerobic (glycolytic) metabolism. Three populations of muscle fibres are identifiable with these histochemical procedures and they are described as slow-twitch oxidative (SO), fast-twitch oxidative and glycolytic (FOG) and fast-twitch glycolytic (FG) (Peter *et al.*, 1972). Alternatively, a more conservative nomenclature, Type I, Type IIA and Type IIB is used instead of SO, FOG and FG. The reason for this is that whereas in animal studies the contractile speed of muscle fibres can be determined as well as their histochemical profiles, in human subjects only the histochemical profiles of the muscle fibres can be precisely determined (Burke *et al.*, 1971; Dubowitz & Brooke, 1973).

The muscle fibre composition of elite endurance athletes shows a high proportion of Type I, i.e. SO (slow-twitch), fibres whereas sprinters have been shown to have a high proportion of Type II, i.e. FG (fast-twitch), fibres (Gollnick *et al.*, 1972). In addition to having more than 70% Type I (slow-twitch) fibres, the muscles of elite distance runners have also significantly greater aerobic capacities than the muscles of sprinters (Costill *et al.*, 1976). As might be expected, the skeletal muscles of sprinters not only contain a higher proportion of fast-twitch fibres than the long distance runners, but they also have greater capacities for deriving energy from anaerobic (glycolytic) metabolism (Costill *et al.*, 1976). The skeletal muscles of endurance athletes also have a greater capillary supply than those of untrained individuals (Inger, 1979). Female track and field athletes have the same patterns of muscle fibre composition as male athletes with the only apparent differences being their smaller areas (Costill *et al.*, 1976). The trend revealed by these studies, on the morphology of skeletal muscles of internationally successful athletes, is that the distance runner tends to have high proportions of slow-twitch (Type I) fibres, with greater capillary and oxidative capacities than the muscles of untrained individuals. The predominance of one fibre population in the muscles of successful athletes is the result of genetic endowment, whereas the large capacity for oxidative metabolism is the result of training (Komi *et al.*, 1977b). Interestingly, many of these studies, on the muscle morphology of successful athletes, have recorded fibre compositions of muscles in untrained subjects which are as extreme as the athletes being studied.

It would be a gross over-simplification to describe the potential for success at distance running or sprinting only in terms of the possession of the appropriate muscle fibre composition. Consideration has to be given to the total mass of the muscle and what proportion of the total area is occupied by the predominant fibre type. A further discouragement to the use of 'fibre-typing' as a screening method for the selection of potentially successful sprinters or long distance runners is the realization that the histochemical procedures yield only qualitative information. The procedures indicate only that a certain proportion of the fibre population is probably faster contracting (FT or Type II) or has greater endurance capacity (ST or Type I) than the other fibre population in the same muscle. There is no quantitative information about how fast the fast-twitch fibres may be or how much endurance quality the slow-twitch fibres possess. It is impossible to compare the quality of fibre populations histochemically, when the fibres are from different muscles of different individuals or even of the same individual. As an illustration of this point, the muscle fibre compositions of a selection of athletes who have taken part in experiments in my own laboratory are shown in Table 4. The samples were obtained from the vastus lateralis muscles of these individuals and treated histochemically as outlined above.

Table 4. Muscle fibre compositions of untrained and trained subjects (muscle samples taken from the vastus lateralis)

Subjects	Activity	I (SO)	IIA (FOG)	IIB (FG)	No. fibres counted
CW	Active, untrained	46·6	14·6	38·8	219
SC	Active, untrained	43·4	11·2	45·4	147
DD	Rugby player	33·3	6·7	60·0	288
BG	200/400 m runner	48·8	13·2	38·0	250
RM	1500/5000 m runner	47·7	18·0	34·3	478
TM	Marathon runner	43·4	10·9	45·7	356

The proportions of Type I and Type II fibres were similar for all of these individuals and yet their exercise capacities were remarkably different. One of the athletes (BG), an international sprinter, ran the 400 metres in 48·0 sec while RM recorded 3 min 56 sec for the 1500 metres and the long distance athlete completed a marathon race in 2 hr 27 min. Each was regarded as being successful at their own athletic event and, at their own levels of participation, would have been identified as individuals having aptitude for these events. It has been suggested that the genetic endowment of the proportions of muscle fibre types appropriate for sprint or endurance events, along with a matching cardio-respiratory system, single out the individual as a potentially elite athlete, whereas national or even international level success may be achieved without such extreme characteristics (Komi *et al.*, 1977a).

Training

While genetic endowment (nature) confers on certain individuals, the potential to be able to run long distances in record times, only through training (nurture) will they be able to realize their potential. At the start of a marathon race, all competitors may aspire to finish first; however, while nature dictates those to whom it is a realistic aspiration, training alone can ensure that all competitors complete the race.

Training increases the ability of the individual to sustain running speeds which demand a high percentage of his or her maximum oxygen uptake, without producing more than a modest improvement in that individual's maximum oxygen uptake (Ekblom, 1969; Gollnick *et al.*, 1973; Daniels, Yarborough & Foster, 1978). Even relatively short-term training will improve endurance capacity without producing a significant improvement in maximum oxygen uptake. The information shown in Table 5 is included as an example of the changes in endurance capacity which can accompany training of only 6 weeks' duration. Training involved the subjects in exercising at 75% VO_2 max, on bicycle ergometers, three times a week and resulted in a five-fold improvement in endurance capacity without a significant improvement in VO_2 max values (Bland & Williams, 1979, unpublished).

Table 5. Pre- and post-training maximum oxygen uptake values, maximum blood lactate concentrations, and endurance times

Subjects	VO_2 max (ml/kg/min) Pre-	VO_2 max (ml/kg/min) Post-	Blood lactate (Δ mM) Pre-	Blood lactate (Δ mM) Post-	Endurance time (min) Pre-	Endurance time (min) Post-
PS	43·9	46·8	11·92	9·24	10·0	52·4
MH	47·0	46·7	13·14	12·76	9·3	120·0
NT	44·3	50·8	12·69	12·63	15·0	65·0
JB	51·1	54·0	10·34	13·93	20·0	50·0
JL	46·9	53·9	11·94	9·68	11·0	105·0
PL	53·0	52·8	10·78	11·99	18·0	80·0
KP	43·1	43·8	8·74	8·80	15·0	50·0
CS	41·0	42·2	9·62	7·42	16·4	70·0
Mean	46·8	49·1	10·92	10·36	14·3	74·0
±SD	±5·2	±4·4	±1·58	±2·54	±3·9	±26·3

Although training may result in only modest improvements in an individual's maximum oxygen uptake, the oxidative capacity of the muscles may double (Gollnick *et al.*, 1973). The increased oxidative capacity can occur in both the Type I (slow-twitch) and the Type II (fast-twitch) fibres (Henriksson & Reitman, 1976). Furthermore, endurance training appears to convert the Type IIB (FG) fibres into Type IIA (FOG) fibres, i.e. increasing the oxidative capacity of the fast-twitch fibre population (Saltin *et al.*, 1977). The greater the oxidative capacity, the greater the endurance capacity of the muscle. Fatigue during prolonged running is associated with glycogen (carbohydrate) depletion in the Type I (slow-twitch) fibres (Costill *et al.*, 1973). Glycogen sparing occurs during exercise after training, because of a shift towards the aerobic metabolism of fatty acids and so this training-induced increase in fatty acid metabolism improves the endurance capacity of the individual (Holloszy & Booth, 1976; Henriksson, 1977). Thus one of the important characteristics of well-trained endurance athletes is their greater ability to meet the energy demands of running with increased fat metabolism, than was possible before training. However, it is important to realize that it is the increased ability to oxidize fatty acids in the working muscles, which delays the early onset of fatigue, rather than the mobilization of fatty acids from the subcutaneous adipose tissue (Williams *et al.*, 1975; Gollnick, 1977).

The proposition that female athletes are better suited for long distance running than male athletes, because the female has a significantly greater body fat content than the male, is not soundly based. As mentioned previously, it is the efficient use of the mobilized fatty acids by exercising muscles, rather than fatty acid mobilization itself, which dictates the amount of energy supplied by fat metabolism. Furthermore, the increasing number of successful female distance runners have low body fat contents similar to those of successful male distance runners (Wilmore & Brown, 1974). To date there does not appear to be any good evidence to suggest that the female athlete has a metabolic advantage over male athletes during distance running (Costill *et al.*, 1979).

Acknowledgments

Dr C. Williams is a Senior Research Fellow, and both he and his work are supported by the Sports Council.

References

ÅSTRAND, P.O. & RODAHL (1977) *A Textbook of Work Physiology*. McGraw-Hill, New York.
BARANY, M. (1967) ATPase activity of myosin correlated with speed of muscle shortening. *J. gen. Physiol.* **50**, 197.
BURKE, R.E., LEVINE, R.N., ZAJAC, F.E., TSAIRIS, P. & ENGEL, W.K. (1971) Mammalian motor units: physiological-histochemical correlation in three types in cat gastrocnemius. *Science, N.Y.* **174**, 709.
COSTILL, D.L., BOWERS, R. & KAMMER, W.F. (1970) Skinfold estimates of body fat among marathon runners. *Med. & Sci. Sports,* **2**, 93.
COSTILL, D.L., BRANHAM, G., EDDY, D. & SPARKS, K. (1971) Determinants of marathon running success. *Int.Z.Angew. Physiol.* **29**, 249.
COSTILL, D.L., DANIELS, J., EVANS, W., FINK, W. KRAHENBUHL, G. & SALTIN, B. (1976) Skeletal muscle enzymes and fibre composition in male and female track athletes. *J. appl. Physiol.* **40**, 149.
COSTILL, D.L., FINK, W.J., GETCHELL, L.H., IVY, J.L. & WITZMANN, F.A. (1979) Lipid metabolism in skeletal muscle of endurance-trained males and females. *J. appl. Physiol.* **47**, 787.
COSTILL, D.L. & FOX, E.L. (1969) Energetics of marathon running. *Med. & Sci. Sports,* **1**, 81.
COSTILL, D.L. GOLLNICK, P.D., JANSSON, E.D., SALTIN, B. & STEIN, E.M. (1973) Glycogen depletion patterns in human muscle fibres during distance running. *Acta physiol. scand.* **89**, 374.
COSTILL, D.L., THOMASON, H. & ROBERTS, E. (1973) Fractional utilization of the aerobic capacity during distance running. *Med. & Sci. Sports,* **5**, 248.
DANIELS, J.T., YARBOROUGH, R.A. & FOSTER, C. (1978) Changes in VO$_2$ max and running performance with training. *Europ. J. appl. Physiol.* **39**, 249.
DAVIES, C.T.M. & SARGEANT, A.J. (1975) Effects of training on the physiological responses to one- and two-leg work. *J. appl. Physiol.* **38**, 377.
DAVIES, C.T.M. & THOMPSON, M.W. (1979) Aerobic performance of female marathon and male ultra-marathon athletes. *Europ. J. appl. Physiol.* **41**, 233.
DUBOWITZ, V. & BROOKE, M.H. (1973) *Muscle Biopsy: A Modern Approach.* Saunders, London.
EKBLOM, B. (1969) Effect of physical training on oxygen transport system in man. *Acta physiol. scand.* Suppl. **328**.
EKBLOM, B., GOLDBARG, A.N. & GULLBRING, B. (1972) Response to exercise after blood loss and reinfusion. *J. appl. Physiol.* **33**, 175.
GOLLNICK, P.D. (1977) Free fatty acid turnover and availability of substrates as a limiting factor in prolonged exercise. *Ann. N.Y. Acad. Sci.* **301**, 64.
GOLLNICK, P.D., ARMSTRONG, R.B., SALTIN, B., SAUBERT, C.W., SEMBROWICH, W.L. & SHEPHERD, R.E. (1973) Effect of training on enzyme activity and fibre composition of human skeletal muscle. *J. appl. Physiol.* **34**, 107.

GOLLNICK, P.D., ARMSTRONG, R.B., SAUBERT, C.W., PIEHL, K. & SALTIN, B. (1972) Enzyme activity and fibre composition in skeletal muscle of untrained and trained men. *J. appl. Physiol.* **33**, 312.

HENRIKSSON, J. (1977) Training induced adaptation of skeletal muscle and metabolism during submaximal exercise. *J. Physiol.* **270**, 661.

HENRIKSSON, J. & REITMAN, J.S. (1976) Quantitative measures of enzyme activities in Type I and Type II muscle fibres of man after training. *Acta physiol. scand.* **97**, 392.

HOLLOSZY, J.O. & BOOTH, F.W. (1976) Biochemical adaptations to endurance exercise in muscle. *Ann. Rev. Physiol.* **38**, 273.

INGER, F. (1979) Capillary supply and mitochondrial content of different skeletal muscle fibre types in untrained and endurance-trained men. A histochemical and ultrastructural study. *Europ. J. appl. Physiol.* **40**, 197.

KOMI, P.V., RUSKO, H., VOS, J. & VIHKO, V. (1977a) Anaerobic performance capacity in athletes. *Acta physiol. scand.* **100**, 107.

KOMI, P.V., VIITASALO, J.H.T., HAVU, M., THORSTENSSON, A., SJÖDIN, B. & KARLSSON, J. (1977b) Skeletal muscle fibres and muscle enzymes activities in monozygous and dizygous twins of both sexes. *Acta physiol. scand.* **100**, 385.

MALINA, R.M., HARPER, A.B., AVENT, H.A. & CAMPBELL, D.E. (1971) Physique of female track and field athletes. *Med. & Sci. Sports,* **3**, 32.

PETER, J.B., BARNARD, R.J., EDGERTON, V.R., GILLESPIE, C.A. & STEMPEL, K.E. (1972) Metabolic profiles of three fibre types of skeletal muscle in guinea pigs and rabbits. *Biochemistry,* **11**, 2627.

POLLOCK, M.L. (1973) The quantification of endurance training programs. In: *Exercise and Sport Science Review,* p 155. Edited by J.H. Wilmore. Academic Press, New York.

PUGH, L.G.C.E., CORBET, J.L. & JOHNSON, R.H. (1967) Rectal temperatures, weight losses, sweat rates in marathon running. **23**, 347.

PUGH, L.G.C.E., & EDHOLM, O. (1955) The physiology of channel swimmers. *Lancet,* **ii**, 761.

ROWELL, L.B. (1974) Human cardiovascular adjustments to exercise and thermal stress. *Physiol. Rev.* **54**, 75.

RUSKO, H., HAVU, M. & KARVINEN, E. (1978) Aerobic performance capacity in athletes. *Europ. J. appl. Physiol.* **38**, 151.

SALTIN, B. (1973) Metabolic fundamentals in exercise. *Med. & Sci. Sports,* **5**, 137.

SALTIN, B., BLOMQUIST, B., MITCHELL, J.H., JOHNSON, Jr. R.L., WILDENTHAL, K. & CHAPMAN, C.B. (1968) Response to submaximal and maximal exercise after bed rest and training. *Circulation,* **38**, Suppl. 7.

SALTIN, B., HENRIKSSON, J., NYGAARD, E., ANDERSEN, P. & JANSSON, E. (1977) Fibre types and metabolic potentials of skeletal muscles in sedentary man and endurance runners. *Ann. N.Y. Acad. Sci.* **301**, 3.

TANNER, J.M. (1964) *The Physique of the Olympic Athlete.* Allen and Unwin, London.

WILLIAMS, C., KELMAN, G.R., COUPER, D.C. & HARRIS, C.C. (1975) Changes in plasma FFA concentrations before and after reduction in high intensity exercise. *Sports Med. phys. Fitness,* **15**, 2.

WILLIAMS, C., REID, R.M. & COUTTS, R. (1973) Observations on the aerobic power of university rugby players and professional soccer players. *Br. J. Sports Med.* **7**, 390.

WILMORE, J.H. & BROWN, C.H. (1974) Physiological profiles of women distance runners. *Med. & Sci. Sports,* **6**, 178.

Biosocial Aspects of Sport

COMMENT

W.L. STEEL

Department of Physical Education, University of Manchester

I have no real disagreement with the views expounded so ably by Dr Clyde Williams, particularly in the limited field of distance running on which he concentrated. As a non-physiologist, I would hazard the opinion that much of the evidence he has accumulated is incontrovertible. I do utter a word of caution against the easy assumption that genetic factors determine potential performance. As T.H. Pear remarked in the wider context of sports performance they are: 'bold spirits who write of the born cricketer as if determinants of hook-strokes or leg-glides had inhabited the germ cells of his privileged parents'.

As a physicist and educational psychologist by qualification I am used to the world of measurements. The outcome in my experience is, that man is not the measure of all things. Or perhaps, more appropriately, that what man predicts from measurement is at best fallible. The test is seen in prediction from the measured facts to the outcome or the event. In this connection one of the most stable and valuable instruments used by the educational psychologist is the intelligence test. But no educational psychologist would consider such a test to be a guaranteed predictor, since so many other things have to be taken into account. At best it may predict success in university studies, for example, to a highly significant correlation of around 0·45. Effectively this prediction leaves about 80% of the variance unexplained, or alternatively the prediction is 80% in error. So its effectiveness in predicting the outcome for any given individual is unreliable.

Yesterday was the day of the psychometrician; today is the day of the biometrician. The psychometrician deals primarily with things of the 'mind' but is limited by his lack of ability adequately to assess all its aspects – emotion, personality, character, motivation, dreams, desires. But man is a body/mind or, more appositely, a mind/body. Now the biology of man, particularly as it concerns itself with prediction of sporting performance, excludes much more than anything ignored by the psychometrician, namely the mind as a whole and, of particular importance perhaps, motivation.

Unless we are aware of resultant deficiencies in prediction we may create a kind of pseudo-science which may earn us the same unfortunate reputation as was gained by Dr Cartwright, a research anatomist of Louisiana University at the beginning of this century. Writing of the American negroes he characterized them as revealing 'a want of muscular activity ...' which '... makes their motions proverbially slower'. He was led to conclude (among other equally improbable things) that negroes suffer from drapetomania, a peculiar psychological state which attacked negroes before they ran away from slavery. The chief pre-disposing symptoms were sulkiness and dissatisfaction!

I make this point about the American negroes because they have been the subject in our time of anatomical, physiological and anthropometrical analysis with a view to explaining their outstanding contribution to American athletic success in the sprints, jumps and hurdles. But they have rarely, if ever, been prominent in the power events, throwing the hammer, javelin, shot or discus. Nor have they been seen as Olympic competitors in the swimming pool even in the sprint events. The facile explanation is that they are so-called sinkers. Yet sinkers have won Olympic swimming medals (see T.K. Cureton – The Physique of Champion Athletes).

I wish simply to indicate that there may be social–psychological reasons why the American negro excels in sport, and that these same social–psychological factors can be used to explain the success of the East Germans in sport. This is not to deny the importance of biological factors. It is rather to expand upon them. Moreover these same social–psychological factors can be used to explain the negative 'symptoms' of Czechoslovakia and Hungary. Why are they now relatively unsuccessful athletically, when they have access to the same scientific information which guides the successful progress of their Russian and German comrades?

It is not inappropriate, since Galton is considered to be the founder of developmental psychology, to seek some psychological explanation of athletic phenomena. For although there may be scientific principles guiding selection of individuals it would be a brave man who would predict, as an Olympic hammer thrower, a man with a withered arm; or as an international full-back a player who had to wear a surgical boot; or as an Olympic gold medallist in dressage a woman paralysed from the waist down. With people such as these, and many others, it is possibly because of, rather than in spite of, their disabilities that they became proficient in sport.

In a similar manner Table 1 illustrates how 'national' groups literally fought for recognition and for a place in American society and having achieved that place tended to disappear from the picture. Now biological factors may influence boxing participation but social–psychological factors determine continued participation. In this respect the figures at the bottom of the table indicate that the new poor, the new strivers, the South Americans held a remarkable proportion of professional world boxing crowns in 1976.

Table 1. Rank order of number of prominent boxers of various groups in USA

Date	Rank 1	Rank 2	Rank 3
1909	Irish (40%)	German	English
1916	Irish	German	Italian
1928	Jews	Italian	Irish
1936	Italian	Irish	Jews
1948	Negro (50%)	Italian	Mexican

| October 1976 | Latin America 15/16 world champions |
| October 1976 | Rest of world 9 world champions |

And as one of these champions said: 'Boxing is hard but there are things which are harder in life'. Or in the words of Roger Bannister in 1956:

> 'Though physiology may indicate respiratory and circulatory limits to muscular effort, psychology, and other factors beyond the ken of physiology, set the razor's edge of defeat or victory and determine how closely an athlete approaches the absolute limits of performance'.

This summarizes, more effectively than I can, my view concerning biological and psychological factors as they affect sporting performance.

Biosocial Aspects of Sport

SEX DIFFERENCES IN ATHLETIC POTENTIAL

ELIZABETH A.E. FERRIS

5 Addisland Court, Holland Villas Road, London

Summary. Attention is drawn to fresh data available on female sporting performance and the narrowing gap between male and female performance in many sports. The author discusses attempts made to compare athletic potential in males and females and postulates the existence of a factor called athletic predisposition. The differences in performance amongst males and females possessing this factor are much smaller than in the population at large.

The misguidedness of the orthodox view

Until a decade ago, the available data demonstrated that there were differences between the average male and the average female in physical parameters and physiological responses to exercise that supported the view that women were necessarily inferior to men in the fields of sport and physical activity due, it was conjectured, to inherent characteristics. The traditional view about women and their capabilities was that they were innately inferior to men in undergoing physical activities. This view, it was maintained, was supported by the data observed and measured.

As far as social attitudes and cultural opinions were concerned, this was no more than what was to be expected. It was a 'fact of life' that women could not perform as well as men in any activity demanding speed, power, strength and endurance, and one only had to look at normal men and normal women to see that women were not physically endowed with the essential features that were required to perform as well at sport and physical activities. Therefore, it was in line with the orthodox thinking of the time, and also with the results from athletic competition, that the manifest physical and physiological indices showed the average female to be less able and less suited to performing in the sporting arena.

In view of the supporting data, it was assumed that there was no need for anyone to question either the data or the orthodox view, and for the most part no-one did. In the late 1960s, however, probably in association with the emergence of the women's movement, an upsurge began to occur in certain areas of women's participation in sport that were previously forbidden to them, in particular in long-distance running. This latter phenomenon was particularly interesting as, above almost any other sporting event, long-distance running was officially and medically condemned as unsuitable for women. For women to take it up, as they did, was to fly in the face of officialdom, popular mores, and, as some thought, nature.

This phenomenon stimulated great interest amongst the sport scientists, especially the exercise physiologists and physical educationalists, with the result that in the last 10 years research on women in sport, of which hitherto there was a dismal dearth, flourished. Analyses of actual performances in sporting events involving strenuous exertion, such as swimming and running, have revealed that when compared with the male records, female records are improving at a faster rate at almost all distances. (Dyer, 1976, 1977; Ferris, 1977, 1979).

Figure 1 illustrates the percentage differences in male–female world record performances in all running events from 100m to the marathon in 1956 (1963 for the marathon; this being the first year that a female world best time was recorded in this event) and in 1978. The trends during this 22-year period are apparent: at all distances a substantial reduction in the differences between male–female performances had occurred by 1978. Figure 2 shows a similar trend in the male–female performance differences in freestyle swimming from 200m to 1500m; 100m freestyle is the only event in which no change was demonstrated. Dyer (1977) has stated that linear regressions of mean differences in male–female performance between 1948 and 1976 predict that male and female performances will be essentially equal in running by 2077 and in swimming by 2056. In cycling, possible equality is predicted even sooner, by 2011. Figure 3 shows the actual world best performances for men and women in the marathon, since 1920 for men, and since 1963 for women. Linear regressions in this case predict equality by the year 1990.

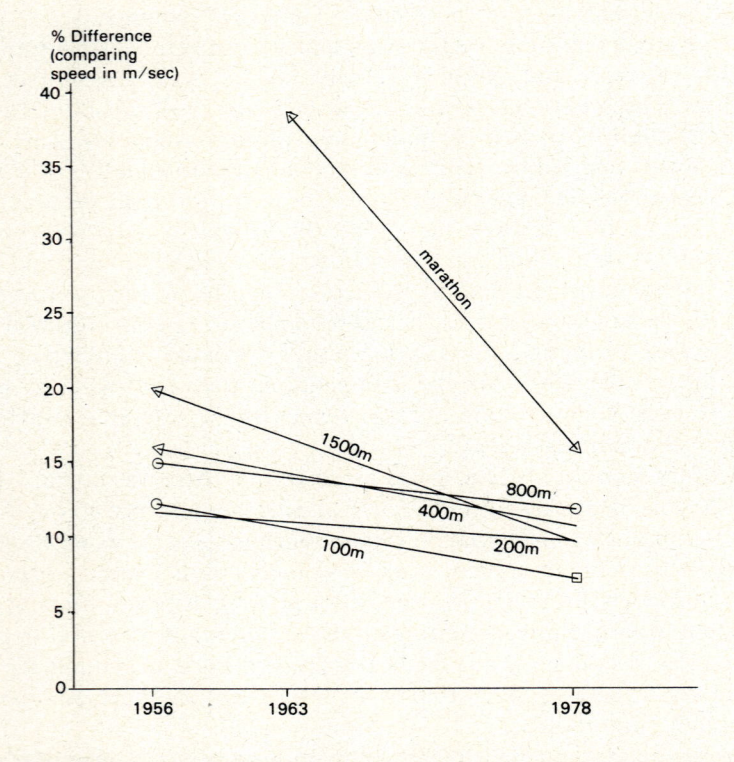

Fig. 1. Percentage differences in men's and women's records and best performances in running (100m–marathon) in 1956 (1963 for marathon) and 1978.

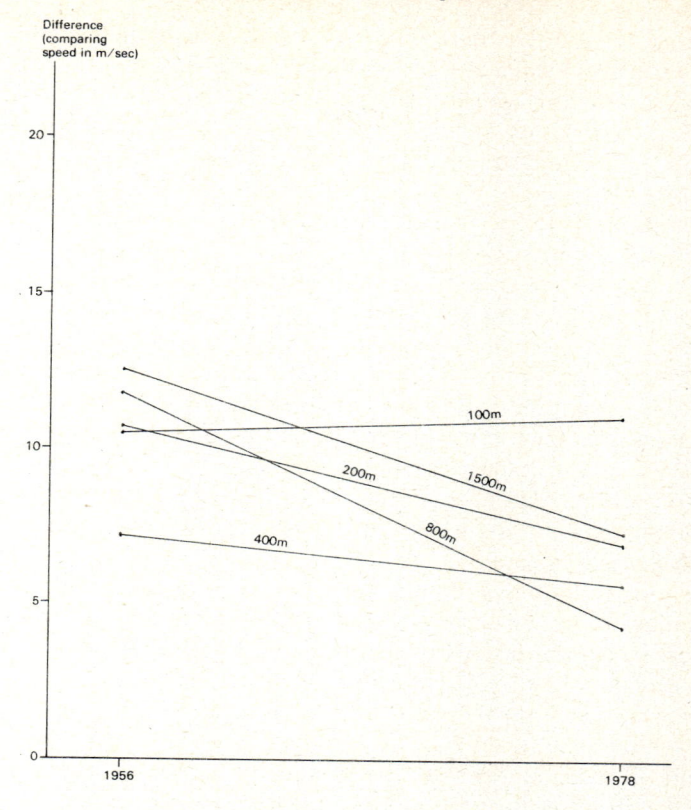

Fig. 2. Percentage differences in men's and women's world records in freestyle swimming events (100–1500m) in 1956 and 1978.

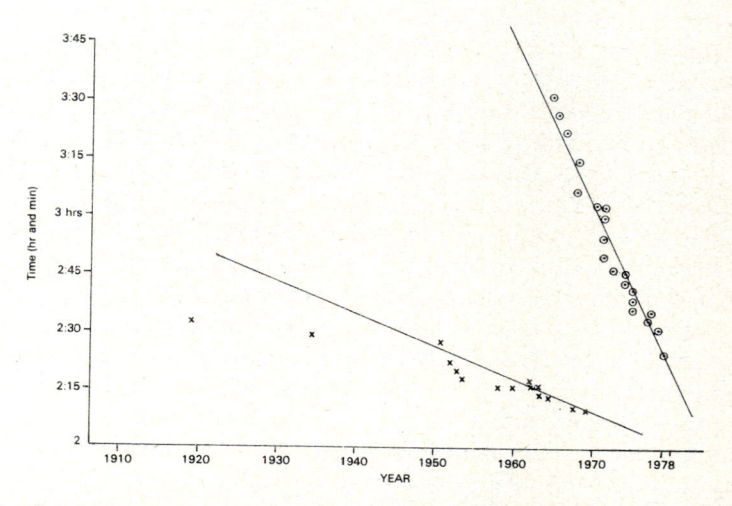

Fig. 3. Trends in improvement in world best performances in the marathon: x, males (Derek Clayton, Australia, 2hr 8min 6sec); o, females (Greta Waitz, Norway, 2hr 27min 33sec).

Physiological research has shown that, contrary to the popular belief which held that females suffer from an inadequate and inefficient cardiovascular capacity to respond to vigorous exercise and that they should be protected from exposure to it, females respond to exercise and to strenuous training in much the same way as men do (Kilbom, 1971; Roskamm, 1976; Cunningham & Hill, 1975; Edwards, 1974; Flint, Drinkwater & Horvath, 1974).

Again, questions have been raised concerning the traditional view that women are considerably weaker than men. Studies have shown that whilst this is true in the upper part of the body, the lower body strength in females, particularly in the legs, when expressed relative to body weight, is only slightly less than in males; when expressed relative to lean body weight, females are actually stronger in the legs than males (Wilmore, 1974). It was also found that with a programme of progressive weight training, females can substantially increase their strength. Wilmore (1974) found that in a relatively short 10-week programme a group of young non-athletic women improved their strength by 30-50%. These relative gains were similar to those exhibited by a group of non-athletic young men on an identical programme. The only difference was that in the women practically no muscular hypertrophy ocurred, whereas in the men the increase in muscle bulk was substantially greater.

In a study on seven track and field women athletes undergoing a strenuous 6-month intensive training proramme which included weight training with near maximal resistance exercises, increases in upper body (bench press) strength of 15 – 44%, and in lower body (half-squat) strength of 16 – 53% were obtained. The absolute values in terms of pounds lifted were considerably greater than the average, untrained male of similar age can achieve (Brown & Wilmore, 1974).

The results of studies on female long-distance runners have unveiled most surprises, at least for those with entrenched traditional views about women and what they are capable of. With respect to body composition, the average female is considerably fatter than the average male of the same age (25% versus 15% fat). This difference in fatness between the sexes is expected, and is considered to be a 'normal', desirable state of affairs. It underlies many of our opinions about what is attractive in a woman's body shape, i.e. soft, well-rounded, curvaceous. Not only does a female's relative fatness constitute a social norm, but it is explainable on a biological basis as the result of the higher secretion of oestrogen, the female sex hormone, in the female. Whether or not this is true, it does give credibility and credence to the belief that not only are women fatter than men, but that they ought to be that way, because it is natural. Studies on female athletes by Wilmore, Brown & Davis (1977) have revealed that long-distance runners have relative body fats that are considerably lower than both the average female and the average male. In fact, several of these women distance runners are competing for leanness with their male long-distance counterparts, with relative body fat values of less than 10%. Costill, Bowers & Kammer (1970) reported an average value of 7·5% fat for 114 male competitors in the 1968 United States Olympic marathon trial. Two of Wilmore et al.'s (1977) elite women distance runners had values of approximately 6%.

With respect to endurance capacity measured as the maximal oxygen uptake (VO_2 max), studies of young untrained subjects reveal what appears to be a substantial sex difference in aerobic power, with female capacity only 70–75% of that in the male (Drinkwater, 1973). In young trained subjects, however, this difference almost totally disappears. In a study of young elite female distance runners the values obtained for VO_2 max were equivalent to those obtained for males of similar age and performance capacity (Burke & Brush, 1979). The mean VO_2 max of 63·24 ml/kg/min was among the highest ever recorded for a group of women. Wilmore & Brown (1974) obtained a mean VO_2 max value of 67·4 ml/kg/min for the three best athletes of a group of mature female long-distance runners; this compares equitably with the value of 69·7 ml/kg/min reported for Derek Clayton, the holder of the world's best marathon performance with a time of 2hr 08min 33 sec (Costill *et al.*, 1971).

These fresh data on women, in particular in the endurance events, that have come to light in the last 10 years, suggest that a re-examination of all the data on women in relation to athletic performance and performance potential is required.

The revolutionary onslaught took place so rapidly that, in the enthusiasm for demonstrating women's potential equality in sport, nobody took the time to articulate a suitable taxonomy within which such data could be properly described and upon which appropriate theories could be constructed.

All these studies illustrate that the conditions necessary for outstanding athletic performance are very similar, or more similar than has hitherto been believed, in highly trained women and men. Therefore, only a small inductive leap is needed to suggest that the gap in performance potential is not as wide as has previously been believed and which indeed had been supported by actual differences in athletic performance, until quite recently. In this paper it will be argued that it is a mistake to infer from the hitherto lower level of athletic performance, a lower performance potential in women.

The problems found when making comparisons between male and female physiological parameters in response to exercise, are reminiscent of those encountered in comparing blacks and whites with respect to intelligence. If the grouping of blacks and whites to be compared does not take into account social variables, the results will not say anything meaningful about the comparative intelligence of the two groups. Instead of simply comparing blacks and whites, one would need to compare (for instance) educated middle-class blacks and educated middle-class whites whose parents had all had similar education and up-bringing.

In order to make a collection of data relevant to the athletic potential of males and females, the samples also need to be matched for suitability for comparison. Data, on the basis of which generalizations have been made about the athletic potential of males and females, have been obtained from studies where the sample groups have simply been males and females, and where the individuals within the sample groups have not been matched for suitability for comparison.

The data in this field of women in sport are in need of re-examination:

(1) to put women and their potential in the sporting arena in true perspective;
(2) to allow for a restructuring of the existing educational programmes in the light of the knowledge of women's capabilities in the athletic field; and
(3) to encourage a rethinking of orthodox attitudes and opinions that have, to date, disallowed women from experiencing their potential in the field of sport and all physical activities.

A presupposition of such a re-examination and re-evaluation of women's athletic potential is a re-classification of some of the terms and conditions which must be adhered to when choosing the relevant population samples. In other words, what is needed is a new taxonomy that will ensure a suitability for comparison between matched samples or groups, that will in turn make relevant sense of the data.

A fresh look at the data

Sport in broad terms requires speed, power, strength and endurance. The physical endowments necessary to be able to demonstrate these qualities include a certain optimum body size, physique, muscle mass and a large cardiovascular capacity. It has been observed that the average mature female, when compared with the average mature male, is approximately 12–13 cm shorter, 16–19 kg lighter in total body weight, 19–21 kg lighter in lean weight, 1–2 kg heavier in fat weight, and with about 10% more fat (Wilmore et al., 1977). With respect to body physique on the basis of somatotype, the average female tends towards endomorphy, or to fatness, whilst the average male tends more towards ectomorphy and mesomorphy, or to slimness and to being well-muscled (Malina & Rarick, 1973). In addition, the average mature female has approximately 30% less total body strength (Hettinger, 1961) and only 75% of the endurance capacity of the average mature male (Drinkwater, 1973; Pollock, 1973).

So, the average woman is shorter, lighter, fatter, and weaker, than the average man, she has less muscles and has less capacity for endurance activities. From these data it has been concluded that the observations constitute the basis of necessary sex differences in athletic potential, with men always having the advantage over women. However, it is now widely acknowledged that the data from which the average values for women and men were obtained, were from sample groups of females and males that had 'lack of suitability of comparison'; the comparison was made between relatively active males and relative sedentary females.

Before puberty, there is no sex difference in performance potential. But it is believed that between the ages of 10 and 12 years, the average female undergoes a substantial reduction in physical activity. At puberty, constraints or demands are placed on both girls and boys to adopt stereotyped sex roles, and these are different for the two sexes. With respect to sport, boys are encouraged, even compelled, to participate in physical activities which are thought to develop characteristics culturally designated as masculine, i.e. strength, independence, self-confidence, self-assertion, competitiveness, etc. The idealized feminine stereotype requires girls at puberty to assume a role that is characteristically nurturing, dependent, passive, non-competitive and not achievement-orientated (Greer, 1970; Bardwick, 1971). Sports and strenuous exercise are considered to produce characteristics that conflict with society's image of the ideal mature woman; so girls, whilst not being actively prevented from participating in sport and exercise, receive little positive encouragement. In general, girls have less sporting choice, fewer opportunities and facilities at school compared to boys, and it is accepted as normal when girls try to avoid games and gym when physical education is a compulsory subject.

As Wilmore (1979) states, 'it is well-known that once one assumes a sedentary life style, the basic physiological components of general fitness deteriorate, i.e. strength, muscular endurance and cardiovascular endurance are lost, and body fat tends to accumulate'. It does not take much observation to notice that males of 25–30 years of age undergo similar changes. These too are related to a reduction in the amount of activity men of this age normally undergo. Thus, it would seem that the average female's sedentary life-style begins at about 12 years, whilst the average male's coincides with the onset of responsibilities, a family and a career in his middle twenties: 'So, what appear to be dramatic biological differences between the sexes, may, in fact, be more related to cultural and social restrictions placed on the female as she attains puberty' (Wilmore, 1979).

The data do not support the view that there are inherent biological constraints which make women necessarily second-class citizens when it comes to athletic potential. A good case could be made that sex differences, when manifested in athletic achievement, are more a function of our cultural context than of any factor that may be deemed biological or inherent.

Misleading statistics

When comparisons of body fat between college-age men and women were made (Wilmore & Behnke, 1969, 1970; Behnke & Wilmore, 1974), in statistical terms the group was not only not homogeneous for fatness but there was a confounding factor that distorted the results; namely, the greater amount of physical activity undergone by the males as compared with that undergone by the females which is determined by cultural norms. It is known that physical activity is associated with a reduction in body fat, the nature and magnitude of the reduction being dependent on the type, intensity, duration and frequency of the activity (Pollock, 1973; Oscar, 1973). Therefore, the lower average value of 15% body fat for the college-age males as compared with 25% for the females, was surely related to the higher amount of physical activity that the college-age male normally undergoes.

The important question is whether it was physical activity that was actually being measured in this sample or, at the very least, are we able to correlate fatness with physical activity from the results obtained? Even if one is able to find a correlation between fatness and physical activity, this alone says nothing about how they are related. In the absence of a theory to explain the data, the correlation (the statistics) illustrates nothing that is interesting and explanatory. It may be that activity causes a reduction in body fat, or a reduction in body fat encourages activity, or that there is an underlying third factor that causes both a reduction in body fat and performing physical activity. It would be interesting to answer the why and how questions with respect to athletic potential.

Athletic potential – a new hypothesis

It has been shown that there may indeed be sex differences in athletic potential and, if so, they may be culturally-determined, biologically-determined or determined by a combination of the two. The questions to be answered are: (1) are there sex differences in athletic potential and (2) if there are sex differences, are they biologically-determined, culturally-determined or the product of both factors. As in the consideration of fatness, conclusions about athletic potential cannot be drawn merely by comparing groups of males and females. It is necessary to separate athletic potential from confounding factors such as physical activity.

Before one can begin to consider the relationship, if any, between sex and athletic potential, one needs to identify what is meant by athletic potential and then to choose a relevant population to study. It is accepted that certain conditions need to be satisfied in order for a certain athletic performance to be possible. For example, in order for the marathon, an endurance event, to be run in under 2 hr 45 min these variables would include: physical factors such as an ectomorphic body physique; a large percentage of slow-twitch muscle fibres; low body fat; physiological components such as a high aerobic capacity; a certain training/conditioning programme covering 80-100 miles per week, and psycho-social factors that allow an individual to undergo the arduous training necessary, and incorporate a will to achieve. Similar profiles could be created for an athlete in any sport, and the conditions would vary according to the requirements which are necessary in order to achieve an arbitrary level of performance in that particular event. However, it would be a mistake to make a direct link between the conditions and the performance, because although the conditions are necessary, they are not sufficient actually to produce that performance, for the following reasons.

Firstly, in marathon running, the data do not support making such a connection. Costill, Fink & Pollock (1976) state that high aerobic capacity, measured as VO_2 max, does not in itself guarantee a fast performance in marathon competition. Two of the best marathon runners in the world, Frank Shorter (USA) and Derek Clayton (Australia) have lower VO_2 max values than other slower runners (71·3 ml/kg/min and 69·7 ml/kg/min respectively), Shorter's best time for the marathon being 2 hr 10 min 30 sec and the world record holder Clayton's being 2 hr 08 min 33 sec. Whilst it appears that both these runners are metabolically economical, according to Costill *et al.* (1976) the explanation for their outstanding abilities remains undefined. The same applies to other quantifiable conditions. So what is the factor, possessed by these two runners but not shared by others who nevertheless satisfy all the required conditions but who do not produce the performance?

The same questions can be applied to totally different activities. What does Isaac Stern have that other violinists, who practise as many hours and have had the same sort of tuition, do not have? What is it that Muhammed Ali has that enabled him at 35 years of age, when boxers are considered to be past their peak, to win back his world heavyweight title from Leon Spinks, a boxer who at the time satisfied many more of the conditions necessary to be able to excel? Fulfilling the conditions therefore does not necessarily result in performance. Furthermore, a certain individual can achieve performance without satisfying all of the conditions and Muhammed Ali is a good example.

Could there be a missing link in our theory? My suggestion is that there is an intervening variable which in the case of athletes, I shall call athletic predisposition. This means that if the conditions are necessary for the performance then the intervening variable, athletic predisposition, would be the sufficiency condition (see Fig. 4).

What can we say about intervening variable in general, and athletic predisposition in particular? Intervening variable, as I have used the term, refers to the circuitry in human beings, the description of which explains why we are innately predisposed to any activity or behaviour. It offers us the functional mechanisms which, as it were, process the stimuli as they impinge on the organism. We cannot examine ourselves to see whether we have this predisposition; it is unquantifiable at present. Hence, the presence of the predisposition has to be inferred. Being inferred, however, does not make it any the less respectable. Science is full of examples of entities that are ontologically as real as tables and chairs, but whose existence has always had to be inferred. For example, the existence of elementary particles is inferred; although no-one has ever seen them, their existence is inferred and accepted because the theory of elementary particles when tested works better than any other in ordering, making intelligible, and explaining the data.

```
      C  ─────────→  I–V  ─────────→  P
```

General

Conditions, or
stimuli, or
inputs

Intervening variable:
a functional state description
of an organism; this processes
the conditions thereby making
the performance the outcome

Performance, or
behaviour, or
outputs

For athletic performance

Physical:
   somatotype
   height
   muscle fibre type
   body composition

Functional state description
of a human being, in which
athletic predisposition
is an innate feature.

An arbitrarily defined
level of performance
which is outstanding in
a particular event.

Physiological:
   aerobic capacity (VO$_2$ max)

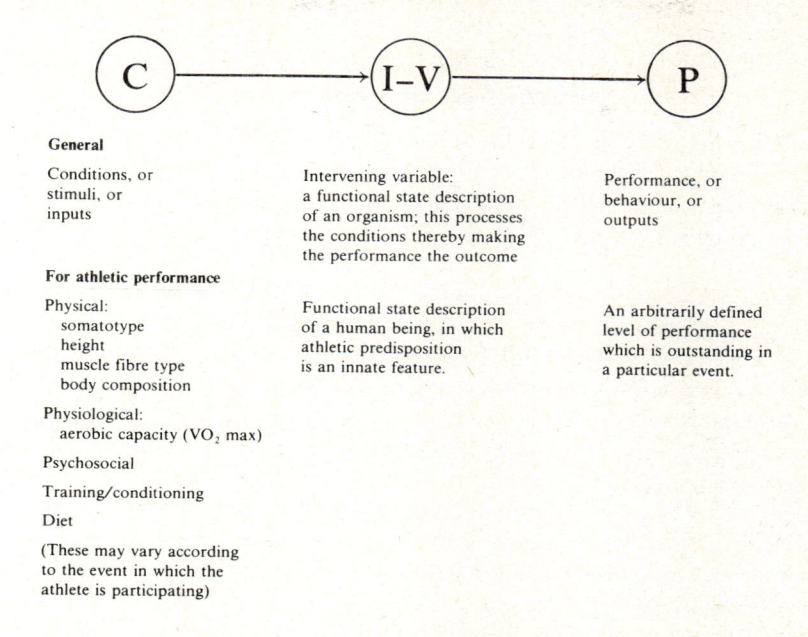

Psychosocial

Training/conditioning

Diet

(These may vary according
to the event in which the
athlete is participating)

Fig. 4. Diagrammatic representation of influence of intervening variable (IV) on conditions (C) producing performance (P), in general terms and in relation to athletic performance.

In attempting to make sense of what athletic potential means, and what sex differences, if any, exist with respect to athletic potential, the theory postulating a feature of the intervening variable, that I have called athletic predisposition, works better than any other because it enables us to delineate that subclass of people, or that population which forms a relevant sample to the issue in question. I have suggested that we set a certain standard of achievable performance – in marathon running, for instance, of 2¾ hours – as necessary for an athlete to be said to have athletic potential. By doing this, we have already delineated a specific relevant sample population (of both sexes).

A precondition for any comparison concerning athletic potential is, however, that the specific feature of intervening variable – athletic predisposition – is present. How does one know if athletic predisposition is present? If all the conditions result in a certain performance, arbitrarily defined as in our marathon example, then the presence of athletic predisposition can be inferred to be present. Can athletic predisposition be inferred without the conditions, resulting in the performance? Not necessarily, given our state of knowledge, but in practice there are good indications that would lead one to expect that athletic predisposition was present. For instance, American college talent spotters go round the black ghettoes in American cities searching for individuals who look as if they have the potential to make good basketball players. The assessment by the talent spotters depends to some extent on physical features, such as height, but it will also include what can be described as a reaction to some unquantifiable predisposition that appears to exist in a particular individual in relation to basketball potential.

So, to summarize, the precondition, athletic predisposition, is an explanatory device which, if not put into the scheme, will not enable us satisfactorily to link the necessary conditions with the performance.

Sex differences in athletic potential?

When attempting to assess sex differences in athletic potential, rather than dividing the world up into males and females, I am proposing that the world should be divided into those who have athletic predisposition and those who do not. This theory highlights the one condition which is essential when one is comparing the sexes with respect to athletic potential.

It is commonly believed that biological differences distinguish the sexes in relation to physical performance and athletic potential. Athletic predisposition is innate, and therefore must be biological. But I suggest that this factor actually distinguishes not between the sexes, but rather between people who are athletically predisposed and those who are not and is neutral with respect to sex. The theory will facilitate the isolation of the relevant sample or population on which the appropriate tests should be done. This should be a subclass of males and females who all show athletic predisposition and who all excel at a specific activity or event. When comparing the sexes in this elite subgroup, it may become clear that sex differences are irrelevant and that males and females are capable of the same athletic potential in this particular event. Another possibility is that it may become evident that there are sex differences in this group, but that these do not correspond with those found in the statistically average male and female. It may even be discovered that females in a specific event may outclass their male competitors.

The data support all these possibilities. Highly-trained female long-distance runners have demonstrated that, with strenuous training they are capable of developing similar aerobic capacity to male long-distance runners. The women's performances are improving at a startling rate and approaching those of the men in these endurance events.

In addition, several workers have suggested that the heat-regulating system in female endurance athletes may be somewhat different and more efficient for this sort of exercise than that in males (Wells, 1977; Weinman *et al.*, 1967; Wyndham, Morrison & Williams, 1965). In cross-channel swimming, women have already shown themselves to be superior to men. The Canadian Cynthia Nicholas's record time of 19 hr 55 min for the two-way, non-stop swim in 1977 cut the previous male-held record by 10 hr, and Penny Lee Dean (USA) holds the England to France swimming record of 7 hr 40 min.

As several investigators have commented, male and female athletes participating in the same event and doing similar amounts of training, are much more similar than they are different with respect to those specific characteristics necessary to excel in that event (Wilmore, 1979; Ferris, 1977). As Wilmore (1979) says, 'With regard to the female athlete, there appears to be little difference between her and her male counterpart in terms of strength, per unit body size in selected areas, cardiovascular endurance capacity, body composition and muscle fiber type'.

Within the subclass of people called athletes, intersex differences are much less important than the differences between non-athletes and athletes of the same sex. One only has to compare a male and female endurance athlete, and then compare either of these with a sedentary non-athlete of the same sex to confirm this observation.

Finally, perhaps it would be useful to make a distinction between physical activity, and manifesting athletic potential by athletic activity. Almost anyone is capable of running a mile, but only a relatively small number of people are capable of running it in a time that would be classified as an athletic as opposed to a physical activity.

This class of people with athletic potential would be relatively small when compared with the male/female division of the whole world population, but it is this class that I am interested in examining with respect to the sex differences in athletic potential. When sex differences in this small class are examined, they do not match the sex differences of the larger male/female class and the descriptions do not match those of the average male and the average female.

References

BARDWICK, J. (1971) *Psychology of Women*. Harper & Row, New York.
BEHNKE, A.R. & WILMORE, J.H. (1974) *Evaluation and Regulation of Body Build and Composition*. Prentice Hall, New Jersey.
BROWN, C.H. & WILMORE, J.H. (1974) The effects of maximal resistance training on the strength and body composition of women athletes. *Med. & Sci. Sports*, **6**, 133.
BURKE, E.J. & BRUSH, F.C. (1979) Physiological and anthropometric assessment of successful teenage female distance runners. *Res. Q.* **50**, 180.
COSTILL, D.L., BOWERS, R. & KAMMER, W.F. (1970) Skinfold estimates of body fat among marathon runners. *Med. & Sci. Sports*, **2**, 93.
COSTILL, D.L., BRANHAM, G., EDDY, D. & SPARKS, K. (1971) Determinants of marathon running success. *Int. Z. Angew. Physiol.* **29**, 249.
COSTILL, D.L., FINK, W.J. & POLLOCK, M.L. (1976) Muscle fiber composition and enzyme activities of elite distance runners. *Med. & Sci. Sports*, **8**, 96.
CUNNINGHAM, D.A. & HILL, J.S. (1975) Effect of training on cardiovascular response to exercise in women. *J. appl. Physiol.* **39**, 891.
DRINKWATER, B.L. (1973) Physiological responses of women to exercise. In: *Exercise and Sport Sciences Reviews*, Vol 1. Edited by J.H. Wilmore. Academic Press, New York.
DYER, K.F. (1976) Social influences on female athletic performance. *J. biosoc. Sci.* **8**, 123.
DYER, K.F. (1977) The trend of the male–female performance differential in athletics, swimming and cycling 1948-76. *J. biosoc. Sci.* **9**, 325.
EDWARDS, M.A. (1974) The effects of training at predetermined heart rate levels for sedentary college women. *Med. & Sci. Sports*, **6**, 14.
FERRIS, E. (1977) Exploding the male myth. *Sunday Telegraph*, 6 November.
FERRIS, E. (1979) Sportswomen and medicine: the myths surrounding women's participation in sport and exercise, I and II. *Olympic Review*, **138-139**, 249; **140**, 332.
FLINT, M.M., DRINKWATER, B.L. & HORVATH, S.M. (1974) Effects of training on women's response to submaximal exercise. *Med. & Sci. Sports*, **6**, 89.
GREER, G. (1970) *The Female Eunuch*. MacGibbon & Kee, London.
HETTINGER, T. (1961) *Physiology of Strength*. Thomas, Springfield, Illinois.
KILBOM, A. (1971) Physical training in women. *Scand. J. clin. lab. Invest.* **28**, Supplement 119, 1.
MALINA, R.M. & RARICK, G.L. (1973) Growth, physique and motor performance. In: *Physical Activity, Human Growth and Development*. Edited by G.L. Rarick. Academic Press, New York.
OSCAR, L.B. (1973) The role of exercise in weight control. In: *Exercise and Sport Sciences Reviews*, Vol. 1. Edited by J.H. Wilmore. Academic Press, New York.
POLLOCK, M.L. (1973) The quantification of endurance training programs. In: *Exercise and Sports Sciences Reviews*, Vol. 1. Edited by J.H. Wilmore. Academic Press, New York.
ROSKAMM, H. (1967) Optimum patterns of exercise for healthy athletes. *Can. med. Ass. J.* **96**, 895.

WEINMAN. K., SLABOCHOVA, Z., BERNAUER, E.M., MORIMOTO, & SARGENT (1967) Reactions of men and women to repeated exposure to humid heat. *J. appl. Physiol.* **22,** 533.
WELLS, C.L. (1977) Sexual differences in heat stress response. *Physician & Sportsmed.* **5,** 79.
WILMORE, J.H. (1974) Alterations in strength, body composition and anthropometric measurements consequent to a 10-week weight training program. *Med. & Sci. Sports,* **6,** 133.
WILMORE, J.H. (1979) The application of science to sport: physiological profiles of male and female athletes. *Can. J. appl. Sport Sci.* **4,** 103.
WILMORE, J.H. & BEHNKE, A.R. (1969) An anthropometric estimation of body density and lean body weight in young men. *J. appl. Physiol.* **27,** 25.
WILMORE, J.H. & BEHNKE, A.R. (1970) An anthropometric estimation of body density and lean body weight in young women. *Am. J. clin. Nutr.* **23,** 267.
WILMORE, J.H. & BROWN, C.H. (1974) Physiological profiles of women distance runners. *Med. & Sci. Sports,* **6,** 178.
WILMORE, J.H., BROWN, C.H. & DAVIS, J.A. (1977) Body physique and composition of the female distance runner. *Ann. N.Y. Acad. Sci.* **301,** 764.
WYNDHAM, C.H., MORRISON, J.F. & WILLIAMS, C.G. (1965) Heat reactions of male and female Caucasians. *J. appl. Physiol.* **20,** 357.

Biosocial Aspects of Sport

COMMENT

MOIRA O'BRIEN

Department of Anatomy, Royal College of Surgeons in Ireland, Dublin

The first point that I want to make is that women athletes are very different from the ordinary non-athletic woman and they differ in their psychological and physical make up. If you are going to succeed you must be very different and you must be able to cope with the fact that you are different. In America particularly, Mary Bacon, as one of the premier jockeys, had a very difficult time – first of all to be accepted and also because of the fact that she wins, which makes it even more difficult; she feels she is a man competing against men, but she has not lost her femininity. I think that is very important because a lot of girls are dissuaded from realizing their athletic potential because they are afraid; they do not want to be different and they are discouraged.

The physical aspects can be divided into two main types: anatomical and physiological. There are definite anatomical differences. For example, most females have a rather wide pelvis; their function is to have children and because of this the pelvis is slightly different. The typical female pelvis has a much wider outlet, the iliac crest is less curved and does not reach as high, so the iliac fossa is shallower and the ala of the sacrum in the female is wider than the body; the opposite is found in the male. The distance between the anterior aspect of the pubic symphysis is wider than the diameter of the acetabulum in the female, while it is less in the male. As a result the distance between the acetabular fossa and the femoral heads are wider apart in the female, and the angle between the quadriceps extensor and ligamentation patella is proportionately smaller.

The quadriceps muscle normally tends to pull the patella laterally and the angulation of the femur in the female tends to increase this tendency. If there has been any injury to the knee joint, the horizontal fibres of the vastus medialis are the first to go; they waste within 24 hr and this is a very important point in that, once they are wasted, the patella tends to tilt so that the medial facet on the patella is not in contact with the femur and this is the start of chondromalacia patella, if not corrected. The treatment for chondromalacia patella is hyperextension of the knee; the horizontal fibres of vastus medialis which are inserted into the patella only come into play during this period. There are still a large number of people who try to correct chondromalacia by quadriceps exercises with a weighted boot; this builds up the main bulk of the quadriceps, but it does not act on the horizontal fibres as it is impossible to hyperextend with a weighted boot.

Another anatomical difference, in the upper limb, is the carrying angle of the forearm. With the arm extended and supinated, the forearm bones make an angle with the humerus of 167° in the female and 178° in the male. This difference is due to two factors; in the female, first, the medial end of the humerus is approximately 6 mm lower than the lateral end and second, to the obliquity of the superior articular surface of the coronoid process which is not at right angles to the shaft of the ulna. The upper part of the humerus is not at right angles to the shaft and this is more marked in the female than it is in the male. The importance lies in throwing events such as the javelin; when the arm comes down, because of the carrying angle, the elbow cannot be brought down as far in the female as in the male and this is one of the factors which limits the throwing power in the female. The other factor is that the musculature of the upper part of the body in females is less than in males; this could be due partly to the fact that, in the past women were discouraged from using weight training. This was because parents and coaches thought that it would lead to muscle hypertrophy. The low level of androgens in the female means that the muscle strength can be increased without the reciprocal increase in muscle bulk that occurs in males.

Of the physiological factors, puberty is most significant. Before puberty, the sex differences are minimal, and in fact females can be stronger than males, particularly as the growth spurt occurs in girls at least 2–3 years earlier than in boys. The age of menarche varies in different countries but in the British Isles and in Sweden it tends to be about 12 or 13 years of age. However, studies have found that in a certain group, particularly swimmers, the very tall thin girls tend to start menstruating at a later age. This does not usually worry them too much but it often worries the parents who wonder if there is something wrong; it is important to provide reassurance that provided the periods start before about 17 years there need be no cause for concern. But puberty is one of the reasons why girls stop taking up exercise at the age of 13-14. With the developing level of oestrogens their body fat increases and some of them are embarrassed at their changing shapes. Also, they are often not expected to participate any more, and this depends very much on the school that they go to. Some schools have an emphasis on sport and if girls attend that type of school participation will increase and improve. If they come from a family where there is a lot of swimming or a lot of athletics then they have a far better opportunity to continue to take part.

Another physiological difference in females is the fact that females tend to have smaller hearts and one reason for this was reputed to be that a lot of the women had given up exercise at a much earlier age. During the past 3 years echocardiography has been carried out on athletes, particularly swimmers, measuring the thickness of the wall of the left ventricle and the effect of exercise. The girls who had done a lot of swimming, and particularly endurance training, showed an increase in the diameter of the left ventricles and had increased end diastolic diameters, that is the diameter of the heart in the resting phase, in comparison with the non-athletes. They also reacted to submaximal exercise in a completely different way to unfit controls. This is very important. The athletes were tested before and after submaximal exercise, i.e. riding a Monark bicycle ergometer until the heart rate levels out, at the steady state; the post-exercise measurement was taken approximately 45 sec after coming off the bicycle. The fit athletes, including the girls, increased their end diastolic diameter after submaximal exercise, while in the unfit controls the end diastolic diameter decreased and, as a result, the stroke volume was reduced. We followed some of the swimmers over a period of 3 years and have noted that there is an increase in musculature and end diastolic diameter and we have only had one case where there was very little increase; this occurred in one of the swimmers who was with a particular club which did a lot of sprint work and did no endurance work at all. Her posterior wall thickness was 0·5 mm less than in the other girls, her stroke volume was smaller and her muscle mass was less. I think this helps to confirm that endurance exercises are very important, but it also shows that the girls can increase their heart muscle just as efficiently as the males. The blood pressure was also measured and in some cases it was rather frightening when immediately after exercise the reading was 250, or even, in one person 300; this must obviously be the stimulus to the increase in wall thickness; blood pressure was highest in the unfit controls. The groups with the thickest muscles were the rowers and the cyclists and, as a group, they tended to do far more training than the other group.

Lastly I want to mention the difference in hormonal levels and the effect of menstruation. A lot of the mythology has disappeared but menstruation does affect different athletes in different ways, and each athlete has to know how she reacts to the various phases of the menstrual cycle. The number of athletes who get dysmenorrhoea is relatively small and this is probably due to the fact that it only occurs with ovulation and a lot of athletes have anovulatory cycles. Whether this is natural selection or not is not known but with the swimmers, particularly during the first 2 years, this is not a problem. Girls put on a lot of weight in the pre-menstrual period due to fluid retention and this can be a disadvantage although nowadays this can be treated adequately with diuretics and progesterone.

Some athletes get secondary amenorrhoea and this can cause problems. Secondary amenorrhoea is often associated with a marked loss in body weight, when the body weight drops dramatically due to a marked increase in work.

There is a difference in athletic potential; the difference is not as marked because there is natural selection; the people who go in for various sports tend to do so because they have the natural attributes that will help them to perform much better than the others.

Biosocial Aspects of Sport

SELECTION AND TRAINING AS THEY AFFECT FACTORS OF PERFORMANCE

JOHN F. CADMAN

The Hockey Association, London

Summary. The changes in the competitive structure of hockey at national and international level over the past 30 years are described. Ways in which the pressures on players have affected their attitudes to the sport, and the efforts made to relate selection and training procedures to the rapidly changing situation are discussed.

Introduction

It is a reflection of modern times that a coach should find himself addressing a conference such as this. Some years ago people would have asked what we had in common but the papers already presented have proved the need for a great understanding by both sports scientists and coaches of each other's problems. One difference between the coach and others is that there will be no scientific jargon in this paper, but there are, no doubt, scientific terms for the situations I describe. I shall attempt to build up a picture, through my assigned topic of selection and training, which has changed considerably over recent years.

Selection

Selection and training clearly go hand-in-hand. Performers are selected for events for which they have already been training or for which their selection means further training. The time at which selection occurs in an individual's life will have varying effects on his life pattern. Selection at a young age may affect school studies; at a later age it may affect university studying, professional work or family life. In addition to the mere selection, the amount of training an individual is required to do for his particular event may well also affect his way of life.

Many of you will be familiar with the selection procedure in the sports with which you are connected. It is therefore my intention to comment in general terms on selection and training over a reasonably wide field and pose some questions, and then to comment more specifically on the problems and developments within my own sport of hockey.

The main methods of selection seem to fall into the following areas: (1) selection on results; (2) selection by choice; (3) selection on potential.

Selection on results

This method might appear, initially, to be the most simple. It is not unreasonable to assume that the fastest runners over 100 metres will be the ones selected to represent their country; that the boxer who wins his area competition is the one who will move on to regional finals and the regional winners will move on to represent their country. On the surface this is a clear-cut procedure.

While this form of selection appears simple to an onlooker, I am certain that Kevin Hickey will add comments that prove the simplicity to be not as great as it first appears. The pressures on competitors in individual sports are considerable, particularly at moments leading up to important races or events, where their futures can be decided by a split second or a single punch. The elation on winning will spur them on to greater efforts in future events while the disappointment of losing must give coaches considerable problems in motivating their charges for further competition.

Selection by choice

This seems, again, to be a method of selection which is becoming more and more evident. We read in the national press that individuals have not yet chosen which athletic event they will compete in at a major international meeting. It is, of course, important that our best athletes should compete in those events in which they themselves, along with their coaches, consider they are most likely to gain success. However, the period of indecision must cause considerable frustration for those athletes whose future remains uncertain until the stars have made their choice. Again, those not selected will have the problem of accepting non-selection while those who fill the vacancies not taken up by the stars are lifted and re-motivated to prove that they also can succeed.

Selection on potential

This method falls into two very different categories: (a) selection at an early age, based on scientific information and (b) selection at a stage when a performer is well into his sporting career, based on known achievements. The latter is particularly relevant to team games.

Early selection. When the words 'scientific selection' are mentioned many of us immediately think of eastern European countries and the selection of 8–9 year-old children for specific events as a result of their particular body type, muscle structure, movement ability etc. In our western society, many of us react adversely to this idea. However, in countries like East Germany and Russia, where there is the possibility that a family might eventually have one of its members achieve the level of Master of Sport and reap the benefits that go with that status in society, one can understand why they find the situation acceptable.

The questions that I want to ask in assessing this method of selection are:

(i) What is the success rate in terms of numbers who represent their country compared with those initially selected? (In the past a figure of 2% has been quoted.)
(ii) What happens to those who do not make it; what effect does this have on them as individuals within their society, and is anybody concerned about this?

If people are dropped from the system because they fail to show the will to win or the ability to perform well under pressure, does this not indicate a weakness in the method of selection as compared with the more traditional methods that are more familiar to us? Or do their claims, that the will to win and the ability to perform well under pressure are already there, justify psychological testing at the early age of selection? If such tests are carried out, can such early judgement be accurate?

However, if all children who show potential go through the selection process, are they not more likely to participate in activities in which they are likely to be successful, as opposed to youngsters in this country who tend to participate in activities that their parents can afford, or which by chance they have the opportunity to experience in a wide physical education programme? Because of the society in which they live, they find themselves in a situation which is normal to, and accepted by, those around them. Are we right, therefore, in criticizing such selection?

Selection by achievement. This is best seen in team games where individuals are picked at one level of performance to go on to another, from a series of matches or trial games. The effects of selection on the training demanded of a player will be considered later.

At this point we must distinguish between selection in a professional game like soccer and an amateur game like hockey. In the soccer world the responsibility for selection tends to be with one person – the manager. He is paid to produce a squad of players from whom he selects a team from match to match. He is judged on results and often heads roll in a world where rewards are high but security in bad times is poor. The crowds supporting a particular team want results. Their behaviour towards a manager's selection and a team's performance will vary from week to week. The most recent example of crowd reaction has been clearly shown at Everton. Cushions were thrown on to the pitch after their 4-0 defeat by Ipswich. The manager's team selection was criticized by the crowd. Two weeks later, after defeating Ipswich in the quarter-final of the FA Cup, his selection was totally right. The pressures on an individual in this type of job must be enormous. The constant worry for 24 hr a day presents a totally different picture from, say, rugby union or hockey, where selection is part of an individual's hobby and his major worries are tied up with his business or profession.

Problems of selection

Having made these general observations I should now like to look at the developments in selection in my own sport. Considerable change has taken place over a period of years which has led to a greater security of tenure for players and allowed them to concentrate on playing rather than on being selected. The pattern I am going to describe probably follows closely that of many amateur sports. My comments will relate to selection at international level, though this is mirrored down the scale. While talking about the selection of players it is also important to look at the selection of selectors, but more of that in due course.

In the late 1950s, which is the time when I found myself involved in selection, we can trace the development most effectively. There had been little change over a number of years prior to the latter part of the 1950s. The England trial teams were selected after a series of divisional matches. No coaching took place and any training was left to the individual's own discretion. The divisional teams were selected after county matches and divisional trials. The first time one met the players in the trial teams was immediately before a game. Each individual had little knowledge of the style of play of those around him. The effect was that players tended to play for themselves and their own selection rather than for the team.

Those who saw the recent television programme 'Better Badminton' will recall an international player of the 1920s saying what a hopeless situation he found himself in when he met his partner in the men's doubles match against Ireland in the dressing-room half-an-hour before the game. So the problem was not confined to hockey.

After the trial game the selectors retired and in due course players were informed of their selection for the first international match of that season. Those selected were requested to report to a particular hotel, if playing at home or in the UK, on the Friday evening before the game. Again, they may not have played previously with those around them. Saturday morning would be spent in going over a few points such as set pieces and a broad strategy, and then into the game. Very little opportunity was given to prepare as a team and the training that each person had done prior to the game would vary, though individuals had been motivated to increase their fitness as a result of being selected. Each game was taken in isolation. Selection for the second international of the season took place after the first game. Changes could occur and players were living from match to match.

The commitment required from players was considerable but it was fitted around their normal day-to-day living and had little effect on the pattern of their social life. Players trained for 2–3 days per week, mostly going out for a run, with a variety of distance and speed work but with very little guidance from coaches. The selectors had the opportunity to retain a team to allow it to develop as a unit or to experiment and make changes, hoping for a better blend next time.

As a player, one important fact stands out on reflection. Each game was played individually but in as much a competitive atmosphere as games today. However, the social environment that developed through after-match dinners and parties led to the formation of deep friendships which still endure today.

During this period no major competitions, other than the Olympic Games, existed. The Olympics were the pinnacle in any competitor's career and the four home countries entered the selection melting-pot together to produce an Olympic squad. For this competition, preparation was more thorough and training weekends were added to the programme, but never at the expense of the programmes of each of the four home countries.

The 1960s and 1970s have seen an explosion in competition with the additon of the county championship, European Cup and World Cup – a demanding competitive environment in which the selection methods and random training of the late 1950s proved completely inadequate. Methods of selection had to change and training had to be organized to prepare players for a far more demanding programme.

The first change was the introduction of training weekends and the selection of a squad of players from whom a team would be picked. Selectors watched preparation during training weekends and worked closely with the team manager and coach. Initial selection to the squad gave players the opportunity to work together, and the selectors the opportunity to experiment to achieve the best blend for the task ahead. Players were motivated to work harder in their own preparation to raise their standards of individual fitness.

The introduction of training weekends necessitated players being away from their clubs but as there were at that time no club leagues their absence was acceptable. Travelling to training weekends required players to request leave of absence from headmasters, employers or their own businesses. In general these requests were treated favourably, there being a sense of pride on the part of employers that one of their employees was representing his country – a fact often used to the benefit of certain companies. Some individuals had to offset holiday time against such absence but the frequency of leave taken was at that time acceptable. In the services those chosen for representative honours were encouraged to take part and postings were often changed to allow ease of training and participation for those selected.

During this period, the early 1960s, the English schools team at under-19 was established. However, the gap between under-19 and full international honours was considerable and many selected for school teams disappeared into the wilderness and were not seen again – a terrible loss to the sport.

The 1970s created a number of additional problems: a further explosion in competition; an increasing reluctance by employers to release players; a more professional attitude to coaching; an increased amount of pressure from home life; little difference in the methods of selection. In the 1970s we saw the introduction of the European Cup, the World Cup, European Under-21 and World Under-21 competitions, club leagues, a club championship, a club indoor championship, and mid-week indoor leagues in addition to the existing Olympic Games and county championships.

The season for those players selected for representative honours has extended to 12 months in the year. Players now experience a tremendous clash of loyalty, often causing conflict in their minds. Clubs are loath to release players selected for the international squad when their teams are playing in the county championship final on the same day. The England selectors, who are already without those players involved in preparation for the Olympic Games require all the players selected to look at their full potential. The effect on the county, who have worked their way through the county championship competition, is considerable as they find that a number of their best players are not available. A similar clash occurred on the evening of the indoor club championships, one of hockey's main television events, when the Great Britain management insisted that players must be at a training weekend, additional to the original programme, leaving club selectors with the problem of filling places, once again those of experienced club members.

For the players the problem is enormous. Do they defy the requests of the Great Britain management in order to help their clubs in a tournament where they have worked hard to reach the national finals, or do they look to their own futures? With these pressures at the back of their minds, can they perform at their best when this type of clash of events occurs?

A further factor which influences the attitudes of players is the apparent decline in willingness by many employers to release individuals. Pressure from unions, profit making and full use of employees' time seem to be paramount in the minds of employers, causing a change in attitude from the early 1950s. In the services, with a far more streamlined force, individuals find it harder to get leave for sporting events. The game of hockey is no exception in this respect.

The more professional attitude of coaches to preparation puts added demands on players' time. For our players even to keep pace with our position in European and World hockey 7 years ago means a far greater commitment to training and preparation. The young married man with a family, having to maintain his position in his job, often finds the pressures unsettling.

There also appears to be a greater pull towards family life. When it meant being away from home for four or five weekends during the winter to play representative hockey there were few problems, but players now find themselves committed to three or four training weekends, plus an increasing number of international matches and new competitions. Their families rarely see them – hence a further conflict of loyalty. We have a greater demand on players' time because of increased competition coupled with a decline in willingness by employers to release them, causing a conflict between commitment to hockey and home life.

The increase in visits to other countries for international competitions has also changed in pattern. Teams arrive for an international weekend in, say, Holland on a Friday evening, play matches on Saturday and Sunday and return on Sunday evening to be back at their university or place of employment by Monday morning. How different from the social atmosphere of those occasions in the early 1960s when we arrived on a Friday evening, played on Saturday, had a magnificent dinner and party on the Saturday evening and returned on Sunday, having made many friendships which last to the present day. I am glad I played when I did.

The selection of the squad is still done in the traditional way by appointed selectors. The squad is then handed over to the manager and coach to select the team for each match. From the coach's point of view this is clearly beneficial as he can select each team according to the job in hand. However, the method of appointing selectors still leaves much to be desired. Names are put forward by divisions and the Council of the Hockey Association decides which names should go forward as selectors.

What qualifications for judging selectors are possessed by those people putting names forward from divisions? What qualifications do the Hockey Association Council have for choosing from those names? Do the jobs go to people who are thought to be good selectors? Is their track record considered? If the answers to these questions are unsatisfactory, how many good players are ultimately not selected? What training or advice is given to selectors before or after they have been given the job? How many of them are aware of what the coach requires? How well do they understand the tactical requirements of the coach when selecting players?

One major problem exists when selectors are nominated by divisions, particularly when, as occurs at schoolboy level, the representation is one per division. It appears that a situation exists where selectors are more concerned about getting as many players as possible from the divisions they represent into trials, rather than looking for the best players overall.

I feel that playing standards and levels of coaching have advanced a great deal over recent years, while the method of selecting selectors has trailed behind.

The opportunity for players to advance from level to level is important. There is now a progression from schools under-16, to under-18, to under-19, to Hockey Association under-21, to full international. Thus players who have proved to be successful in one age group will be known and may well have played alongside the others who are selected for higher age group squads. The system allows for players to be included or discarded according to variations in their achievements. This progression does, however, produce problems, particularly when fixtures clash between the under-19 and under-21 groups. Should players be encouraged to advance to the higher level when the clash occurs? There seems to be a pull from the selectors of the younger group to retain players to ensure their teams are at their strongest, as opposed to the view that the youngsters should have the opportunity to progress as fast as possible. Is the age group or the individual more important? I believe the argument should be in favour of the individual.

At present, as a result of serious clashes in the past, the matter of selection is now decided between the managers of the under-19 and under-21 groups. This, from the individual's point of view, is sensible in that it does not cause a conflict of loyalty in his mind. This means that a player, often at a time when important examinations are on the horizon, does not get further over-worked and find himself worrying about the consequences of a decision that he might be required to make. Evidence, however, shows that the school's section retains the services of the player. Thus it would appear the age group benefits rather than the individual.

There are sensible reasons why different decisions should be taken in other sports. Rugby, for example, for physical reasons could decide that players should remain within their age group. In non-physical contact games, however, it is difficult to justify the decision not to allow individuals to progress.

These are some of the developments and problems in hockey. In the individual sports, particularly gymnastics and swimming, other problems arise which are not often experienced in team games. These relate to the time demanded of very young competitors, who have to fit training in with school studies and availability of facilities, so that they have little time to involve themselves in the social activities of their peers. Others may wish to comment on the detrimental effects or otherwise that result.

Early opportunities

Thus far we have discussed the selection of individuals at representative level. It is relevant to look briefly at the selection of activities in schools, where a person's sporting life begins and may be the reason for his eventual selection at high level. This comes better under the heading of initial opportunity. What are the factors which lead to an individual becoming involved in a sport for which he or she may eventually be selected for representative honours? There are at least four, though others may be added to the list.

The school curriculum must take a prominent place in the opportunity offered to an individual. Here the seeds of interest are sown which develop either through a depth of coaching at school or through activity being followed outside the school environment. Some of us may be concerned at the wide variety of activities offered within a school curriculum, where the time allowed gives very little insight into each. Some activities are not possible within the individual's home environment and therefore cannot be pursued when he leaves school.

Parental influence is often a factor, either through encouragement to follow the interest of the parent, for example at the rugby or hockey club, or through financial backing perhaps best seen in the horse world. One recalls seeing in golfing magazines the young Sandy Lyle following his father around a golf course.

Outside influences, where someone takes a friend along to his club, or the media motivate individuals to follow a particular sport, are another factor. Women's gymnastics, for example, received a tremendous boost as a result of Korbut and Comaneci who motivated many youngsters to participate in the sport.

Finally chance, and the most topical example must be that of Robin Cousins, who at the age of 9 took shelter from the rain and walked into an ice rink at Bournemouth.

Compared with the eastern European countries this is a totally haphazard method of entering sporting activities. Our top sportsmen come out of the area of recreation into the competitive world and return to the field of recreation – a pattern wholly acceptable in our society and one which I doubt we would want to change.

Training

Training will be interpreted as preparation for a given activity. I have mentioned the 1950s, when players were left to their own devices. The development that has been outlined has seen enormous changes in the attitude to preparation and along with it increasing demands on competitors.

Athletes, swimmers and boxers for example, have always been used to training. The change here has been the influence of sports science, in conjunction with coaches, on the type of training and the programmes for preparation. The actual amount of time spent in training for an event has perhaps not increased but it is now better planned and used more beneficially.

The amount of time put into preparation by young gymnasts would frighten most club hockey players. However, my knowledge of training in individual events is as an observer and a parent, whereas my knowledge within the game of hockey is, I hope, founded on stronger roots.

Before commenting on hockey I should like to make some observations as the parent of a primary school and club gymnast. The subject in question competes in two different types of competition – BAGA grades and school. The former is a four-piece competition, floor, vault, bars and beams and the latter a two-piece competition, floor and vault. This involves two evenings per week, $1\frac{1}{2}$ hr each evening, two mornings for $\frac{1}{2}$ hr and five lunch-time practices of $\frac{1}{2}$ hr, a total of $6\frac{1}{2}$ hr per week, at the tender age of 11. The school, at which she finds herself a leading competitor, is motivated by success, while at the club the motivation appears to be one of maintaining and possibly bettering the standard of her colleagues. This is all sheer hard work, a great challenge but little fun. Ask a potential adult hockey international to commit himself to such a programme and there are problems. Why? The current generation of youngsters, because of developments in coaching, is brought up to see preparation as an important factor in participation. This is now spilling over into the team games, with the development of mini-rugby and mini-hockey. The adult of today participating in hockey was brought up on a recipe of participation. The problem for many of our team-game players is that they play too much and prepare too little.

However, attitudes have changed. Competition has given clubs the taste of possible championships and for some the possibility of relegation. There has evolved a need to prepare. This need, however, has to be weighed against the historical attitude that the game is for recreation. Coaches involved in planning preparation programmes obviously find it easier to motivate those who have reached representative level and the very young.

The new generation of players coming up through the game and now participating in mini-hockey and colts competitions is being bred on a diet of coaching and competition and, in the course of time, they will expect that pattern to continue into their senior hockey. This is not a problem in other European countries, particularly Holland and West Germany, where hockey has been based on club competitions over a number of years.

Training that does exist in clubs varies enormously from well-prepared programmes, normally designed by a club member with a PE background, to haphazard training with little real meaning. Let us consider what constitutes a training or preparation programme. Clearly fitness and skill form a large part of the work. To coaches, the five S's – stamina, strength, speed, suppleness and skill – figure prominently. Each programme contains these ingredients in varying proportions according to the result required. Added to these must come (a) the psychological aspects of preparation such as motivation and personality profiles (the latter, to the majority of coaches a very new departure), and (b) tactical awareness of the individual within a team.

Teams are made up of individuals with differing reactions to each situation. Each team can be said to be as strong as its weakest member. The job of the coach is to blend the individuals into a united and effective team. Failure to do this can lead to clashes of personality which may adversely affect the performance of the team. It must be remembered that each individual will be fulfilling a different role within the team and their fitness requirements differ considerably. For example, a goalkeeper and a centre forward each needs to be motivated in different ways.

At representative level the attitude to preparation has seen the greatest change. The Great Britain and England teams now bring in individuals to look after physical fitness, medical treatment and back-up of players and often a physiotherapist to deal with pitch-side problems. This more professional approach is now influenced by sports scientists as the need for higher levels of fitness required to participate and succeed in the more intensive environment of competition develops away from the situation experienced in the early 1960s.

Other countries, particularly Pakistan the World Champions, West Germany, Holland and India, pour much greater financial resources into their hockey than we do in England. The attitude of their governing bodies appears to be that the game at grass roots reacts and thrives on success at the top. A great deal of time is spent on preparation and training for major events. In this country the attitude seems to be that international squads must not be seen to be receiving too large a slice of the cake. Hence management is restricted in what it can do in terms of team preparation – another reflection of the recreational attitude to the game.

Coaches can see the need for improved training methods and their influence may be felt lower down the scale. Gone are the days when training could be left until a player had reached representative level.

The influence of sports scientists is perhaps showing the greatest beneficial effect in sports like rowing and swimming, where coaches and sports scientists work closely together. The requirements, in terms of biomechanics and the effect of the build-up of lactic acid for example, can be easily measured and recognized in these activities. In team games, the requirements of the game in terms of individual players are more difficult to measure.

However, the pattern of training programmes for hockey has changed considerably. Our present training programme is based on our team's requirements for the World Cup, commencing in December 1981, and is planned back from that particular event. Intermediate peak points are established and cycles of training, containing the five S's, have been drawn up.

The effect of improved preparation must be to raise the standards of team performance in this country, but we must be realistic. At the moment the amount of work our players are able to do is merely maintaining our position in world and European hockey. Players want to achieve international honours but few have accepted that to do this a dedication to training, far in advance of anything they have experienced before, is necessary. In athletics, swimming and gymnastics it is well established that a considerable amount of training has to be undertaken in preparation for any event.

We realize that to motivate players checks have to be made but these have to be fitted into very busy programmes on the occasions when squads meet together. We need to test levels of improvement, not forgetting that the ultimate test of any hockey player is his performance on the field within the team unit.

I should like to make one comment on the influence that sports science appears to be having on sport. We seem to be becoming almost too concerned with testing. I see the testing of players falling into two very distinct areas: (a) tests required by sports scientists to continue their research, out of which it is hoped that improved training methods will come that will raise levels of performance in the future, and (b) those simple day-to-day tests that coaches can use for quick checks on the progress that their players are making.

The explosion of competition, which has led to the need for more intensive and scientifically based preparation, plus a certain reluctance by some employers to release individuals, has resulted in international players of today having to make considerable sacrifices. Their dedication and attitude has become far more professional than in the early 1960s. But the rewards are great and just as worthwhile for those competing today as they were 20–30 years ago.

Biosocial Aspects of Sport

COMMENT

KEVIN HICKEY

Amateur Boxing Association, London

I would like to pass a few comments on the excellent paper my colleague has ably presented and perhaps point a few arrows in the directions I feel we are going in this country. I feel strongly that we are looking for a philosophy for British sport and all the sports scientists and coaches have a part to play in contributing towards a cohesive unit rather than a fragmented programme which is unfortunately the case at present.

I believe John Cadman's opening statement about selection by results is valid and one must look at the process of selection very carefully with perhaps a word of caution in that the achievement of qualifying in a certain time and a certain place has to be evaluated against what pressure was applied. One can be running either against opposition or against the clock and the psychological pressure and success at international level, with which we are concerned, is perhaps a different matter. The difference between international competition and club level performance is so vast that comparison is meaningless. The problems that each present are so completely different that to try to combine them and hope to answer all questions is an impossible task and would result in achieving neither.

First, there is the question of selection by results. Different countries have different approaches and when I advise the selectors on the make up of international sides I am always wary of domestic performances because the pressures are not the same. When one considers a country like Russia where they have 300,000 boxers then one understands their reasons for selecting entirely by results.

Considering selection on potential – I spend 3 months of the year behind the Iron Curtain, and I see a great deal of the East Germans and the Russians. One must accept that the society and the sport on which it is based have to be in balance. One cannot look at the Eastern Europeans and at their sports fields and try to copy a system which is unsuited to our society. The communist system of control and the programme of preparation and selection that follows would be totally impractical in our society. Perhaps we should concentrate on keeping the square pegs in the square holes. They may have arrived at their choice haphazardly, and their physical attributes of movement and speed may lend themselves to be better suited to another activity, but in the context of our society efforts should be diverted towards providing incentives, goals, and preparation facilities so that in their chosen activity sports people can maximize the potential which they have.

Nevertheless, in Eastern European countries there is an enviable, fundamental, acceptance of sport, and this is in line with what Dr Joan Bassey was saying; that there is a complete acceptance of the role that sport plays in contributing to the physical and mental well being of society. It follows therefore that time is given to this end and I never cease to be amazed at what one sees in this connection. On a recent visit to Kiev, at 5.30 in the morning when out for a run with the squad, there were 25 older women having a game of volley ball in the adjacent arena. In the UK perhaps that would not work, and perhaps we should never ever achieve that level of control.

It follows that there is pressure on coaches of a kind that is not experienced in this country; I know of one Rumanian coach who proved too successful, as measured by his results in the Olympics and European championships. Russia sent two coaches to investigate the Rumanian methods and they toured Rumania for nine months. This is part of the pressure which is part of their society.

On the other hand, in our country, we have coaches who perhaps would like to have these pressures. Maybe we would like to have the perfect system which must go with it. If you have the system you can then have this factor of accountability but I feel that we are a long way short, in any sport, of having the ideal system. It will be interesting to see the results of the Sports Council's programme in connection with four sports and to see how that develops as a model for sport on an international level.

The consequence of our system, which has so many loopholes, is for some coaches, at all levels, to rationalize failure, not accept that we have limitations and that we have to do the job as best we can according to what our society will allow. The rationalization procedure will continue and there is always another excuse for a poor performance. Somewhere between the two, the accountability and the rationalization, there lies a balance which I think we need to aim for in this country.

As an example of the need for properly qualified selectors, referred to by John Cadman, I can give a practical example within our system. In 1976 the Olympic Boxing Team went to Montreal with seventeen members and if it had not been for the intervention of the Sports Minister then an inappropriate team would have been selected; the coach having been invited to leave the room before the final selection.

Changes are needed. In terms of the time needed for training squads, there are growing problems for participants in being in the right place at the right time and with difficulties of being allowed time off from work. We find that with sponsorship, which is a fact of life, and with television showing far more sport, people are becoming increasingly nationalistic. This is something which again society will reflect and the next decade will show the effect of the difficult 2 or 3 years we may be facing. In boxing there is perhaps less of a problem than in other sports and this may be accounted for by the social economic group from which most boxers come.

There are certain factors which I suggest are the areas which, as coaches, we should discuss in relation to our national or Olympic teams. I consider first the competitor's technical make up – his ability as a boxer; this includes his range of skills, his tactical perception and his ability to cope with a variety of opposing styles. With experience, one knows that a certain society will produce a particular style or approach to the sport. Even among the Eastern Europeans, and boxing is one of the strongest sports in Eastern Europe, there are the Hungarian, the Rumanian and the Russian styles; each is different and each reflects that society. This is a fascinating subject and one in which one never ceases to learn. But I would add to the the technical make up, something which is perhaps part of the essence which is beyond the measure of sports medicine or sports psychology and that is flair. It is the magic, the gold medal touch which cannot be coached into the performer. It is there, and the coach with experience can recognize it and it is of enormous significance.

Other factors to be considered are the current form of the performer and his aptitude for the big occasion. No matter how physically or mentally prepared a competitor is, when the pressure is on and he or she steps into the international arena a psychological block can occur; and if, in spite of efforts to rectify it, the block remains, then that competitor should not be put into that situation. The psychological make up of a performer, Dr Kane's anxiety level, is very important. For the success of the squad system, which is a basic essential for all sports, the personality and sociability of the individual have to be carefully assessed. In the atmosphere of an Olympic village where the media are focusing the attention of the world, there is the type of existence which creates a tremendous amount of pressure and different people react in different ways. Unless we know our individuals, unless the personality and sociability factors are taken into account, then we may create additional pressures which should have been anticipated beforehand.

The physical preparation and the physical profile of the individual, the five 'S' factors which have been mentioned, are all part of the international profile basic to his need. Experience should be assessed in terms of progression from the home countries through Western European, Eastern European, multinational and major nation events. Each leads on to the next and each requires a different type of experience which may eventually lead to international success and an Olympic medal.

The other factor which was mentioned is maturity and I agree with the idea that in contact sports this may be a slightly different problem. There is a need in selection to assess both the physical and mental maturity of the individual. One is looking for the actual physical hardness and the mental stability; the better the performer knows himself then the better he is able to cope with the pressures which undoubtedly will be magnified when he steps into the international arena.

One last point is perhaps peculiar to boxing and to sports where you have to make a particular body weight. It is known that to make the weight over a period of 10 days is a different matter from making the weight on one occasion. For judo, for example, and boxing, where you have to weigh in for the relevant category according to the day that you compete, this produces a tremendous problem. There are many medals lost at Olympic level simply because of the weight factor. For the domestic programme where the performer is required to make the weight once a week the tapering of the dehydration process causes no problems whatsoever. But in Olympic competition there are problems, because of this gradual drainage. A matter of $\frac{1}{2}$ kg can make the difference; at 57·5 kg he is strong and fit, but at 57 kg you can push him over with a feather. The sports scientists could be thinking about this type of practical problem which would be invaluable from the point of view of the coach. In weight lifting the weight has to be made only once, so there can be a reduction of weight of up to 6-8 pounds overnight; diuretics are used widely and rather indiscriminately. Turning to the training side and the comparison that John Cadman referred to in terms of the standard of performance one can look at the events where you can quantify performance without problems. One can see improvement and that the standard has been raised significantly. In subjective assessment it is not quite the same and boxing is one of those sports. Film of the 1964 Olympic Games shows the boxers showing signs of fatigue in the semi-finals but in 1976 their superb condition was simply taken for granted. However, the difference between the medallists is not the physical preparation but the technical and, perhaps even more important, the psychological preparation and this is what will be even more apparent in the 1980 Olympic Games in Moscow.

The Eastern Europeans do a great deal of training at altitude, but, for some sports, scientists in this country have divided opinions about the benefits. As a coach I listened to sports scientists but I must also find out what works in practical terms. If I see something that does work, my job then is to say this is the method to use, if it is repeated and the pattern is shown. Preparing at altitude, where a lot of money is spent behind the Iron Curtain, does produce a supreme physical specimen which takes us four or five times as long a period in training. I want to know from the sports scientists and sports medicine experts why altitude training does work.

The last point I want to make is to the individual's need to progress; as John Cadman said, the individual in our society is absolute, and it is difficult for the coach to cater for the individual in a squad system. There is a contradiction in having 25 people who are working to a set programme and you know, either through information provided by sports science or through your own reading of one individual, that he is lacking in certain physical departments. Psychologically, it is difficult to adjust his training programme so that he feels that he is doing exactly the same work load as the rest of the squad. If he feels that you have cut down his schedule then problems will arise because then he will realize that he will be less fit at the end. So the individual rate of progress must be objectively measured and the role of sports science in providing information which can be objectively applied is vital as far as coaching is concerned.

In closing I support strongly that there can be no substitute for the experience of competition. Success at international level is a highly complex process and the whole person is greater than the sum of his parts; a lack of one feature may be compensated for elsewhere, and he will be successful simply because of this, so we must build up the total picture of an individual. We need to move towards a British sports policy which is truly a policy based on what our society needs and, given the control which our society will allow, we must prepare our athletes accordingly. If they fail, it should not be through lack of opportunity or preparation.

GENERAL DISCUSSION

A question arose from John Cadman's reference to the gap between schoolboy internationals and the level of senior team competition and it was suggested that it should be the policy of national sports associations to reinforce a coaching structure within universities and colleges to maximize the potential of young players of proven ability, rather than have such players attracted away to outside clubs or lose them altogether. A related problem was that colleges and universities did not necessarily participate at a sufficiently high level of competition to make demands on these individuals' ability and potential.

Comparisons were drawn between the school-based competitive structure of some sports in Britain and the more successful structure, based on adult competition, found in some other countries. The position of a particular game as a national sport was also a determining factor in the amount of time and resources devoted to it.

It was agreed that the academic theoretician and the sports practitioner had much to learn from each other and that research and its application needed to be directed along appropriate lines.

The view was expressed that selection in sport should be looked at in economic terms and that the full realization of good structure and planning within a sports organization was sometimes frustrated at management level, leading to a loss of potential sports talent in Britain. Mr Hickey replied that, unfortunately, economic factors, rather than structural programmes, would shape the pattern of British sport in the next decade. Ideally, through consultation and discussion, a practically-orientated programme should be worked out which would help to answer the coaches' questions yet satisfy the organizations which distributed money for research. A co-ordinated approach to the Sports Council by all the sports bodies concerned would help to modify present policy but, nevertheless, any changes would have to be acceptable in the wider context of society as a whole.

It was suggested that flair, as mentioned by Mr Hickey, could be equated with the innate predisposition referred to by Dr Ferris, and it was agreed that this was an intangible quality for which, at present, there was no scientific explanation.

IV

HAZARDS OF SPORT

Chairman: Peter Sperryn

Biosocial Aspects of Sport

INJURIES AND PHYSICAL STRESS

JOHN E. DAVIES

Sports Injuries Clinic, Guy's Hospital, London

Summary. After classifying injuries, and giving examples of the ways in which they can arise, treatment, rehabilitation and the value of exercise are considered. Having given a review of the effects of increasing leisure time and sports participation, the value of legislation, education, protective clothing and close supervision in preventing the occurrence of injuries in sport are discussed.

As this conference is concerned with the biosocial aspects of sport and my brief is to discuss the biosocial implications of injuries and the physical hazards of sport, I found it easier to prepare the lecture by referring to the traditional and proven methods of medical teaching – namely the formulation of a correct diagnosis and the proper management. Biologically and clinically, an accurate diagnosis is made by proper examination and history-taking with particular reference to symptoms and signs. Sociologically, within the concept of the biosocial aspect of sport and injuries sustained, the same proven method applies. Within our society the symptoms and signs with regard to an increasing sports participation and resulting injury rate are well-established but the method of management and treatment is questionable. Can the National Health Service, which has finite resources, absorb the increasing demands of injuries in sport, which now exceed injuries from road traffic accidents in the UK? It has been confirmed, by studies at Leeds, Southampton and Glasgow, that, in 1979, of the 60,000 people in Glasgow who attended casualty departments, 3500 cases were due to sport injuries, which was more than the road traffic accident cases. The DHSS have not hidden their thoughts and their policy regarding this particular problem, as they will make no firm commitment towards sports medicine in the UK. So the question arises whether this phenomenon should be catered for outside the National Health Service, within the sector of private medicine.

A DHSS handbook, published a few years ago, set out guidelines for positive action to promote health. It suggested:

> action which individuals could take in relation to the health and well-being of themselves and their family; action in planning and reorientating local and national services to give a greater emphasis to prevention within whatever resources can be made available; prevention is the key to healthier living and higher quality of life.

Turning to preventive medicine – people are living longer and there is increasing leisure time; more and more people are taking up sports and the injury rate is increasing. The relevance of preventive medicine can be summarized as follows:

(1) prevention and health are everybody's business;
(2) curative medicine may be increasingly subject to the law of diminishing returns;

(3) longevity, increasing leisure time; fitness and health;
(4) prevention and management of injuries; avoidance of complications which could result in disability;
(5) education

The success stories of preventive medicine are well known: through vaccinations, immunizations, improvements in public health standards and lower infant and maternal mortality, we now have people who obviously do not attract the diseases that they did 30 or 40 years ago. To illustrate the educational role: the Royal College of Obstetricians was estabished around the 1930s and total infant and maternal deaths have decreased rapidly over the last 40 years; this must be due partly to the fact that the doctors are better educated. In sports medicine a few individuals have been informing and educating the medical profession, as well as lay people, in relation to the need for increased knowledge about sports injuries in this country.

Apart from education, preventive medicine in relation to sport lies in the prevention of injuries and the prevention of complications after injury by adequate treatment. The practicalities of prevention include consideration of risk factors. In coronary heart disease, for example, the following risk factors apply: obesity, lack of exercise, high blood pressure, high blood fat levels, family history and smoking, and the more of these risk factors that are present, the greater is the risk of coronary heart problems later in life. Similarly, to eliminate the risk factors in sport one needs to have injury surveys, properly designed and with statistical advice. Three years ago, a sports injuries survey of rugby football was undertaken at Guy's Hospital (Davies & Gibson, 1978) and the results highlighted the large percentage of injuries which were probably caused by foul play. Several other surveys in rugby union have been carried out before, in the UK and elsewhere, but none has looked at the case of deliberate fouls in relation to injury. In addition, other areas of risk which we have studied were: (a) playing position – was there any one particular player at risk; (b) phase of the game – was there any part of the game which carried a greater risk of injury. The overall findings were that a total of 185 players entered the survey; 151 injuries were reported among 98 of them (53%) during the season. Forwards sustained significantly more injuries than backs, the prop forward being the position most at risk in this particular survey. The standard of rugby, players' body weights and presence of joint hyper-mobility were not found to affect the risk of injury in this survey. The leg was the most common site of injury. Head and neck injuries tended to occur while play was static and on wet pitches. Scrummages did not account for any neck injuries in this survey. It may be relevant that referees had received explicit instructions at the beginning of the previous season to prohibit the collapsed scrum because of alarming reports of neck injuries. Almost half the injuries occurred during the last quarter of the game, which is as expected when people were more fatigued.

The most alarming point is that foul play may have caused as many as 31% of all reported injuries. Twelve per cent were caused by deliberate punches or gouges, whereas the remaining 10% were due to the player being kicked. In a few cases the players concerned were unsure whether they had been kicked deliberately or not but an injury did result. As these percentages of increased violence were deliberate attempts to harm opposing sportsmen this was an ugly indictment of rugby football as played today. Vigorous prohibition of deliberately dangerous play is clearly needed to reduce the very high rate of injury in the sport. This is only one of several facts which emerged from the survey. Another interesting fact which emerged was that only one quarter of the injuries sustained during foul play resulted in a penalty being awarded. The authors commented that this is perhaps a case for linesmen adjudicating at the top level of rugby, or for two referees to be put in charge. Having carried out the survey and evaluated the results then obviously recommendations should be made and some action may follow. In fact this particular survey has, in 1980, for the first time led to linesmen at senior and international representative level of rugby being allowed to adjudicate. This should lead to a reduction in the foul play occurring on the blind side of referees. Other measures, such as padded posts, use of mouth-guards and suitable boot studs all help to reduce the risk of injury.

Classification of sports injuries

For the purpose of this paper, sports injuries will be grouped into three classes: (a) psychological, (b) soft-tissue and (c) over-use injuries.

Psychological injuries. It is not surprising that the majority of sportsmen have problems due to the intense pressure and competitive nature of the sports they are involved in. For instance, a first class golfer travels around the world and suddenly he comes to face a situation where one putt could mean the difference between £5000 and £15,000; this is a tremendous burden for any man to take. On personality, it is important first to clarify one or two things which, to the layman, might sound odd or even unlikely. We tend to think of people as being very much alike and if somebody has a personality rather different from ours we believe that this is due to his upbringing and with a bit of persuasion he can be made to be much like anybody else; in fact, this view is fundamentally erroneous. The worst difficulty for a sportsman is when his emotional instability interferes with his play (Eysenck, 1979). It is not only the neurotic person who experiences anxiety, depression and other emotions resulting from continued lack of success or adverse effects such as wrong line calls in tennis or bad refereeing decisions in football. Such emotional reactions interfere considerably with success and an individual with a personality which makes him prone to such reactions is unlikely to be very successful. On the other hand, almost complete absence of emotional responses is also bad and, up to a point, emotion can either mar a person's performance or act as a useful drive. It is very important in sport that a doctor, as far as he can, liaises with the coach who probably understands the athlete better than anybody else. Coaches, in particular, should know far more about the psychological phases of personality differences, particularly as they are related to success in sport, and should also be acquainted with methods of behaviour therapy and modification which can be used to alleviate bad effects of certain personality traits. Reference has already been made to motivation in relation to the recent England–Wales rugby game; there may be 'dominant' and 'subordinate' races and a highly charged audience but also, of any 30 rugby players two or three may already have had problems in the past and have bad disciplinary records. This is a selectorial rather than a coaching problem, but one must accept that there are certain players who can be motivated very highly and who play extremely well whereas others, perhaps with an underlying psychopathic personality, have to be handled extremely carefully in emotionally charged situations. So there is need to be careful in motivating players; this is the responsibility of the coach who ought to know his players very well.

Almost all sport imposes an intense strain on the mental and physical wellbeing of players (Pattmore, 1979). Such are the pressures of fame in competition that some sportsmen say they really want to kill their opponents. Brian Close in his book *I Don't Bruise Easily* says that on one or two occasions 'I felt so completely out of my depth that I even contemplated killing myself'; this is the kind of pressure found in cricket.

The delivery speed of Jeff Thompson, the Australian fast bowler, has been timed with the use of cameras at 99·6 miles per hour. As his bowling hand is concealed behind his back until the last moment, this makes him a very difficult bowler to anticipate, or 'pick' as the batsmen say; by the time the batsman's central nervous system is processing information about the delivery he has approximately half a second to determine what his response should be. If the ball deviates after pitching, as it often does, he has considerably less then half a second and it is possible to produce figures to prove that he should begin playing his stroke before the ball is delivered. Many technically accomplished batsmen, under this kind of pressure, have failed for want of psychic gifts! But seriously injuring a batsman does not apparently fill fast bowlers with pleasure; usually they are overcome with remorse. It is suggested that physical injury to a batsman, though serious, is perhaps less crucial than the threats to his emotional stability which are part and parcel of a professional sportsman's lot. Many batsmen have made themselves physically ill through trying to resolve the contradictory pressures of their task, especially if asked to bear official responsibilities such as captaincy. Some are struck down by mysterious physical maladies which clear up as soon as the crisis is past; they are not malingerers, their illnesses are real. This is the psychosomatic aspect of sports injuries.

Soft tissue injuries. These can perhaps be initially prevented and certain complications can be avoided if the right treatment is given. Treatment by ice, compression and elevation (ICE) has been well tried over the last few years by many people and it is interesting that Galen and Hippocrates, centuries ago, could not agree on the use of heat or cold in the management of sprains or strains.

The role of exercise has been misunderstood until recently but in the last few years a great deal of work has been done on this, especially on the use of exercise with ICE therapy in the first 48–72 hr after injury. The value of exercise lies in: increased blood flow; increased rate of healing; stretching of scar tissue; avoidance of adhesions.

Injuries can be prevented by the use of protective clothing. Who would have thought, a few years ago, that batsmen would ever wear helmets? This may perhaps be found in rugby union over the next 10 years, but it is doubtful. Occasionally the wearing of protective clothing can itself cause injury and the helmet has caused real problems in American football. About 2–3 years ago it had to be modified and, even now, these enormous men weighing 260–270 pounds charge into each other using various techniques whereby the helmet is used as a direct weapon against the other man's chest or abdomen, causing internal injury.

Over the last few years progress has been made. For example, it obviously makes sense for a rugby prop forward to wear a gum shield and the dangers have been eliminated provided the shield is well fitted and made by the player's own dentist; ungoverned use is not advised.

Over-use injuries. These are summarized in Table 1. It is not surprising that we find tissues breaking down under stress when we consider the muscular effects on top athletes in training (Geoff Capes may lift 6 tons of weights in one session). It has been estimated that the man who runs 150 miles a week gets 5 million foot impacts per year, and it is not therefore surprising that his feet hurt and he has problems with shin soreness. Improved design of running shoes, for example, is important here and people must have correct, comfortable, shoes for their particular activity.

Table 1. Classification of injuries caused by over-use

Bone	Stress factor	
Tendon sheath	Tenosynovitis	Achilles and patellar
Tendons	Tendonitis	Adduction
		Bicipital
		Supraspranatus
Bursa	Bursitis	Achilles
		Infrapatellar
		Trochanteric
		Subacromial
Musculo tendonous areas	Shin soreness	Tennis elbow
	Anterior tibial syndrome	Golfer's elbow
	Forearm splints	Javelin's elbow
	Hamstring origin	Baseballer's elbow
Joints	Talotibial exostosis	
	Chondromalacia patellae	
	Foot strain	

Muscle tears can be caused by over-use. Some recent work on hamstring injuries by the Americans shows that there must be a correct balance between the quadriceps muscle at the front of the thigh and the hamstring at the back. Without this correct balance there is increased risk of injury to the hamstring muscle. This is therefore a preventive factor to be taken into consideration and a factor which doctors would be wise to check in patients with recurring hamstring injury.

Over-use can lead to incapacitation at an early age. A recent review of sports injury and osteoarthrosis has been carried out by Adams (1976). Some of the points made which are relevant to this paper are:

(1) osteoarthrosis is often reported in former sportsmen but causal connections have not been established;
(2) injury affecting the muscle ligaments around a joint will affect normal joint action and thus impose greater stresses in the cartilage and bone;
(3) adolescents are more prone to injuries, because of immaturity, weakness, hypermobility and lack of co-ordination;
(4) those previously injured are more prone to further injury;
(5) the man most likely to develop osteoarthrosis is the professional sportsman who continues to play although injured.

Selection is another important factor; obviously, a 13-year-old boy who is 6ft 2in tall with a long neck should not be put in the front row of a rugby scrum. The same applies to other, less obvious, incompatibilities. A boy who was quite an able runner until he reached the age of 13 or 14 started to develop problems in both knees; this was due to an anatomical disparity of having an abnormality in both knee caps which were medially displaced. Some people can obviously be selected because of their size, weight, height etc.; others, with an abnormality, may need to be considered extremely carefully to ensure that they do not enter into sports for which they are not suited.

Another preventive aspect of sports medicine relates to back pain. Billings, Burry & Jones (1977) reviewed 100 sports people who came to the Sports Injuries Clinic at Guy's Hospital with back pain and found a high proportion (30%) of people with a stress fracture at the base of the spine. The majority of people with this stress fracture took part in weight training which was frequently unsupervised. For young people, between 14 and 19 years of age, this is a preventive factor about which physical educationists need to be extremely careful.

A good example of over-use is in the adolescent javelin throwers, where too much throwing can result in a fracture, or a lack of fusion in the epiphysis of the olecranon. If this is happening in elbows in adolescence one wonders what is happening in the spines. Exercise is good for you but even the popular sport of jogging can cause injuries. A recent review of sudden deaths in sport (Fentem & Bassey, 1979) came to the conclusion that there was no increase in sudden death during sport. Exercise on the whole does you good but there are problems and these are what we see at the hospital clinics.

Some of the manoeuvres in the more esoteric sports such as ski jumping and hang-gliding defy description but bring feelings of satisfaction and well-being through personal expression, self-fulfilment and freedom. Society itself has created some of our problems for us. A few years ago there was the skateboard boom and accident and emergency departments throughout the country were treating people for broken arms etc., but at least they were protected in part when they wore protective clothing.

In conclusion, let us return to the earlier question of whether the National Health Service can cater for the injury boom which man has created for himself. A recent critical article said that sports medicine was a pseudospeciality, which was dangerous, meddlesome and wasteful (Pringle, 1980). The author, an orthopaedic surgeon, made the point that the grouping of patients according to the origin of their injuries was artificial and he felt that the main emphasis in this field, as in industrial medicine, should be on prevention. He also made the point that NHS resources were being diverted towards treating and rehabilitating sportsmen at the expense, indirectly at least, of the remainder of the population. He suggested that those taking part in sport should have compulsory accident insurance which would cover the expense of private treatment.

I firmly believe that the future development of the involvement of the medical and physiotherapy professions in the diagnosis and treatment of injured sportsmen and sportswomen will evolve predominantly in the private sector and less so within the National Health Service. What is important, however, is to ensure the involvement of registered medical practitioners and chartered society physiotherapists in any private medical insurance schemes for the diagnosis and treatment of sports injuries thereby eliminating the unqualified 'back street' sports injury clinics which appear to be emerging at present.

References

ADAMS, I.D. (1976) Sports injury in osteoarthrosis. *Practitioner,* **224**, 61.
BILLINGS, R.S., BURRY, H.C. & JONES, R. (1977) Low back injury in sport. *Rheumatology and Rehabilitation,* **16**, 236.
DAVIES, J.E. & GIBSON, T. (1978) Injuries in rugby union football. *Br. med. J.* **2**, 1759.
EYSENCK, H.J. (1979) Personality in sport. *Medisport,* **1**, No. 7, 23.
FENTEM, P.H. & BASSEY, E.J. (1979) *The Case for Exercise.* Research Working Paper, Sports Council, London.
PATTMORE, A. (1979) How sport became death or glory. *Now,* 2–8 November, 19.
PRINGLE, R.G. (1980) Sports medicine is a pseudo-speciality. *World Med.* **22** March, 29.

Biosocial Aspects of Sport

COMMENT

GREG McLATCHIE

Monklands Hospital, Airdrie, Scotland

The theme of my comments, following Dr Davies's talk about preventive medicine in sports medicine, is related to my own close involvement in the martial arts. They are of biosocial importance, therefore their study is important and, in this branch of sport, the injuries are almost totally preventable. Some years ago, a pathologist reported an interesting case of a young soldier who was murdered; his injuries were so peculiar that the authorities felt certain they must have been inflicted by some blunt instrument. However, it was revealed in court that his assailant was an expert in karate techniques and the severe injuries in the region of his neck had resulted from the classical karate-chop. This was reported in 1959 as a curiosity case.

The techniques involved in karate require the acquisition of very quick reflexes with remarkable muscular co-ordination; they include striking, blocking, and thrusting by means of the foot, the knee, the leg, the hand, the elbow and the forehead. Obviously, these must be controlled movements because often the fighters wear no protective equipment at all and things do sometimes go wrong. The forms of karate are of three types. The traditional type is like sword fencing in which the attacker makes his attack, tries to withdraw it just before it reaches its target but, once hitting, it can be at speeds of up to 40 mph; when his opponent is moving it is difficult to judge where his head is going to be, so although, in theory, there is supposed to be no contact things often can go wrong. Semi-contact is a further development of that theme; some areas of the body, such as the testicles and the face, are exempt from attack but the head can still be kicked if the attacker can manage it. Finally, there is full-contact karate which causes the most anxiety because it is very similar to Chinese kick-boxing but, because it is not called boxing, it is under no form of statutory control whatsoever. I believe that very shortly we are going to see, yet again, the punch-drunk syndrome – in people who are not boxers but who are fanatical practitioners of full-contact karate. This is a very popular sport in the United States and it is gaining popularity in Britain also.

Let us consider the incidence of injuries in karate. A traditional karate contest lasts for about 2 minutes. I studied 744 contests in the year 1974–75 and there were 147 injuries which gives a ratio of about one injury per five contests, i.e. one injury every 10 minutes in competition. Sites of injury are the target areas but virtually the whole body is an injury site. During the last 5 years I have studied over 6500 contests and the following are all injuries which I have seen personally, and they illustrate the problem which exists.

Concussion and depressed skull fracture are very common. Eye injuries, fractures of the cheek bones and of the middle part of the face are also common; the latter cause rupture of the ear sinuses within the face producing a kind of spongy feeling to the skin called subcutaneous emphysema. Fracture of the nose, culminating in bleeding, is a standard injury, as also are dental and mandibular injuries. Why are these injuries so common? Part of the reason arises from the Japanese philosophy that one accepts pain stoically and we have a sport in this country which is now extremely popular, practised by over 50,000 individuals who have carried on, to some extent, the same Japanese philosophy, and this is the major problem with prevention of injury in karate. First of all we have to educate the participants that this type of injury really is not acceptable. Of these injuries to the face, I should like to give one recent case report on a young man, a university student, who was blind in his right eye since birth. He was very inexperienced, yet, at his second or third karate lesson he was allowed to take part in competition and he was kicked in the other eye, in which he is now only partially sighted. Under no circumstances would this have been permitted in boxing and it is totally unacceptable.

Injuries to the neck have produced paralysis. I have seen one case of a ruptured trachea and one man who was struck by a spinning kick and sustained a dislocation of the cervical vertebrae. A hardened fighter can obtain phenomenal speed, the speed of a gymnast, and produce forces of up to 650 pounds per square inch with a rotating kick. Because he has rotated, through almost 360°, once the movement is initiated, he cannot see where his opponent is by the time the blow lands, so there is no way to control it. I should like to see such techniques banned.

Injuries to the trunk, rupture of the liver and of the spleen have all been reported. Acute traumatic pancreatitis can develop through injury to the pancreas, which lies behind the stomach and is very important both in the production of insulin and as a digestive gland. If the digestive juices leak outside the limits of the pancreas itself, it actually begins a process of autodigestion. This is a very serious condition and can be fatal. Fractured ribs and burst lungs are quite common from kicks in these regions.

One must remember that the original intention of karate was to maim and kill armed opponents, so choice sites, such as the middle of the upper arm to make a swordsman drop his sword by injuring his radial nerve, or sites at the head of the fibula to hit the superficial peroneal nerve and make him fall down, were very common. Perhaps you have seen people break bricks with karate blows so it is really quite easy to break long bones. Dislocation and fractures of the fingers are very common. The superficial injuries that occur in training are mainly the soft tissue ones; there is virtually no person in karate who has not had a bruise or a knee problem or some sort of pain or injury, perhaps a simple thing like tennis elbow, from punches not directed at hitting any particular target.

How can this be prevented? There are two basic remedies. First, there should be prevention by control, both immediate and remote. The immediate control of any fight or sporting contest is in the hands of the referee but he only has rights in as much as a governing body of any sport will allow. So the governing body represents remote control. The referee has no power at all unless he is totally supported by the governing body and it is the responsibility of these bodies to lay down categorical rules so that there can be no room for misinterpretation. This would lead to a reduction in the sort of injuries we see.

Dr Davies pointed out that protective clothing in cricket is now a fairly common sight. Until 5 years ago, karate carried no protective clothing at all but, with the help of the Martial Arts Commission in London, participants now wear pads on their fists and their feet, gum shields and groin guards.

The other measure of control which is being introduced at major international competitions is weight classes and we would also like to see the outlawing of uncontrollable techniques such as the spinning back kick. And I must stress the importance of medical cover. Any combat sporting contest should have a doctor present, as well as first aid people.

Padded flooring is another particularly important safety feature. If the fight is taking place on a concrete floor a concussive blow to the chin alone would probably allow the victim to recover within a few seconds. However, if he falls back unconscious, he strikes the back of his head on the floor; we have had three cases in the neurosurgical institute in Glasgow because of this type of injury, and I am sure it is equally common elsewhere. Padded flooring is now being introduced into competitions and yet the recent European Junior Championships in Paris were fought on a hard concrete floor, as also were the Senior Championships in Finland.

There are injuries similar to boxing injuries which should preclude any further participation in the sport for some time. Head injuries are probably the most important and I would extend this beyond the realms of combat sports. It seems reasonable that if a fighter is concussed he should not fight again for perhaps 3-4 weeks, but this should also be so in football and this is beginning to be a cause for concern. A recent paper from the neurosurgical institute in Glasgow (Lindsay, McLatchie & Jennett, 1980) reports studies of head injuries in sport and it was found that boxing is not now the major cause, in our area, of the problems related to what was once called punch-drunkenness. The minor trauma of heading a football or of being concussed on the rugby field, and then being allowed to wake up and continue to play the game, could all contribute to this problem of traumatic encephalopathy. An international footballer, apparently knocked out for 10 minutes in a match, should not have played again in an international match only 1 week later. The player is certainly under pressure, but he is also at risk of suffering a more substantial head injury with cumulative brain damage. Aural and eye injuries should also preclude participation in a combat sport until recovery is complete.

Do these preventive measures help? The injuries sustained in the study of 744 contests in 1974–75 were compared with those found in a series of 1022 contests the following year when protective clothing, head guards and groin guards were used; a considerable difference was found, both in number of injuries and in anatomical distribution. There is always a level of injury which is probably acceptable; we cannot stop everybody from injuring themselves but I think, as doctors, we could certainly reduce injury to a minimum. And it is not even the practice of medicine; it is the practice of common sense and the education of trainers and coaches.

Reference

LINDSAY, K.W., McLATCHIE, G.R. & JENNETT, B. (1980) Serious head injury in sport. *Br. med J.* **1**, 789.

GENERAL DISCUSSION

The question was asked why it was that, although scoring in boxing was based on landing blows on an opponent, neither amateur nor professional boxers used any form of protective head gear or clothing. Mr McLatchie thought that this was related to the attitude of the public, who did not like to see padded fighters but positively enjoyed the spectacle of boxers being hurt in the ring. This was a matter for re-education and, in the meantime, referees should follow the excellent example of medical control set at the Olympic Games in Montreal when men who were obviously beaten were not allowed to accept further blows. Head injuries occurred too easily by accident, without encouraging deliberate exposure.

In answer to a question about the steps being taken to improve the rules governing karate, Mr McLatchie praised the actions of the Martial Arts Commission which he thought was one of the governing bodies most enthusiastically active in their efforts to reduce injury through a programme of research into the extent of the problem and the establishment of a regional medical service with education as an important area of responsibility. Personal involvement as a former participant had led to an awareness of the problems and, internationally, colleagues had been co-operative. Some opposition had been encountered but dismissive attitudes were gradually changing to a greater appreciation of the need for improvements. Similar efforts and a realistic acceptance of the facts were needed in all sports.

Kevin Hickey differentiated between professional boxing, which was a form of show business entertainment and therefore perhaps difficult to justify in moral terms, and amateur boxing where medical safeguards were constantly being improved. Skill, particularly in defence, was an important element in the prevention of injury and the introduction of too much protective clothing could lead to over-reliance on this and detract from the importance of developing improved technique. Mr McLatchie agreed that skill was an important factor and said that 80% of the injuries found during his study had occurred at grass roots levels of karate, indicating the need for adequate supervision and coaching. Amateur boxing was not now regarded as a major cause of serious injuries in sport and provided an excellent example of a high risk sport where injuries had been reduced to the lowest level by statutory control. It was hoped that similar progress would be made within the martial arts.

The question was raised of the special vulnerability to injury of adolescents at the time of the growth spurt and reference was made to the particular problems of gymnasts and the importance of selecting people with appropriate physical characteristics. Weight lifting had been shown to cause lesions of the epiphyses of the spine and, in general terms, it was felt that certain people at certain ages should not be allowed to try certain movements. Education of coaches and parents was the means by which this could be implemented.

Biosocial Aspects of Sport

USE AND ABUSE OF DRUGS IN SPORT

ARNOLD H. BECKETT

*Chelsea College, University of London,
Manresa Road, London*

Summary. An account is presented of the increasing use of drugs in sport, the attempts to test for and control the drugs used, and the devices used to evade detection. The author's view is that all the drugs being used at present can be detected, provided that sufficient funds are available for organizing tests and that national federations co-operate fully.

The problem

The abuse of drugs in sport is not a new event. For centuries there have been attempts to alter performance by using drugs. However, it is only in the past few decades when drugs have become more potent that the dangers and problems involved in drugs in sport have been clearly seen. The death of the Danish cyclist Knut E. Jensen in the Olympic Games in Rome and the hospitalization of two of his cycling colleagues began to focus world attention on the problem. A further jolt was given to the international complacency when the British cyclist, Tommy Simpson, died in the Tour de France. However, these events were only the tip of the iceberg. Questionnaires filled in by competitors at the Olympic Games in Tokyo showed how much drug misuse had pervaded top sport; even if some of the replies were discounted, the measure of the abuse was great. This was later confirmed, in the presentation at one of the Senate sub-committees in the USA by Harold Connolly, triple Olympic gold medal winner in the hammer event.

The introduction of anabolic steroids into medicine and then into sport had far reaching effects and increased greatly the number of competitors involved in drug misuse. At the Olympic Games in Tokyo, some of the doctors involved in sports medicine became sufficiently concerned to demand action.

Planning for action

By early 1960, some countries had become sufficiently concerned about drug misuse to begin to plan Acts of Parliament to attempt to deal with the problem. This was the case in Belgium and in France. This plan for action was co-ordinated with the outcry by the doctors at the Tokyo Olympic Games. In the early 1960s therefore, dope control in sport was started in an extensive way on cyclists, especially in Belgium. In the first year of the tests a very high percentage of competitors were found to be positive on drugs which could be identified and an even higher percentage were found to have abnormal constituents in the urine, which at that time could not be identified but almost certainly represented drug misuse. In these early days of testing in cycling, therefore, probably more than 80% of the professional cyclists were involved in drug misuse. In the United Kingdom, my own research group became involved in the problem after we had presented at the international conference some of our research information on drug absorption metabolism and excretion of amphetamines. It was obvious that very sensitive methods of analysis were now available, and we were asked to contact the sports authorities; this then lead to our involvement in dope control during the 1965 Tour of Britain cycle race – the 'Milk Race'. The International Cycling Federation had not only introduced rules to ban drugs, but had made arrangements that at certain international events there should be testing. In the following year the football authorities acted and we were asked to carry out a dope control at the World Cup soccer finals held in the UK. Other international federations were also considering action, and the International Olympic Committee, itself, made the move of commencing a new medical commission (see Table 1). The plans were started in 1966, and in 1967 the commission began to function under the chairmanship of Prince de Merode of Belgium. The intention was to plan for international action to attempt to deal with the serious problem of drug abuse in sport.

Table 1. IOC Medical Commission

Established: Athens 1961		Chairman, Sir Arthur Porritt
Re-established: 1967		Chairman, Prince A. de Merode
Responsibilities:	1.	Guidance and approval to the host country on medical and paramedical installations, organization and facilities at the Olympic Village and sports sites
	2.	Doping control
	3.	Sex control
Additional responsibilities:	(a)	Medical Counsellor of IOC
	(b)	Contact organisation for the 'Olympic Solidarity' movement
	(c)	Links closely with the International Sports Federation

Action

It was essential, in any action, to be able to deal objectively with the problem. This meant that the abuse had to be proved by methods not involving denunciations. Thus some means had to be found of establishing unequivocally that the abuse had occurred and this pushed matters in the direction of suitable analytical techniques.

The question then, was which biological fluid should be used. Because drugs are present in higher concentrations in general in urine than they are in blood, and because collection of urine involves less invasion of the integrity of the individual than does taking a blood sample, the emphasis for testing was therefore on urine.

It is interesting to trace the influence of the International Olympic Committee Medical

Commission and understand some of its philosophy. First it was important to try to ensure that we had clear principles which could be accepted by all those supporting any attempt to curtail drug abuse in sport. We took a pragmatic approach to this problem (see Table 2). Furthermore we realized that competitors had to be allowed medication. Some would have colds, and would require treatment. Some would have travelled long

Table 2. Why should some drugs be classed as doping agents?

Moral argument		Pragmatic arguments
Their use contravenes the basic characteristics of sport – the matching of the natural capabilities of the participants	(a)	Competition should involve competitors, not pharmacologists and physicians
	(b)	Competitors should not be used as guinea-pigs
	(c)	The use of some drugs can cause aggression and loss of judgement – hazards to other competitors, spectators and officials
	(d)	Danger of bad examples to young people
	(e)	Danger of drug dependence

distances, and therefore would require sedatives if they were to sleep properly. Some would compete, and yet they would be asthmatics; treatment was therefore needed to enable them to compete under conditions which were the best for them by removing the disadvantageous effects of their asthma. However, we had to attempt to draw a line which would allow medication and yet not allow those types of material which could cause serious problems in sport. This policy is shown in Table 3. Once the principles were established, then it was a matter of ensuring that we had all the analytical techniques available and functioning correctly. Furthermore, we had to ensure that those involved in

Table 3. IOC Medical Commission policy on dope control

	Policy
1.	To prevent the use of those drugs in sport which constitute dangers when used as doping agents
2.	To prevent drug abuse with the minimum of interference with the therapeutic use of drugs
3.	To ban only those drugs for which suitable analytical methods could be devised to detect the compounds unequivocally in urine (or blood) samples
4.	To ban classes of drugs based upon the pharmacological actions of members of the classes, but not to attempt to produce a complete list of banned drugs

dope control realized that dope control itself was much more than the collection of samples and their analysis; the procedure is outlined in Table 4.

Results

The introduction of dope control in sport soon had a big effect in curtailing the misuse in those sports which had planned testing, and in those events where testing was occurring. Unfortunately, not all federations agreed to act in the early stages of dope control. Furthermore, many of the sports writers were doubtful of attempts at dope control in the early stages. They argued that some of the tests were not reliable and that tests were interfering with the rights of the individual. Soon, however, they began to realize that the tests were fair and accurate, and that there was a good measure of support for them amongst the competitors themselves.

Table 4. Dope testing – general aspects

1. Selection of athletes to be tested
2. Control of sampling: Bottles
   Codes
   Urine collection
   pH measurement
   Subdivision of sample
3. Transport and control of samples: Sealing
   Codes
   Laboratory receipt
4. Reporting of results
5. Repeat analysis on duplicate sample: Method
   Observer
6. The use of control 'positive samples'

By the time of the Munich games in 1972 much of the problem of the misuse of stimulant drugs was under control (see Table 5 for classes of drugs with examples). However, because we had no suitable tests for anabolic steroids, the misuse of these compounds was escalating in a dramatic fashion. Normally most people think of the use of anabolic steroids in connection with the 'heavy' events. They think of them as being used along with the high protein diet in the attempt to increase bulk. However, it should be realized that anabolic steroids are the result of chemical modifications of the male hormone testosterone with the attempt to reduce the masculinizing effects but to maintain the anabolizing one. But, the compounds produced, i.e. the anabolic steroids, do retain a substantial amount of the masculinizing effect. Thus they cause increased aggression and competiveness. It is for this purpose that they are used in many sports in addition to the effect of increasing weight in some sports, when a high protein diet is taken. When it was realized that the control of the stimulants was very effective there was an increase in the use of anabolic steroids. Much work was involved to devise tests for these, and Professor

Raymond Brooks, of St Thomas's Hospital played an important role in developing radioimmunoassay methods. However, such tests could only be used as screening tests, since, in dope control, we had decided that the actual drug itself had to be identified unequivocally before action was taken.

Table 5. List of doping substances, defined by the IOC Medical Commission (Munich, May 1971)

Psychomotor stimulant drugs	Sympathomimetic amines	Miscellaneous central nervous system stimulants	Narcotic analgesics
Amphetamine	Ephedrine	Amiphenazole	Heroin
Benzphetamine	Methylephedrine	Bemigride	Morphine
Cocaine	Methoxyphenamine	Leptazol	Methadone
Diethylpropion	Related compounds	Nikethamide	Dextromoramide
Dimethylamphetamine		Strychnine	Dipipanone
Ethylamphetamine		Related compounds	Pethidine
Fencamfamin			Related compounds
Methylamphetamine			
Methylphenidate			
Norpseudoephedrine			
Phendimetrazine			
Prolintane			
Related compounds			

This list is not complete, other substances may be added.

In the case of the stimulant drugs and narcotic drugs, after the first few years of testing, we had reached agreement that no positive results should be declared unless mass spectrometry had been carried out and the compounds identified unequivocally by what is equivalent to taking a fingerprint. In the case of anabolic steroids, therefore, we delayed action until we were able to have definitive tests. These were well developed before the Olympic Games in Montreal in 1976, and there, for the first time, we went into action with the decision to test and also to act. Despite the fact that we had announced that we were testing, there were eight positive results in the Olympic Games in Montreal and two gold medals and one silver medal were withdrawn as a result of the tests and the establishment of the misuse of anabolic steroids.

Within a year or two of this work, when testing for anabolic steroids was more widespread, avoiding action was then taken by competitors and their advisors. It was realized that if taking of anabolic steroids was discontinued, then positive results could only be obtained for about 2-3 weeks. Thus some competitors using anabolic steroids discontinued their use before any main event that would be subject to testing. However, their performance went down because stopping the anabolic steroids led to depression and lack of competitiveness. To cover this gap, therefore, injections of testosterone were used with the intention that, since testosterone was endogenous, we would not be in a position to act. Analytically we can see the material, but as yet, we cannot act because it is an endogenous material and we cannot distinguish between the injected and the normal hormone. Nevertheless, within a few years, it will be possible to detect this misuse.

Other competitors changed to the injectable anabolic steroids, not realizing that these would be mobilized slowly from the site of injection and that we would be able to test for them for months. Such a misuse led to the recent disqualification of some of the top middle distance women runners when they were caught for drug misuse at the Balkan Games in 1979. Unfortunately, the IAAF Council has failed, by reinstating those disqualified to enable them to compete at the Moscow Olympic Games; thus its integrity in the fight to clean up athletics has been weakened.

The result, therefore, of dope control has certainly produced a curtailment of what was an escalating problem, but has not solved the problem. There still are loopholes, but one by one these will be plugged.

There has become an increased sophistication in the attempts to circumvent dope control. In the early days, rather crude procedures, such as placing urine under the armpits in plastic bags and then getting this urine into the bottle, were used. This was obviously an easy thing to counteract since one had to ensure that it was observed that the urine came from the right individual. More recently, in the anabolic steroid field, if competitors have come along to an event where they found there was to be testing before the event started, then some have used big doses of diuretics to try to 'wash out' the anabolic steroids quickly while using legal arguments to delay the tests. When finally they had to appear for testing, they have taken large amounts of liquids along with diuretics and hoped that the urine would be so dilute that the laboratory would not detect the presence of anabolic steroids.

In recent years there has been a realization by many federations that they must follow the lead set by the International Olympic Committee Medical Commission in ensuring that the laboratories carrying out the analysis linked with dope control had the appropriate expertise and equipment. Because of lack of attention to this point, some federations have disqualified competitors incorrectly, using information where the presence of the drug was not established unequivocally. Unfortunately, some medical commissions of the federations have not had amongst their members people with enough detailed scientific knowledge. Right from the start of the plans by the International Olympic Committee Medical Commission, there has been much stress on not only that justice be done, but that justice is seen to be done. For instance when a positive result has been obtained on the first sample, then the analysis of the second sample is carried out in front of observers from the country being challenged.

Latterly, the International Amateur Athletic Federation has made important rules on ensuring that laboratories can carry out the work of dope control effectively and have started a laboratory accreditation scheme. In this scheme the laboratory seeking accreditation supplies information on its apparatus, the skill of its personnel and the reference compounds available to it. Without an adequate supply of reference compounds of drugs considered in the banned list, and also drugs which may give results comparable to some compounds of the banned classes, it is impossible to carry out effective analytical procedures. If the appropriate criteria have been demonstrated for the laboratory, then the IAAF sends ten urine samples from subjects who have taken drugs of the banned classes. The laboratory receiving them has to get the correct results before it is accredited. Furthermore, there is an updating of the accreditation every 2 years, when new urine samples containing drugs are sent. This ensures that all aspects of analysis and dope control are carried out correctly.

The future

Although much has been accomplished by dope control, the fight against the misuse of drugs has not yet been won. Some battles have been lost, some have been won; probably many lives have been saved by dope control, but the fight will continue. Some individuals are determined to win at all costs and some people supporting them are under such pressure that they too will do anything to the competitors under their care, irrespective of the consequences, in their attempt to win. Thus the problem of drug misuse will not vanish.

Some countries have taken very strong stands and are carrying out routine dope control throughout the year at events other than the major ones. This is especially important in trying to deal with the problem of anabolic steroids misuse. However, not all countries act in this way. Thus, competitors from countries which do not act are in a position to overwhelm those from countries where the competitors are tightly controlled. Unless something is done internationally on this matter and political agreement reached, then inevitably a split between the controlled and non-controlled countries must occur. It is devastating for those competitors who are under control to realize that many of the international standards being set, and the qualifying distances being demanded involve competitors who have achieved these standards under the influence of drugs. So much is at stake in international competition and so much is at stake for competitors, for whom success can alter their lifestyle, that the pressures are intense.

The various devices and techniques used to attempt to circumvent dope control have already been indicated. Undoubtedly the sophistication in this approach will continue. If only we could rely upon all doctors and coaches involved in sport to take a strong line against drug misuse then we could bring matters under control. Unfortunately, this is not the case and drug misuse involves far more than the competitors themselves. For instance it is well known that in weight lifting and power lifting some competitors use diuretics to reduce their weight before they come for the weigh-in. Immediately afterwards, dextrose and salts are infused to bring the person up to his normal weight and strength; this infusion is done by some doctors who are thus condoning this terrible misuse of diuretics. The β-blocker drugs have also assumed some prominence in drug misuse in some sports, such as pistol shooting and in ski jumping. Undoubtedly, attempts will be made to use any drug which will alter performance, especially if it is thought that at that point in time there are no controls for that drug. Corticosteroids are now being misused extensively, and although the international cycling federation has banned these drugs, the possibility of using the natural hormone cortisone will do much to undermine their regulations.

The fight against drug misuse has allowed protection of many competitors to occur. Unfortunately however, the drug misuse is now spreading to younger age groups. In some countries it is involving the younger teenagers who, having heard about gains which may come from using drugs, have begun to experiment with them. Even parents have been known to give drugs to their children to give them a chance of being picked for certain prestigious teams.

It is only correct to consider the drug misuse of sport in the correct perspective of drug misuse in society. Many countries really are now drug-ridden societies, and therefore, one can hardly expect sport to be exempt from the prevalent opinion that there is a pill for all ills and a pill to allow one to act in all sorts of ways. Sport, however, should have higher ideals than those which obtain in society as a whole. Sometimes, it requires courage to act against this drug misuse in sport. Today the technological facilities are available to deal with most of the problems. Many federations have had the courage to act. Unfortunately, the international federations have not the right to deal with problems occurring in member countries. If those countries are not prepared to act then, unfortunately, the whole plan dealing with drug misuse must be in doubt. It is now time for the politicians to show courage, before sport becomes destroyed by drugs as well as by politics.

Biosocial Aspects of Sport

COMMENT

RON PICKERING

40 Woodstock Road, Broxbourne, Herts

I was delighted to hear Professor Beckett take such a strong moral stand, which I should like to reinforce, on the question of drugs in sport.

The historical background suggests that the philosophy behind doping is as old as man himself who, given the power of thought, has never been able to accept his mental or physical limitations. The first recorded doping incident was in the Garden of Eden when Adam and Eve ate the forbidden fruit – not because they were hungry, nor because they were curious, but because the serpent deceived them into believing the fruit would make them god-like. Throughout history, anomalies, double standards and hypocrisy have always been present in sport. In 1904, the Englishman, Fred Lotz, representing America, ran in the marathon and he ran most of the course but about 9 miles from the finish he decided he could not continue, so he took a lift in a car. However, before he reached the stadium his friends persuaded him, for a joke, to run into the stadium, which he did; but he ran to the finish line and then, of course, the joke backfired. It was realized that he had cheated and he was banned for ever. However, the winner of the gold medal was Tom Hicks, who was supported throughout the race by professional trainers who, with the aid of stimulants, forced him to run on, despite collapsing while still some way from the stadium, and, sadly, he never ran again. So there were problems even then.

The death of the cyclist Tommy Simpson was the watershed and, as far as I am concerned, one of the reasons why we are doing all this testing is to safeguard the athlete from the dangers that he may be tempted to put himself under. Mr McLatchie horrified me with his account of karate injuries, and I would still choose athletics rather than karate, the Manx TT races or mountaineering, which are inherently more dangerous.

We should understand that the generation we are talking about have as their idols not C. B. Fry nor the Corinthian Casuals but current pop stars, and they do not always understand the standards by which we would like to operate, however strongly motivated we are by idealism. These same young people are growing up to question the double standards which exist in sport – such standards as the reinstatement of the athletes who were found guilty of breaking the laws yet will now appear at the Olympic Games in Moscow. And Rick Demont, of America, who won his Olympic gold medal in 1972 in the swimming, only to find that he proved positive in a doping test. He said he had taken ephedrine in nose drops given to him by his doctor because he suffered from hay fever. As a result he was banned for ever and lives with that stigma. (Professor Beckett later pointed out that the actual situation was somewhat different. It was not nose drops but fairly extensive oral use, prescribed by his doctor in California. He had been warned not to take the material and it had not been prescribed by the American team doctor).

First, let me comment briefly on some of the things which are not only acceptable but are recommended by athletes' coaches, physicians, doctors, trainers and other advisers. There are the nutritional aids – vitamins A, B_1, B_2, B_6, B_{12}, C, D, E, and K – often given in injections and known to have a euphoric effect; the doctors may question their usefulness but the fact is the athletes think they work. Niacin, folic acid, iron, calcium, potassium, phosphate, citrates, bicarbonates, gelatine, pollen, wheatgerm – the list could continue. We are being helped now by sports scientists but, with these aids, problems and complications are also found. For example, glycogen overshoots are common in marathon races. Liquid pre-game meals prevent dehydration but if there is too much dehydration there is a way of putting back the liquid. There are physical aids. An athlete does not need to warm up by a run round the track; we can warm him up with hot and cold applications. We can give him oxygen, before or after the race. This was sometimes needed for survival when the Olympic Games were held at altitude in Mexico City in 1968. Now the benefits from negatively ionised air are being advertised widely and there are ultraviolet light, ultrasonics, altitude training, acupuncture, Zen therapy, and, for horses, neurectomy. That is the society in which young competitors are growing up and they find it very confusing.

Track and field athletics are involved first of all with the anabolic steroids. Professor Beckett said that this was known in 1968 but there is evidence to suggest that the problem was known about at the time of the Olympic Games in 1964. Dr Martin Lucking and I came across a clear case of steroid use at this time, and tried to draw attention to the dangers we foresaw. Sadly, although the British Amateur Athletic Board took a considerable lead, and despite our fears of dangerous side-effects, they were not banned until 1975. It is appalling that a whole generation of athletes grew up with these substances not banned because members of the medical profession remained unconvinced of these effects; the compounds were not recommended but neither were they condemned and, in today's language, not to condemn is the equivalent of condoning. This is intended only as a warning because, as Professor Beckett said, other drugs are now being used and other sports now have problems. Gymnastics, which is the most aesthetically satisfying and beautiful sport of all for women, has now become, in my opinion, a sport for stunted dwarfs. I think we should be looking carefully at this, although I have been told that there is no serious medical problem. Apparently there is no drug known to delay the onset of puberty but we do know that there are problems which perhaps should be investigated.

So, on the one hand, there are the mitigating circumstances; they may not be acceptable but are a partial explanation. Young people today do not necessarily share the same standards; they want objectivity and further information. Most of the evidence, as far as they are concerned, has stayed on some university library shelves and has not been handed on to those who have to deal with the athletes at first hand. These are controversial topics. We know, for example, that altitude training led to altitude training camps which led to improved oxygen transportation which led to blood packing. This is not yet banned, and perhaps need not be. But these are problems, serious social problems, and I am trying to protect sport.

You may ask why I think that sport should not reflect society but should have Utopian ideals. It is because I think that sport has always been a sanctuary and should remain so. It is one of the few forms of human expression that is based entirely upon ideals and today, at grass roots level, our sports have never been stronger. Particularly among track and field athletics, there are more people running, jumping and throwing for fun than there have ever been. There are more people attempting for the first time in their lives to run a marathon course; there are 50 million people in America taking up jogging and in the UK we have more young people taking up sport at club level than ever before. Therefore, I think it is extremely important that the shop window, that area which represents the elite, the best, the greatest, the example for everyone to follow, has to be based on idealism. We should strive for the Utopian model because I think this society will be judged on its standards of civilization by the next one and we should, at all times, have their interests at heart.

Biosocial Aspects of Sport

COMMENT

WILF PAISH

British Amateur Athletic Board, 70 Brompton Road, London

In a situation such as this I am very aware of a conflict between two aspects of my personality: that of a coach dedicated to one's athletes, and that moulded by years of training as a physical educationist with the associated philosophy of sport for enjoyment and where the 'win at all costs' idea is totally alien.

While I know that there are several hundred compounds reputed to have been used by sportsmen, I will restrict myself to the issue of androgenic hormones, since I believe that these have had the most profound effect upon sport. Some people here today will certainly find what I have to say offensive because they have probably been sheltered from the world of top-class sport. My contribution will be to ask a series of provocative questions, offer some answers, and so provoke discussion and deeper thought.

Why is the topic of drugs included in a conference of this nature? Do you, as the organizers, believe that sport is riddled with drug takers? I can assure you that this is not the case. I meet thousands of good, honest athletes each year who never take anything more than a little iron or ascorbic acid. There is evidence only that a few top-class athletes (in the Greek sense) take anabolic steroids to aid their performance. Furthermore I believe that it will be impossible to legislate against this. As long as the rewards for success remain high, and as long as there are those who are politically motivated, there will always be those who are prepared to cheat. What is more, I am convinced that they will always remain two steps ahead of the detectors, as many are backed-up by an equally efficient screening system.

However, sport has embarked upon a campaign to stop this abuse. This raises the question 'why test'. Presumably to catch a person who is cheating. Does sport pursue the same efficient tactics to catch those who cheat other rules, such as breaking the amateur code and the associated criminal offence of tax evasion? I think not. To support this double standard, sport would suggest that testing is done to protect the health of current and future competitors. I have seen little, if any, evidence to support adverse side-effects upon fit, healthy, young men. I know of men who regularly took these preparations as long ago as 1964. They still appear to be very fit and they have produced healthy families. I also know of one man who has confessed to taking steroids most days since 1964 and he is still competing at international level. These preparations are taken by mature adults, some of them doctors, endocrinologists and biochemists, who must be aware of any possible side-effects. As informed people they are prepared to take this risk for their sport. In many countries these drugs can be purchased over the counter without prescription. I think it unlikely that the manufacturers would permit this to happen with a dangerous drug.

To return briefly to detecting the criminal. I know of men who have been given a 'clean bill of health', following doping tests, who have taken a form of stanozolol up to and including the day of competition without having to resort to a diuretic. I do not know of any informed athlete who has been caught out by the tests. In view of this I personally question the effectiveness of testing in terms of catching the criminal and one might also question any health hazard associated with its therapy. Many sportsmen would suggest, that like smoking, it could rest as the choice of a mature adult since the drug, unlike nicotine, is not addictive. So the validity of the test, and the motives for testing are certainly open to debate.

Anabolic steroids have been used in sport since 1952. Presumably, some of those early abusers are approaching old age. So why is not more known about the long-term side-effects on such people? This is where the possible dangers must rest. Because administration has been illegal, very few people have been prepared to admit to taking them. Hence 28 years of documentary evidence on the health of takers, has been missed. Is there any chance of catching up on this lost time? Would it be wrong to devote some of the money used in testing to research in this area?

Why is it so few sportsmen or women have been detected? Again, it is a situation in which the criminal is better informed than the police force. But here remains the greatest danger of all, and the reason why I believe that testing is far from protecting the health of the participants. The fear of being caught is forcing some athletes to resort to drugs such as pure testosterone, thyroxin, ACTH etc., which cannot be detected by present methods. These drugs, when compared with a mild dose of an anabolic steroid, must be viewed with horror.

Many people who are involved believe that international sport has taken over from war. In the present situation let us hope that it remains so. I wonder where, in the rank order of bullets to atom bombs, would drug-taking fit. However, I doubt if many administrators would be prepared to accept this comparison, although many sportsmen do.

It is impossible for us, as more mature people, to put ourselves in the place of current top-class sportspeople. In most sports there will be a generation gap. The situation is such that few participants consider the taking of this preparation as cheating. They will emphasize that it is not a magic pill, but one which will act as an ergogenic aid. Although there is a euphoric effect associated with it, the compound is not taken as a stimulant, but rather as an aid during training. For there to be true effective legislation against its use there would need to be spot checks, on the world's athletes, at any time of the year. If the political barriers involved in such an exercise could be removed then I am certain that all athletes would rejoice as few, if any, are habitual drug takers.

You might gather that I condone the use of steroids but how can I? To me it is a simple rule of cheating in much the same way as a deliberate trip in football, or handling the ball in a rugby scrummage. Because it is a rule then every effort must be made to enforce it. With highly motivated people, it is not sufficient to suggest decreased libido when takers know the opposite to be true; or suggest that it has no effect upon rats when competitors become bigger and stronger than ever, or even suggest that the expensive, sophisticated tests will catch you. I believe the true cancer to be the rich pickings for the successful. Will it remain one of those rules which will be impossible to enforce fully?

You might suggest that I should be more open in my condemnation of the taker, but it is easier said than done since I am realistic and close enough to sportsmen to know how difficult it is for them to share my philosophy. I also felt that to stimulate an unbiased discussion I might be the only person close enough to the 'cutting edge' to give the other person's view. For me it is a simple moral decision and I believe that there are moral issues in sport far more significant than drug abuse.

GENERAL DISCUSSION

The discussion was opened by Professor Beckett, responding to the suggestion that drug abuse in sport was not a serious problem. He described a legal action brought by an American football player who was awarded substantial damages for injury resulting from playing while under the influence of amphetamines and barbiturates prescribed by the doctor in charge of his team. It had then become apparent that amphetamine abuse was widespread in American professional football, a sport which previously had been thought to be free from drug problems and where participants were under the strict control of medical advisers. Professor Beckett was of the firm opinion that controlled use of drugs in sport was not possible because there would always be the temptation to increase the dose to try and obtain increased effect. He was sure that it would soon be possible to test satisfactorily for the misuse of even endogenous substances such as testosterone. Dr Sperryn commented that the extent of drug taking, as also the side effects, was at present unknown but the Sports Council had allocated funds for an epidemiological survey. Other speakers also expressed their fears about the abuse of drugs, but it was appreciated that Mr Paish, in his chosen role of devil's advocate, had highlighted the real difficulties faced by people involved in the practicalities of sport.

The discussion then turned to the subject of sex tests and it was suggested that different standards were applied in the approach to drug testing and sex testing. Before action could be taken against an athlete on grounds of drug use, unequivocal tests were clearly necessary and in any uncertainty the athlete was given the benefit of the doubt; over femininity tests, however, at least one speaker felt that the opposite was true and any doubt operated against the athlete concerned. Professor Beckett felt that, taking together the chromatin test, chromosomal mapping and the physical examination, the tests were definitive and provided protection for the true female but this view was not wholly accepted by the discussants. Although protection was the intention, it did not in practice work like that and a strong plea was made that men also should have to undergo the indignity of sex testing, with the possible hazard and unhappy effects of disqualification. It was later suggested that the femininity test embodied a very narrow definition of sex, and disqualification was a harsh penalty for an innocent offender; the necessity for submitting all women participants to this procedure was questioned and it was thought that perhaps it need be used only for individuals about whom doubts had been raised.

Returning to the problem of combating drug abuse, it was suggested that, for real progress to be made, random testing would have to be introduced. Professor Beckett agreed and pointed out that opinion was moving in this direction although the principle was not yet universally acceptable; eventually, eligibility of a country to compete would depend on its acceptance of random testing. However, among those present, there appeared to be little support for the suggestion that this principle should be confirmed by governmental legislation, perhaps because it was felt that this might lead to governmental interference in other areas of sport.

Another speaker drew attention to the fact that many of the problems considered at the meeting had culminated in discussion of moral issues, some of which were potentially more hazardous than taking drugs and might be more appropriate areas for legislative action. The allocation of resources needed to be considered carefully so that, for example, the moral issue of drug abuse did not receive an undue proportion of the limited funds available. Practising sportsmen might feel that other areas of sports medicine, or improved facilities, deserved more support. The role of legislation to support the corporate moral view on particular issues was further discussed in relation to freedom of choice in a democratic society.

In practical terms, it was agreed that clearer guidance was needed for those athletes who had a genuine need for medication. For asthmatics, for example, recent advances in anti-asthmatic drugs had widened the range of acceptable treatments available but a general permitted pharmacopoeia and permitted circumstances when bona fide treatment could be undertaken were required, at all levels of competition, and this information should be available to participants through team doctors and efficient team management.

V

TRENDS IN SPORT

Chairman: Roger Bannister

Biosocial Aspects of Sport

CITIUS, ALTIUS, FORTIUS?

JOHN WILLIAMS

Farnham Park Rehabilitation Centre, Farnham Royal, Bucks

Summary. Factors leading to improvements in human sports performance are considered. The positive and negative effects of social and economic changes and the application of scientific and technological developments are discussed.

Introduction

Prediction of likely improvements in human sports performance in the years to come demands an understanding of the history of sport's development and its world role. Initially sport evolved from training for the hunt or for war, and so glorified essentially masculine characteristics. It evolved as a civilized recreational occupation in Western Europe at about the time of the Industrial Revolution, but it is only in the twentieth century that general sports participation has become a world movement. At the highest level, this was initiated by the development of the Olympic Games of the modern era under the guidance of the Baron Pierre de Coubertin and was later greatly facilitated, particularly during the latter half of the twentieth century, by the development of easy and quick means of travel. Increasing emancipation of peoples worldwide, the end of colonial systems and the upsurge of nationalist aspiration in the developing countries all contributed to the development of sport at the highest level. From its very origins, sport has inevitably been competitive and this competitive element has become progressively more refined. Most sports have as their objective some form of winning rather than simple participation. Under this stimulus, competition records (that is to say, indices of performance) have shown a steady improvement. For example, marathon runners nowadays are running the 26+ miles at a faster pace than that achieved in the 6 mile races at the turn of the century.

When will it all end? The answer is, of course, never. As long as human beings engage in competitive sports performance, records will be broken. As time goes by, these records will be broken perhaps less often and by smaller margins. But it is axiomatic that anything that one man can do, another man can sooner or later do, and do fractionally better.

Improvements in performance

Various specific factors can be identified as contributing to the steady improvement in human sports performance. One is quite simply the size of the population engaged. In general, it is true to say that the broader the base of the pyramid in terms of population size, the higher will be its peak in terms of elite performance. This generalization is, of course, subject to a variety of caveats. For example, it presupposes that the general characteristics of the population increase are uniform. Where the population increase occurs because of an influx of more athletically gifted people, the peak of the pyramid will be correspondingly higher whereas, as is in fact the case, the influx tends to be on the whole of less athletically gifted people so the rate of increase in height of the pyramid is slower. Much of the increase in the world's sporting population is to be seen in the developing countries where nutritional, educational and other standards may not yet be as high as in the developed and athletically sophisticated West. Even so, there appear to be very significant geographical factors operating and it has been seen repeatedly how some countries develop remarkable talents in particular sports; the ability in world competition of squash players from Pakistan, and of those of Indonesia and Malaysia in badminton, offer outstanding examples.

Many elements contribute to the ability of any particular individual to perform well in sport; these may be inherent in the genetic background of the individual, may derive from his social and environmental situation or may be added in the form of different types of education or training programmes. At the very highest performance levels (to which this paper chiefly refers) differences in these elements, with the exception of the genetic, may be largely irrelevant since the most promising sportsman or woman can often obtain appropriate training and competition even if in some community or country other than his or her own (as witness the best British swimmers training at American universities).

In predicting the limits in performance in sport, it is necessary to appreciate the nature of the sport itself. Fundamentally sport is a controlled clinical trial in which the individuals or teams compete against each other within a rigidly maintained framework, the object being to assess the comparative capabilities of the competitors on a direct and objective basis. It is for this reason that, for example in track and field athletics the dimensions, weights and shapes of the implements are clearly defined. Occasionally, as in the case of throwing the javelin, problems arise because the very improvements in performance in the event tend to make it impossible to contain it within the arena! If this continues, there will have to be some modification in the rules of the event which would actually change it and so start a new line of competition rather than continue the old. Any rule change which significantly modifies a sport, inevitably interrupts and shifts the curve of human performance and record breaking.

An important factor which influences the extent to which human performance records are bettered is the number of actual opportunities for performances in the record class to be achieved. It may be only under certain combinations of ideal weather, track state and make-up of the field of competitors that, for example, the world 1500 metres record can be broken. Ease of travel and communication facilitates the gathering together of an appropriately selected field of athletes, new technology facilitates the availability of appropriate quality running surfaces and the sophisticated environmental engineering in new sports halls which controls temperature and humidity will improve the climatic and environmental conditions in which races can be run. Improvement in the opportunities for world record breaking will inevitably accelerate the pace at which record breaking takes place, at least temporarily. This was, for example, very obvious in the Olympic Games in Mexico City in 1968 where many of the events were facilitated by the less dense air at altitude which produced less wind resistance in the sprint events. World records in these events took a sharp up-turn at this point but have subsequently levelled out and the curve has resumed its normal trend.

Heredity

Among the specific individual factors which contribute to increases in top level sports performance, the most fundamental is heredity. It is often said that to be a great athlete it is necessary first to choose one's parents properly. There is little doubt that the physical endowment of high quality athletes as a result of an appropriate genetic make-up is of the utmost importance. Attempts at breeding a 'master race' have been made in the past; now the process of natural selection due to the tendency for young athletes of both sexes to get together and subsequently pair off in marriage is ensuring that families are being produced in which both parents have been both highly successful and gifted athletically. Inevitably, this will sooner or later produce generations in which the appropriate athletic genes are more highly concentrated. This, together with an appropriate sporting background in which the new generation is brought up, will contribute materially to raised sports performance. It seems that specific genetic engineering may already be in practice in certain areas where success in sport is politically highly desirable. Even so, however, the best laid plans may come undone. Tragically, from time to time the best stock may be distorted by the development of relatively minor but athletically crippling congenital problems while in any case there can be little guarantee that the new generation will have the same psychological approach to sport as their forebears. The significance of psychological drive in achievement in sport cannot be underrated. There is, as yet, no means of ensuring that the individual, however physically gifted, will be equally psychologically equipped for coping with all the stresses of top class athletic performance.

Sex differences

It is here interesting to consider the extent to which women may aspire to parity with men in athletic performance. As already indicated most sports glorify essentially masculine characteristics; some however do not, and among these may be included gymnastics, diving, trampoline and ice skating, all of which require those elements of co-ordination, skill and grace which are normally regarded as essentially feminine. Whatever the social or emotional arguments may be, unless something biologically bizarre occurs women athletes will never quite compete on equal terms with men in those events which demand predominantly masculine characteristics, however hard they try. Inevitably, a masculine male is more masculine than a masculine female! Certainly, as the size of the female athletic population increases and comes closer to that of the male athletic population, and as women's opportunities for participation in sport improve, the differences between men and women in sports performance will become less marked, but except in those events where there is obvious physical equality, for example, in certain forms of equestrianism, in shooting and possibly in sailing, women will always be to a degree at a physical disadvantage.

Environmental factors

Environment, particularly control of environment, is a 'key' factor in improved sports performance. Some indication has already been given of the type of environmental engineering which can provide optimum conditions for athletic activity. An essential component of the environment is the equipment used by the competitor, particularly in highly technical events such as rowing, sailing and the Alpine sports. The classic example of improvement in performance related to technical developments is the pole vault record. The replacement of the old bamboo pole by fibreglass, and the development of the new techniques needed to utilize the characteristics of what now must be regarded as little less than a catapult have revolutionized the event. Similar revolutions may be seen or expected in a wide variety of other technical sports where developments in new equipment and the skills required to use them will produce an, in some respects, artificial upward surge in performance. One of the important practical problems created by this new technology of sport is expense. The racing of large sailing boats has always been a rich man's sport but the cost of developing an America's Cup challenge has now become almost astronomical. To a lesser extent this is true in many other sports. New boats for rowing and new 2- or 4-man bobsleighs for the ice-run are becoming almost prohibitively expensive. Their development calls for the deployment of a wide range of technologies which are progressively available to fewer and fewer individuals or teams.

An interesting negative factor in the development of sports equipment is the subjective response of sportsmen and women on the one hand and of manufacturers on the other to new developments. Fads and fashions play an important part in the design and promotion of sporting equipment, particularly in the mass market. The innate conservatism in many industrial organizations producing sports equipment is self-destructive insofar as important new developments are frequently neglected because they are likely to meet with sales resistance!

Education and training

Educational and training facilities can have either a positive or negative influence on the development of high-class performance. Just as fads and fashions in equipment and clothing may demonstrably inhibit sports activity, so too can such fads in training. A classic example was the enthusiasm for altitude training in the early and middle 1970s. While the effects of altitude may (and as Mellerowicz showed often do) add to the training load in the untrained individual working submaximally (and so increase the training effect) the increase in physiological load due to altitude on the individual who is already training maximally, can only result in a reduction of the individual's capacity to accept a training load in another direction. Take as a simple example the case of the individual who engages in only moderate training but who regularly races over 3 miles at a 5 minutes per mile pace – he would benefit from the increased training load if he carried out his usual training programme at altitude. However, the established international 5000-metre runner whose training load is already as heavy as he can carry will find that any attempt to maintain the same training load at altitude will be impossible. Over and over again, training fads have bedevilled the development of athletic potential, particularly at the highest level. It is only necessary to remember the transient enthusiasms for isometrics, for vitamin E and for the Astrand diet to realise to what extent sportsmen and their coaches will find themselves going up blind alleys in the search for success.

It is often remarkable what success is achieved in the face of relatively inadequate technical back-up, but where a high quality back-up is available improvements in sports performance become readily apparent. In the German Democratic Republic, for example, sport is a matter of national interest and the back-up services for the sporting elite are highly organized and effectively run. This is not to suggest that there are any particular secrets of training techniques or psychological manipulation that are exclusively available in the GDR, but rather to point out that the sports organisers in that country have a single-minded application to the provision of any facility which can be shown to better sports performance. Inevitably, the ruthless pursuit of such a policy will tend to detract from the recreational and fun element of sports participation but perhaps these elements should not be considered in the context of elite sport anyway. It might be expected that programmes of this type would produce high drop-out rates amongst the sportsmen and women concerned but where motivation is intense and where some real attempts are made at selection and monitoring right from the beginning of the elite sports training programme, this is comparatively rare. This is not to say that such a programme of systematic development of the sporting elite is necessarily to be regarded with any particular approval but in terms of producing gold medals it certainly works. Whether a similar programme is possible in more developed Western European countries where individual freedoms are more highly cherished and more vigorously defended is a different matter. Certainly, present systems of sports administration in the United Kingdom tend to militate against the single-minded East German approach. It is only when governing bodies sink their differences, both internal and amongst themselves, either voluntarily or under compulsion, that the best logistic support for elite sport becomes possible: an essential component is a corps of fully professional administrators, coaches, scientists and physicians whose continuing office depends upon success. It might be argued that the latter element of such a system operates in professional football where the working security of managers and coaches is very much success dependent. However, that degree of corporate co-operation and co-ordination required to produce a high quality national football team is missing, as evidenced by the reluctance of the clubs forming the Football League both to make players freely available for international competition and more important training, and to reduce the size of the leagues and the extent of the competitive season.

The result of over-playing has been seen in English professional football for many years; it is apparent in English county cricket to some degree and is beginning to become a problem in Rugby Union football. Top class performances can only be expected of elite players if they have sufficient time between competitions to recoup their mental resources and to maintain their training. A constant programme of competition without adequate opportunity for proper maintenance training inevitably leads to deterioration in performance. It has been noted on previous occasions in athletics, for example, that the response to objective fitness testing indicates that track and field athletes are in some ways at their fittest at the beginning of the competitive season and to a degree lose fitness as the competitive season goes on. The concentration on competition at the expense of training is a noticeable cause of lack of success in many sports, for example lawn tennis. Young players who survive only the first few rounds of competition too often fail to spend the rest of the time after they have been knocked out in perfecting their fitness and skills. In this context a key part of the programme of rational training is a reduction in competition with more time for training. The motor racing Grand Prix circuit illustrates a suitable type of programme with sufficient breaks during the season to allow the impetus to be maintained; the relatively small number of Grand Prix races assists in this.

An essential component in the application of scientific method to sports training is the availability of adequate data. There is a wealth of published information on all the technical and technological aspects of sport; the great difficulty for sports administrator and sports scientist alike is in assimilating what is available. Thus the need for data banks with adequate retrieval systems and effective material handling is becoming essential. The United Kingdom National Documentation Centre at Birmingham has been a very considerable help, and with the advent of ever more simple and readily available software it should be possible to provide print-out terminals for data retrieval systems more widely. Associated with such data handling services is the possibility of more accurately determining norms for high quality athletes in a whole variety of different sporting events. It can be argued that where resources for the development of elite athletes are limited they should be applied to those most likely to benefit from them, i.e. to become outstandingly successful. Basic scientific selection at an early stage will itself facilitate this process but such selection is only likely to be effective if adequate norms are available. Multi-factorial analysis of elite sporting profiles must be carried out to indicate clearly the relative importance of the various determinants of performance.

Even with all the most desirable attributes for high quality sports competition success cannot be guaranteed in the face of possibility of injury or other accidental problems. The curve of human performance has not yet reached its asymptote and projections based on past performances indicate that improvements in record standards are still to be expected across the whole spectrum of sport. What at the same time is becoming clear is that such improvements are unlikely to be obtained by the sheer quantity of sports training practised. One of the determining factors in survival in elite sport now appears to be the extent to which the athlete is able to withstand physically the training pressures on his body. The incidence of over-use injuries in the top sporting population is steadily increasing and is a cause for concern. This is particularly the case in children, where over-use injuries affect the skeletal system rather than, as in adults, muscles and tendons; the former are more likely to give long term problems.

It now seems probable if not certain that significant improvements in performance will not be obtained by simply multiplying the training loads on the young or developing athlete. There is now a pressing need to discover those factors which determine the effectiveness of different types of training programmes so as to maximize the benefit of the subject's preparatory work and minimize the risk of break-down due to tissue over-loading.

Effect of drugs

In this context, it is essential to be aware of the limitations of other methods in seeking to modify physical performance capacity. Here the doping controversy rears its head. It must be agreed that, although the effect of any drug (particularly hormone preparations which directly modify the structure as well as function of the human body) is not accurately predictable in each individual case, in general specific groups of drugs (whether natural or synthetic) tend to have a broadly similar effect. Thus anabolic steroids and related compounds contribute to the development of the massive physique required for power events such as the throwing events in track and field athletics and weight lifting, judo and rowing. If chemical manipulation is uniform in its effects and uniformly utilized it becomes an integral part of the 'environment' of the sport and so largely irrelevant. The simple equation, sportsman plus steroid equals sportsman plus steroid can be reduced to sportsman equals sportsman by simply removing steroid from both sides! The use of drugs is, therefore, only relevant to the outcome of any sporting competition if it is unilateral. It was interesting that when anabolic steroid testing was first introduced to international athletics at the Rome European championships, the medal and place table for the shot put was much as might have been expected from the comparative rankings of the competitors, but their actual performances were collectively about one metre down on their previous bests for the season; the reason for this interesting phenomenon is not hard to imagine! If drugs are standard in their effects they become part of the controlled element in the competition and, therefore, irrelevant in the context of the results. If by their unilateral use they become part of the uncontrolled element of competition, the competition itself is denatured. It ceases to be a competition between sportsmen and becomes a competition between pharmacologists. The addition of a turbo-charger to a racing car, while not affecting cubic capacity of the engine, materially affects the performance of that car, and therefore the nature of the competition between a turbo-charged car and one which is not. The competition is no longer fair.

Psychological factors

Of rather more concern from the sports ethical point of view is the extent to which improvements in performance will be produced by psychological manipulation. There is little doubt that with extreme motivation, humans are able to achieve levels of physical performance both in feats of strength and of endurance which would be regarded as normally impossible. Such feats have been seen regularly in survival situations. There is no doubt that under appropriate motivation the human body is able to withstand the stresses both physical and psychological imposed by high grade physical performance. The extent to which this 'over-drive' facility can be released at will in athletes is yet to be discovered and the potential of appropriate motivation is yet to be fully exploited. (Many aspects of motivation are understood, for example the commercial gains to be made by success. It is interesting too that in Grand Prix racing an individual who has been a world champion is often less aggressive and less effective in his driving than an aspirant to that status.) There seems little doubt that future gains in sporting performance will increasingly be achieved by psychological manipulation, and what must be of concern are the methods by which this manipulation will be achieved. Will sport still be sport?

Future prospects

Looking to the future, it is apparent that the upsurge in human performance as measured by records in sporting activity has not yet reached its asymptote. That records will continue to improve is not in doubt. For the scientist and the sociologist there will as ever remain conflicts between the effectiveness of the methods used to obtain higher, faster and stronger performances and their social and ethical acceptability.

GENERAL DISCUSSION

The discussion opened with a question about the effect of drugs on indirect competition, such as the setting of qualifying standards and world records. Dr Williams' view was that if all people were taking drugs then this would make them equal and the drug-taking irrelevant, but that the use of anabolic steroids did lead to the setting of qualifying standards which were impossible to achieve without the use of these drugs. Either drugs became acceptable and therefore part of the controlled situation or they were part of the uncontrolled situation and therefore cheating. It was also important to bear in mind that something which was entirely acceptable within the philosophy, religion or culture of one country was not necessarily so in another, for example, the Moslem view on alcohol, and it was the basic common factors which had to count. Another speaker agreed that if all competitors possessed the same advantages there was equality between all and suggested that this applied not only to drugs but also, for example, to the spikes on running shoes or even to training; such factors did help to raise the absolute level of performance and this the competitors liked. But Dr Williams doubted whether there could be an absolute level of performance because of the intervention of uncontrollable factors such as wind and humidity, and it would be self-defeating for athletes to want to compete only under perfect conditions. He was of the opinion that the basic object of competition was the competition of man against man within strictly defined rules and circumstances and that interest in timed performances existed only as a measure of performance against other participants. Fundamentally, the rules made competitive sport a civilized activity and among the controllable elements it was no more difficult to exclude drug-taking than to define the size of the circle for putting the shot or the type of spikes permissible on running shoes.

While agreeing in large measure with Dr Williams, the Chairman suggested, however, that athletes did use timed performances to see whether they had themselves reached a new peak. Even the outstanding athletes, for whom there was no real competition, would deliberately seek the best conditions in order that their own absolute performance might improve, despite the fact that these conditions changed the end result. Other speakers felt that a distinction should be made between breaking the generally accepted basic rules applied to any sporting activity and yet still trying to make the best of training methods. The Chairman pointed out that it was necessary continually to re-define legitimate variation of a previously established factor such as new materials for running tracks which could lead to faster running; from a personal angle, he said he would have felt very disillusioned when trying to achieve the first 4-minute mile if other competitors had been enjoying advantages denied to him. Nevertheless, athletes were constantly striving to improve performances, and technical advances, such as the Fosbury flop in high jump or the introduction of the fibreglass pole in vaulting, were examples of human ingenuity and such overt developments were then available to all participants. The responsibility for re-defining the rules was an important aspect of the sports administrators' work.

A student teacher raised the problem of education and questioned whether the awareness of moral issues was being communicated to children in schools and other young competitors. The response of a practising teacher and athlete was that, with recent changes in sport, it was vitally important that there should be corresponding changes in the philosophy of sport and of sports education on the part of teachers already in schools, whose attitudes might be outdated, and among those responsible for training the next generation of teachers.

Finally, the importance of the correct diagnosis of sports injuries, both at school and club level, was considered briefly. Incorrect diagnosis led to incorrect treatment and thence to delayed or incomplete recovery. It was agreed that there was room for improvement in this area and that, ideally, specialist medical cover and advice should be made available to all participants.

Biosocial Aspects of Sport

WHITHER SPORT – THE NEXT DECADE

G. C. LAMB

Badminton Association of England, Bradwell Road, Loughton Lodge, Milton Keynes, and Rugby Football Union, Twickenham, Middlesex

Summary. Recent changes in attitudes, within and towards sport, and their effect on the future development of sport are discussed. Social, political, commercial and legal influences are also considered.

I want to pose the question 'Is British sport likely to progress in the next decade – or merely change?' and perhaps highlight some of its major problems and some solutions. Change does not surprise most of us because we have grown up in an era of change. But it was not always so. Before the present century the world altered slowly and the young were truly the novices. Experience was the consolation prize for survival into middle age but today, experience can be a fallible guide. Although not all today's scientific marvels are new, what is new is their proliferation. The first simple television sets for example were on sale in 1936; today there are nearly 200 million highly sophisticated sets in use in the world. Similarly with sport in general. In earlier times, sport was something only the landed gentry enjoyed – usually on their grouse moors or whilst fishing and hunting. Over the intervening years this aristocratic conception has been democratized and sport as we know it today is very much a creature of the 20th century, or even of the last 50 years. It is a field of activity in which millions regularly participate whilst, on occasions, hundreds of millions observe. What we accept as normal today, our grandfathers living at the turn of the century could never have imagined as being possible. In the years of lethargy and neglect following World War I public sports facilities in Britain were on the whole extremely poor and for most people, apart from a relatively small minority, personal leisure time existed mainly with unemployment. The years since World War II have seen dramatic changes; so much so that nowadays the need for sport has to be seen in relation not only to the greatly increased amount of leisure time available to the majority of people, but also to the continually improving facilities. Modern sport ranges from relatively uncommon pursuits to the mass spectator sports. It covers a wide diversity of interests encompassed by a variety of classifications such as land, air or water sports, professional and amateur sports, indoor and outdoor sports, spectator sports and solitary sports; sports where the contest is against standards of time or weight as opposed to sports which match team against team; sports which use no equipment and those which do; sports which require special surfaces and ones which can be played on almost any type of open space.

Sport has become a world-wide social phenomenon and its roots have spread directly or indirectly into the lives of most of us. As a result it is no longer the whim of individual escapism but is linked with some of the great problems of our civilization, such as urbanization and delinquency. Moreover, the effect of competition – particularly international competition – upon the development of each sport has been no less remarkable. Levels of individual performance are rising progressively year by year – so much so that the records set in one Olympiad are sometimes below the qualifying standard required by the time the next Games take place. In addition, the values attached by modern society to international competition are strong and explicit. Success in this field is often given a political dimension, so that the world's peoples find, in the achievements of their athletes, a meaning that often transcends the sport itself, and the achievements of individuals are of great significance to the average man in the street. The significance of these individual and team achievements may be transitory but new faces, records and skills replace them and then the cycle starts again. Through the activities of the media and of commercial sponsors each new situation is exploited to the full and the overall popularity of sport in Britain is unlikely to diminish in the foreseeable future. It is in the light of this modern concept of sport, with its explosion of opportunity and achievement, that we must view the future of whatever sport we play. Sport is important because it forms values and attitudes as well as keeping one fit. It is a form of education whereby the participant can know, express and eventually surpass himself. It enables him to discipline his actions and increase his efficiency. It frees him of certain physical limitations and develops a taste for initiative and responsibility. It is a source of health and through individual development has become a vital part of our social organization which contributes towards human progress. Sport can mean more than merely escapism or a relief from monotony. It can be not only the preparation for but also an eventual determinant of manhood. The attitudes and values, formed from the realization that competition provides the opportunity to lose as well as to win and to discover that to lose does not mean the loss of self esteem, are permanent and provide a rich social interaction throughout life.

In these terms, it cannot seriously be argued today that there is anything incompatible between the aims and values of sport and what ought to be the overall aims and values of the nation as a whole. I believe they are complementary and that it is because our predecessors saw this relationship between sport and the national ideal so clearly that they went out of their way to encourage a sporting ethos in a way that no longer pertains. There is much in the atmosphere surrounding sport today that invites derision, yet older societies than ours have been able to make the distinction between the values of physical fitness and athletic endeavour and the occasional excesses of spectator behaviour or press exaggeration. The real lesson that our predecessors have demonstrated is that recreation is an essential and universal characteristic of life which should not be denied its right to expression and fulfilment. If this same realization were to become re-established in a national sense it could help to arrest our slide not only into sporting mediocrity but also into mass indiscipline. It is not because all forms of sport should be seen as a sort of Olympic Games in which we seek to win medals in order to show our prowess or to gain transitory fame, but because it has much deeper significance for us than that. Sport at any level brings its return in terms of self-awareness, self-discipline and the capacity to work with others; sport at representative level contributes to the community building process; sport can foster great national pride and consciousness; if these are accepted then we should all strive to translate these virtues through sport into the fabric of everyday life.

How best to do this is the first great problem of sport today. We hear much about the virtues of competitive sport, of an increase in the numbers of Olympic sports, of every sport having its own World Cup. Surely we have to set our own national house in order first for sport has more to offer than the selective, gladiatorial type of infrastructure as is now seen in American professional sport. Tony O'Reilly has said: 'I like to win but I don't mind losing – the nation's honour isn't all that important'. But is this true? Do you believe it? This apart, is there not at least room for doubt as to whether, say, the principles of amateurism and the basis of the controlling structure of our sports – framed as many of them were 100 years ago and written for a different age – are adequate for today. Even if they are not does this mean we can readily scrap them overnight? The conflict in rugby, for example, between amateurism and professionalism – never entirely dead – has raised its head yet again in recent years. Veiled hints of inducements ranging from pound notes in the boots, to jobs in French restaurants, profits from ghost-written memoirs and newspaper articles have abounded. Jay Gould was presented with a house by his admirers in Wales all those years ago yet we in rugby have not really ever come to terms with the existence of the Rugby League or even of the Amateur Rugby League, and I for one take a lot of convincing that the RFU's arguments over this latter body are either sound or ethically based.

For example, it is often claimed that rugby football epitomizes the virtues just described as well as any type of sport and it might seem sacrilegious to question whether its ethos has actually changed. However, today we live in an age of greater violence and dissent than ever before, where 'discipline' is out of fashion. In the 1920s and 1930s, the mass of people in Britain were disciplined by circumstance. The grim facts of unemployment shaped their lives. After the Second World War, the establishment of the welfare state began to release people from discipline by circumstance and this worked well enough for an older generation who knew what it was to be dominated by fear. But, for succeeding generations, the fact that there first had to be some kind of discipline was either overlooked or deliberately defied. Self-discipline is needed most of all – a man's control of his own actions and attitudes of mind – yet as J.B. Priestley wrote: 'So many people today seem to imagine they have been freed from harsh conditions to do whatever they please and they have left behind the challenging rocks of discipline by circumstance, yet cannot reach the shining plateau of self-discipline'. There is evidence from the numbers of players disciplined on the field that these attitudes are reflected in rugby. The restoration of self-discipline by the players themselves and by those who select them is essential but equally we need men of quality and character to control this game of physical contact. I believe that the control of games by referees has changed in emphasis in recent years and now needs to be exercised more on the individual player than on the game overall. The reasons why this is so need to be understood before remedial action can be prescribed and undertaken on a wider scale.

The essence of control lies in the success of the referee in imposing the laws of the game, so far as he is compelled to do so, in a manner which commands respect, ensures safety, enables the game to flow, culminates in a fair result and has regard to the skill and spirit of the game. Why should the situation regarding control and discipline be worsening? There is evidence, from the schools upwards, of a greater degree of enquiring, questioning and challenging, of a desire to test the limits of laws as written and to seek a way round them rather than to play to the spirit of the game. In consequence there is a greater need for players to be taught self-control. The present day attitudes to discipline and responsibility manifest themselves on the games field, are witnessed by the unseen television audience and will, in consequence, be emulated, particularly at the lower levels. The media are not slow to focus on adverse incidents. More frequently nowadays players express personal dissent and have less concern for the team of which they are a part. On the other hand the pressures on both teams and individuals are more intense, and the stakes and rewards are higher. Demands are now differently and more finely balanced between those of the game itself, the individual players, the spectators and the media. Thus the biggest problem for officials today is control of dissent as expressed in a variety of ways. It cannot be ignored and indeed it is now specifically identified in the laws as an offence. This direction of officials is an unacceptable erosion of their authority and although the referee should be capable, by dint of his own personality, of dealing with such dissent he must be able to fall back on the support of the laws. Firmness, fairness and consistency are the key attributes of the successful referee but the role of the captain of the team in controlling the behaviour of his players requires re-emphasis.

What are the other possible remedies? An oppressive attitude at school could discourage the desirable physical and emotional development of the pupil and lead to him dropping out from active playing on leaving school. However, licence or laxness on the part of officials at school games is bad and it is at this stage that the discipline and the spirit of the game must be taught effectively, particularly by example. Courage on the part of administrators to impose tougher penalties when and where they are justified is a prerequisite for success. So is the need for effective, administrative and disciplinary procedures. Immediate impact is the prime requirement of any penalty; mere cautions or enquiries after the game are of little consolation to the side that has lost the game because of the original offence. If the laws are bad, if they fail to reflect the spirit behind them, if they can be evaded then they should be re-written but constant changing of the rules and the introduction of experiments can be confusing and irritating, both to players and to referees. Moreover we need adequate recruitment, induction training to acquire experience, mental and physical alertness and regular monitoring of performance by assessors who are both guardians of standards and mentors. Invitations to club representatives to attend pre-season discussion meetings with referees could lead to better agreement and understanding of law interpretation and uniformity. Player/coach participation in referees' conferences could prove mutually beneficial. Grant-aid from the Sports Council for full time professional coaching and training of officials is a possibility which deserves investigation. The approach of the media is important and we must somehow bring them to condemn rather than in a sense condone the unwelcome dissent or professional foul by their treatment of it. The conclusion of the RFU Conference for Overseas Unions at Bisham Abbey in 1979 was that 'The overriding sense of this Congress is that the Rugby Football Union should take up with the International Board the necessity for positive action in order to reduce the incidents of violence in all matches played but more particularly in those matches which are publicized to the world rugby community through the medium of television, films, radio and the press. The desire of the Congress is that all games played under the jurisdiction of the International Board should be examples of the true spirit and ethos of the game.'

The dilemma of racism in sport is one which is likely to continue in the forthcoming decade. It is relatively easy to speak out against apartheid, for it is a subject which arouses violent discontent, debate, protest and conflict. The Soviet invasion of Afghanistan made it unlikely that there would be any move to expel Britain from the Moscow Olympics, and any measures taken against athletes of other sports because of the actions of the rugby authorities would be imposing guilt by association to a degree which the International Olympic Committee ought to find unacceptable. The Government have fulfilled their obligation under the Gleneagles agreement by taking practical steps to discourage contact or competition by their nationals with South Africa. There is an argument against sport with South Africa which says that it has not progressed far enough in the direction of multi-racialism. There have been improvements of great significance, although opponents of sporting links with South Africa claim that normal sport cannot be played in an abnormal society. My assessment of the future is that South Africa has the opportunity to show that her strategy of apartheid is based on the principles of trusteeship and not racialism. If she takes council only of her fears and pursues the narrow tactics of white self-interest this opportunity may never occur again. This could lead to a full resumption of the normal sporting links with South Africa for which I believe the sporting and, in particular, the rugby world yearns so strongly.

Sponsorship

As all sports become more difficult to administer financially, sponsorship has become the order of the day and is likely to increase. The degree of expansion will be determined mainly by the rewards sponsors can obtain from television and the press, and the acknowledgment that these organizations are prepared or permitted to give may well decide its future. Sponsorship mainly supports large competitive events and those with mass interest have sponsors looking for them. The demands made by sponsors vary but it is a commercial transaction where charity is seldom seen. Sport has to produce an idea or a product worthy of the sponsor's money and here television is the dominating factor. Every governing body is aware of the benefits to sport from sponsorship, and the dangers at least in the existing agreements appear to be few. Most sponsors believe they get value for money but they are sometimes disappointed and companies will withdraw from sport if it is a failure. The product must be right for the sport and *vice versa*. Once the International Rugby Board had amended its earlier ruling that 'commercial sponsorship was contrary to amateur principles' the way was clear for sponsorship and there are many with ideas, plans and money to spend on this major spectator sport with its considerable TV appeal. The four home unions have made it clear however that no interference with the game or its administration is to be tolerated and there must be no exploitation of players and clubs although the danger of tinges of professionalism and of perks to players are there and must be guarded against constantly.

Sport and the law

The issue of law and order – the effective enforcement of the rules by which any society lives – is beginning to cause anxiety in the world of sport. As sport becomes more a part of everyday life for millions of people and the staging of major, international events takes governing bodies into the realms of big business and financial management there is an increasing need for a greater understanding among all concerned of the requirements and constraints of the law. In an increasingly complex world, sport can no longer exist in a vacuum sustained by its own rules and administrative regulations. Sport belongs to the real world and its rapid development in recent years has made ignorance of the law among decision makers unacceptable. The implications of the judgment in the Kerry Packer case made headlines throughout the world whilst the prosecution in the Newport Crown Court in 1978 for a broken jaw in a rugby tackle was another example. Edward Grayson in his book *Sport and the Law* said 'tackle fairly and there is no problem. Tackle foully but accidentally and there will be no legal liability; but tackle foully with deliberation or recklessness and there is no doubt what the consequences would and should be – a criminal prosecution and a claim for damages'. The Safety of Sports Grounds Act has created heavy legal and financial commitments for sports administrators. Insurance against certain legal liabilities, against theft and damage can cost thousands of pounds per annum. Disciplinary procedures in the case of players sent off the field are now an everyday part of the rugby scene but these domestic tribunals must proceed in a manner which is not contrary to natural justice, namely the obligation to hear both sides of a case equally and fairly. The 1978 World Cup soccer final saw much hysteria regarding alleged doping and today we have the problem of reconciling sporting law for the protection of equal competition and athletic health with state laws unconcerned directly with sport. The impact of the European Economic Community on British customs and habits is beginning to be felt, for example in economic equality between the sexes. Women compete against men on horseback, in boats and at athletic and gymnastic competitions. However, contrary to what might have been thought, the law has been brought into the sporting arena by those concerned with sport for more than a century. In the last 2 years courts and tribunals have been asked to consider not only rugby violence but soccer sex equality, a County Cricket Club dismissal notice, the Jockey Club's disciplinary powers, a boxing manager's licence and a football company shareholders' dispute.

Cricket is a game which has become synonymous with a code of conduct. The word cricket has now entered the English language as a synonym for fair play; accepting the umpire's verdict as final; of playing hard to win – but not at any price. The MCC has long presented an authoritarian image but the administration of the game is both complex and comprehensive. The village green and Lords have a lot in common even though the TCCB and the National Cricket Association have their own separate affiliated memberships. But the problems to which I have referred in other sports also beset cricket. Should there be 1-day or 3- or 5-day matches? Sponsorship and money pull across other loyalties. Bouncers and helmets are commonplace. Walking before an appeal is now regarded as weakness; bowlers kick down stumps and abuse umpires. Pitches are invaded and 'gentlemen' no longer take precedence over 'players'. Kerry Packer has left his mark for all time and as a result – and to quote Lord Denning – 'A man is not to be shut out from his profession at the whim of those having the governance of it'. However, the game may yet be spared some of the worst excesses of those sports which are involved in international arenas if the governing structure becomes sufficiently responsive to today's needs.

In conclusion, sport is with us to stay. It will increasingly dominate a great part of the lives of large numbers of people. The days of benevolent dictatorships governing our sport have gone. Social and political influences affect professional and amateur participants and administrators alike. Money from outside the sport is available as never before and influences our attitudes in a way we may come to regret. A declining few still participate for fun and enjoyment. Facilities are grossly inadequate. However, sport is still worth some sacrifice which many are prepared to make.

Biosocial Aspects of Sport

THE INTERNATIONAL SCENE

TOM McNAB

9 Corder Close, Westfields, St Albans, Herts.

Summary. The development of the Olympic Games is reviewed. The factors which contribute towards success in sport at international level and the achievements and influences of different countries are discussed. The effect of commercial sponsorship on international sporting events is outlined.

To set the present international scene, one must first go back in time to the industrial revolution and the development of the railway system during the 19th century. Large numbers of people would crowd into a stadium as early as the 1860s to see two men run against each other, and many would travel miles to see boxing matches of over 100 rounds. The social habit of large numbers of people watching sport, was well established long before public schools, universities or governing bodies came into being in the late 19th century. It was from public schools and universities, from about the middle to the end of the century, that governing bodies gradually developed but the sports themselves had existed in primitive form much earlier. Indeed, professional runners were going to America to compete against the best American professionals in the 1840s and professional foot-races were being held in Australia in 1801. The international sporting scene had therefore developed much earlier than is suggested by middle class biased history books.

A major development arose in 1896 with the start of the Olympic movement, with less than 400 athletes competing in the primitive Averoff Stadium in Athens. In 1900, in Paris, the Olympic Games included professional and amateur participants, competing in separate groups. The Paris Olympics had fishing competitions, competitions between teams of firemen, and most of the athletics events were held among the trees of the Bois du Boulogne. In the 1904 Olympics most of the world's athletes could not go to St Louis in the USA for the Olympics because it was too far, and because the games lasted for 3 months. The American organisers also decided that athletics, gymnastics and swimming were not sufficiently interesting so they had an 'Anthropological Games', bringing savages from all over the world to compete against each other in such events as mud-throwing and pole-climbing. In 1908 the Olympic Games were held in London and the English made them into a successful conventional modern sports meeting. This was further developed in 1912, when, for the first time, athletes prepared in advance for the Olympics, which were held in Stockholm. In 1910 the Swedes brought an expatriate Swede, Hjertberg, back from America, to Sweden. He spent a year preparing coaches and trying to develop a coaching scheme, without much success. So he concentrated for the rest of the time, with the few coaches he had developed, on preparing the Swedish team for the Olympics, with considerable success. This was the first attempt at modern national team preparation.

The performance of the British entry at the 1912 Olympics was disappointing and was felt to reflect poorly on Britain's standing as head of the Empire. So, it was decided to launch a national fund to establish national coaching schemes for swimming, athletics and cycling and in 1913 the first national athletics coach was appointed; he was W.R. Knox, of Canada, a professional athlete and he spent several months working for the Amateur Athletic Association until the First World War started. So the idea of having a coaching scheme in order to develop a national team existed long before 1947 when Dyson and the AAA scheme began. Similar schemes were developing in other countries. For example, Germany apopointed, for the 1916 Olympics, a German/American, Prinstein, to take care of their team. Thus the idea of coaching schemes and the preparation of national teams entered early in modern sport but the first major development following the First World War was in 1936. In 1933 Hitler had come to power. In 1935 he decreed that any German civil servant or anyone connected with the government with a possibility of being selected for the national team should be given unlimited time off work to prepare for it, and people who were not involved in government were also given great freedom to prepare for the Games. Such thorough preparation had never happened before. It is often thought that Germany 'failed' in the Olympics of 1936 but quite the opposite is true. The Germans led the whole world in the aggregate points tables, for the first time in history, after dismal performances in 1928 and 1932.

Had there been no World War II, national coaching schemes would undoubtedly have developed but, just as happened in 1916, there were no Olympics in 1940 or 1944. The first major change came in 1952. Until then, all of the participating nations competed under basically the same social, economic and political systems. The capitalist nations shared a similar philosophy which was to allow athletes to rise to the top freely without the intervention of such things as coaching or specialized facilities, simply as the product of a recreational system. But 1952 saw the arrival of the communist Russians with a completely different philosophy. This, I think, has been central to many of the problems we have been talking about today, of societies who do not have the same political assumptions as our own, and who look upon games and sport as an extension of political activity and this has destroyed the commonality of philosophy which had existed in the pre-war period. This commonality can still be seen today in such meetings as the Commonwealth Games where one finds participants with similar attitudes and these games are, as a result, refreshing and enjoyable. But the summer Olympics are a different world, one of athletes obsessed with success, who have been preparing for years, and whose only concern is for a few moments on the track.

In Smolinsky's East German technical book on track and field athletics, the first part is entirely concerned with politics and the whole book is concerned with sport as a political tool and an expression of political belief. There is nothing comparable in British sports literature. This is the central problem and we must face the fact that our athletes are competing against people with a totally different set of political and moral values.

Any sports system, capitalist or socialist, operates on a basis of either chance or planned performance. The factors involved are economic, social, political and ideological conditions, philosophy, training systems, physiology, hygiene, nutrition and biomechanics and the mind sciences of psychology, psychiatry and neurology. Only when all of these important factors operate with some degree of unison, and cohesion can sports success be achieved. I believe that the success of the Russians in the 1950s and early 1960s, came from putting these factors together for the first time, albeit in a primitive manner. They started to put to the service of sport a whole series of disparate disciplines which had previously existed separately.

The example of East Germany illustrates my point very clearly. When East Germany first competed as an individual country in the Olympic games in 1968 they achieved only very modest results. At the Olympics of 1976 the position had changed considerably. In the men's events, East Germany came third, but in the women's events they led the points table with as many points as the first three nations behind them put together. Thus, the USSR, West Germany and USA together could not reach East Germany's total, which is quite remarkable in a sport which has existed in an organized fashion for 50 years. In the combined scores, East Germany led the tables, which was a massive advance from 1968, when they were not recognized as a world force. This change has come about because they have suddenly brought all the necessary elements together in a far more organized way, coupled, to some extent, with the German love of discipline. They are a people who like systems and like being organized. Communism is an ideal system for success in sport, which requires a disciplined structure and organization.

In Britain today, we are beginning to come to terms by trying to co-ordinate these factors but in a capitalist society this is much more difficult to achieve, given our basic political and philosophical beliefs. Nevertheless, the advances in British sport have been significant although they have not come solely as a result of government activity; they have come from disparate sources.

World survey

Russia is at present almost static in terms of sport development. They gave away many ideas to their satellite countries in the 1950-68 period and the satellites, particularly East Germany have learned extremely well. It is interesting that in some areas the communist nations compete against us on even terms. For example, in soccer, the UK has some of the best club sides in the world and good national sides, so it has been shown that it is not beyond our capacity to compete with a reasonable chance of success. East Germany is outstanding in track and field athletics, swimming and a wide range of sport but they spend approximately 1·2–1·5% of the national product on sport which is about half of what is spent in the UK on the National Health Service. In our democratic society it is inconceivable that we should spend such a sum on sport.

Nevertheless, we could learn a great deal from East Germany and similar countries. The tradition in the UK is too insular. Other nations are benefitting. Indeed, there are more coaches in Iraq who have been trained in East Germany than British coaches. These coaches may lack practical knowledge but they are well trained people. The British spend a great deal of time talking amongst themselves but should start to look outwards to see what other nations are doing and to have their coaches come into the mainstream of European thinking.

So, the East German situation certainly has been very impressive, but the extent to which a democratic society could use it as a model is somewhat limited. Italy is a country with no great sporting tradition but has a small elite, in track and field events particularly, who are well taken care of. West Germany may have reached as far as it can at present, and is possibly the most effective user of funds within a capitalist society. They have good research facilities, a good sports medicine programme, good club systems and good national coaching systems. There, I think, we must look for a most reasonable model. The French have used great rationale and great intelligence but, unfortunately, I fear the French are, in the main, unsuited by nature for competitive activity. There are a few exceptions; one sees brilliant performances in training or in minor competitions but in major competition they rarely achieve the results. Another central problem in France is undoubtedly the lack of a sound physical education system at base. Finland is a country where track and field athletics are popular and well organized; long distance running is their main strength and, in general, Finnish results are out of all proportion to their numbers, albeit without a highly centralized system. The United States is devoted to college athletics and professional sport and adult structure is almost totally lacking. The wastage in the United Stated is on a dimension which is impossible to understand without experiencing it. The physical skills of the Americans are remarkable, but a structure within which they can be effectively expressed in adult sport is present only in professional sport, i.e. basketball, baseball, golf, tennis and American football.

In the West Indies, Cuba is the one country which has a communist regime and it has produced, as a direct result, the most remarkable sporting development in the last 10 years. They produce a very wide range of performers in athletics and an excellent boxing team. Their results are out of all proportion to the size of the country and are unlikely to be repeated in any other Caribbean country without the same system.

Australia and New Zealand suffer from the same problems as we have and generally they are following our ideas of 5-10 years ago, whilst the Canadians have focused effectively on gymnastics and have a good gymnastic team.

The big future surge is, of course, likely to come from China where there are 600 million people now beginning to think seriously about sport. However, if even they tried to compete successfully in a wide range of sports then they will have difficulties. They must try and focus, if they want success, on a narrow range, just as the East Germans did in the late 1960s, and this may mean sports like diving and gymnastics.

Another aspect of the international scene in the last 20 years has been the export of sports expertise to the under-developed countries of the world, particularly by the communist nations. Correspondingly, Arabs and Africans have been going to Leipzig and Moscow to be trained as coaches. One of the developments of the future ought to be for the capitalist nations to try to help the underdeveloped nations in sport; first, because it would be a good thing to do and second because this would help to cement good relationships.

Sponsorship

The major factor that has come to affect sport in western society in the last few years has been the development of television. The first Olympics to be televised were in 1936 at Berlin but coverage extended to an area of only a few square miles, with only primitive pictures. By 1960, from Rome, television cassettes were being sent all over the world by plane, and today, by satellite, approximately 2/3 of the world's population is capable of seeing the Olympics live on television. This development of television, particularly in capitalist countries, has meant that sporting events have become attractive to sponsors and the biggest single source of money now available to sport in the capitalist world is undoubtedly direct sponsorship through commerce. For the next World Cup, 40% of the money will come from television and the other 60% will come from commerce in one form or another. So this contribution of commerce to sport is crucial to the development of western nations. Equally significant in Britain, since 1965 has been the restriction by the government on advertising by tobacco companies. This has meant a movement of money into sport which otherwise would not have existed. If the government now refused to allow sponsorship of sport by cigarette companies then sport would lose approximately 30% of its income which would be a substantial loss.

Future of the Olympic Games

One cannot, at this time, ignore the question of the present controversy over the Moscow Olympics. There has resulted massive dishonesty on all sides. One good result has been that intelligent minds have been focused on the Olympic movement as a whole and this can only be advantageous. People are beginning to look carefully at the nature of the International Olympic Committee, its aims and philosophies and are trying to evaluate these against reasonable criteria. The Olympic movement has therefore been forced out of its cocoon and exposed to outside assessment. When people say that sport and politics do not mix they are saying that sport is not a part of life, that it is somehow separate from life, indeed that a sportsman is not a citizen. On the contrary, the sportsman is at present in a privileged position by having an opportunity to make a public gesture about Afghanistan and it would be a pity if individual performers were not to take advantage of this privilege.

Finally, it has been said that, because the Olympics may be in jeopardy, we are facing a crisis for all international sport. I think not. The Olympics are particularly vulnerable because of their size, and 7 years ago the British Association of National Coaches suggested that they should be reorganized into smaller units. For instance, combat sports, ball sports or individual sports, could each be allocated to particular countries with relevant interests, expertise and the facilities. As things stand at present it is becoming increasingly difficult for any single country to organize the games in entirety and they are becoming extremely susceptible to political pressure. The Olympics must change because what does not change in the end dies; there must be adaptation. Recent events have forced a re-examination of the entire organization and this could result in beneficial changes.

GENERAL DISCUSSION

Dr Vaughan Thomas opened the discussion with a considered assessment of the difficult problems raised for the potential participants in the Moscow Olympic Games by the Russian–Afghanistan political situation. He felt that, among the conflicting persuasive arguments of the various factions, the real basic problem was a moral dilemma which could be solved for British participants only in terms of the moral standards accepted in Britain. Participants at the Olympic Games could be grouped into four categories. The largest group were the people who followed the Olympics with interest and participated by so doing and whose decisions could be represented only by the democratically elected government of the country; the government's decision to withdraw support was a logical outcome on behalf of the nation on moral grounds but without compelling a certain course of action for others. The second category comprised the officials of the governing bodies of sport, whose prime responsibility was to organize and administer sport, at domestic and international level, so that competitors could compete; it was not part of their function to make moral judgements on behalf of the competitors themselves although the officials, of course, had the right to withdraw personally. The competitors formed the third category, and each one had to make his own simple moral decision – to go or not to go. The last category, the entrepreneurs, had a vested financial interest in the games but similarly had to make their own decision in moral terms.

Further views on the mixing of sport and politics were expressed by other speakers in relation to activities other than the Olympic Games where the establishment of guiding principles would be helpful. It was suggested that if a sport wished to demonstrate its total independence of action, free from any form of governmental intervention, then it could not expect to receive any form of funding by government. Ambivalent attitudes existed which required analysis and debate by the people actually involved in sport. Governmental disapproval of the activities of certain sporting bodies should not lead to a loss of funds used, for example, for coaching and development. The Chairman pointed out that, by the charter of the Sports Council, the money given for sport was totally free from restriction but, like any other body within the country, the Sports Council was required to take account of foreign policy decisions at any particular time.

The Chairman further suggested that the problems which had arisen over the Moscow Olympics might lead to changes in the type of competition which the Olympic Games represented; for example, a reduction in the amount of nationalism, the elimination of team sports which already had other international competitions, the fragmentation of the games to different sites or the alternative of a permanent site in a neutral country. A world sports centre, which while not isolated from the problems of society was at least buffered against them, had its attractive aspects.

Another speaker suggested that western democratic nations should show their displeasure collectively by withdrawing from the games but it was thought that this required concerted governmental action whereas the decision really should rest with the athletes concerned and that if a majority of athletes within a country wanted to attend the games this would demonstrate effectively the existence of that freedom of action which was denied to individuals under non-democratic regimes. It was generally agreed that the non-participation or restricted involvement of different countries, coupled with general public attitudes and behaviour, was likely to lead to a disturbed Olympics in which competitors might find it difficult to produce their best performances.

CLOSING OF CONFERENCE

ROGER BANNISTER

When Sir Alan Parkes told me of the idea of setting up a Conference of this nature, I welcomed what seemed to me to be a most timely initiative. Sport has now a firm place in academic studies in Britain, and departments in which sociology, psychology, physiology and pharmacology are being brought to bear on sport are rapidly increasing in number. They may not be increasing in the same way as in some other countries, but we have to accept that differences in approaches to sport reflect differences in national character.

The proceedings of the Conference and the discussions on many topics which we have had in the last two and a half days will be recorded in book form by the Galton Foundation under the same title *Biosocial Aspects of Sport* and will, I hope, evoke wider discussions and, perhaps, help to solve the many and varied problems facing sport.

I will close the Conference by thanking Sir Alan Parkes and his staff, his advisers, the speakers, who must have given a lot of time and thought to their presentations, and also those who have contributed to discussion of the proceedings of a valuable and highly topical Conference.

SUBJECT INDEX

Aptitude
  athletic predisposition. 123–126
  biological basis of. 103–112
  flair. 147
  psychological make-up. 145
Athletic potential
  athletic predisposition: a new hypothesis. 123–126
  flair. 147
  of young performers. 146
  sex differences in. 126–127
Attitudes and values. 23–27, 171–173, 175–178, 188–189, 191

Behaviour
  interactional model of. 61–67
Biological characteristics
  and performance. 113–115
  of the endurance athlete. 104–105

Coaching
  of young performers. 70
  role of the coach. 141, 144–146
  structure of. 146
Competition
  indirect and between individuals. 188
  psychological preparation for. 86–89, 145
  structure of. 146–147
  value of experience. 146

Disease
  medical checks for sports participants. 99
  role of sport in prevention of. 80–81
Drugs
  effect on performance. 186–187, 188
  use and abuse. 149–156, 157–164

Economic factors
  and pattern of sport. 137, 147, 184
Endurance athletes
  characteristics of. 104–109
Enjoyment
  a balanced approach. 99
  and meaning of sport. 91–93
  exercise for fun. 81
  for women. 44–45

Environmental factors
  and improved performance. 183–184
  influence on choice of sport. 104
  leisure facilities. 52
Equal opportunities
  EOC. 39–45, 52
  for men and women. 52
Experience
  value of competition. 146

Football hooliganism. 17–21

Genetic endowment
  contribution to sports performance. 183
  of athletes. 103–109, 113

Hazards of sport
  a balanced approach. 99
Health *see* **Ill-health, Mental health, Physical health**
Historical aspects
  development of Olympic Games. 197–198
  development of sport. 29–31
  of violence in sport. 7–10

Ill-health
  amelioration by exercise. 79–80
Information
  availability of data. 185–186
  communication with young people. 188
Injuries
  and sport. 151–162
  classification by type. 153–157
  injury-proneness. 86
  in karate. 159–160
  in rugby, survey of. 152–153
  preventive measures. 154, 160–162
  psychological. 167–168
  to young people. 162
International scene
  achievements of different countries. 199–200
  historical aspects. 30–31
  preparation programmes in Eastern Europe. 143–144, 198–199
  problems of drugs. 163–170

Karate
  incidence and prevention of injuries. 159–161

Legislation
  against drug abuse and other moral issues. 163–170, 177–178
  by sports governing bodies. 160–162
  EOC and sex discrimination. 39–40, 52
  racial discrimination. 194–195
  sport and the law. 195–196
Leisure
  availability for women. 35–39

Martial arts
  role in society. 52
  injuries to participants. 159–162
Media
  newspapers and radio. 31
  role in sport. 23–27
Mental health
  contribution to sports performance. 85–89
  definition of. 84
  fulfilment through sport. 65–67
  obsessionality. 85
  treatment of mental illness by sports participation. 89–91
Motivation
  achievement. 62–64
  and performance. 113, 187
  effect of meditation. 98
  intrinsic. 65–67
  mental rehearsal. 89
  problems of. 153
Muscle
  capacity for improved performance. 72–78
  composition and biochemical reactions of. 107–109

National Health Service
  and treatment of sports injuries. 151, 156

Obesity
  brown adipose tissue. 99
  effect of exercise. 80, 98
Obsessionality. 99
Old age
  extension of physical capacity in the elderly. 78–79

Olympic Games
  future prospects for. 201
  historical development of. 197–198
  problem of drugs. 163–168
  problems associated with the Moscow Olympics. 201–202
Oxygen uptake
  and exercise. 72–75
  needs of athletes at different events. 105–107

Performance
  biological characteristics for success. 103–111
  comment and discussion. 143–147
  correlation with personality. 59–67
  effect of drugs. 166–167, 188
  improvements in and future prospects. 181–187
  psychological factors. 114–115
  selection and training. 133–142
  sex differences. 117–122, 129–131, 183
Personality
  comment. 69–70
  interactional approach. 61–67
  personality traits and sports behaviour. 57–61
  relevance to sporting performance. 55–68
Physical health
  a balanced approach. 99
  extension of physical capacity
    in normal adults. 72–78, 98
    in the elderly. 78–79
    in the physically handicapped. 79–80
  prevention of disease. 80–81
  promotion of. 151–152
Physically handicapped
  extension of physical capacity. 79–80
Progress in sport
  improvements in performance. 181–187
  technical advances. 183
  the next decade. 191–195
Protective clothing
  in prevention of injury. 154, 160, 161–162
Psychological factors
  effect on performance. 113–115, 183, 187
  mental rehearsal. 65, 85–89, 98
  preparation for competition. 86–89, 145
Psychological problems
  of women athletes. 129
  psychological injuries. 153–154
  specific problems and treatment. 85–89

Index

Referees
   control by. 15, 160, 193–194
Role of sport
   and enjoyment. 91–93
   fulfilment of the personality. 44–45, 65–67
   in life. 69–70
   in promoting health. 71–81, 99, 143–144

Selection for competition
   by results, choice or potential. 134–135, 143
   early opportunities. 139
   economic aspects. 137, 147
   factors to be considered. 143
   problems of. 135–139
Sex differences
   anatomical and physiological, effect on performance. 129–131
   in athletic potential. 117–128
   in long-distance running. 111, 120–121
   in performance. 117–122, 183
   sex roles. 41–42
Sex tests
   for women. 49–50, 177
Social bonding
   and violence in sport. 5–22
Sponsorship, commercial
   and the BBC. 25
   benefits and dangers. 195
   effect on international events. 200–201
Sports Council. 1, 144, 147, 194, 202
Sports science
   influence of. 141–142
   usefulness and application of research. 147
Sports medicine
   comment. 97–98, 156
   treatment for medical needs of participants. 178
   treatment of injuries. 156
Stress
   physical, and injury. 151, 154–156, 186
   psychological. 65, 86–89, 97–98, 153–154

Technical advances
   effect on performance. 183–184, 188

Television
   role in sport. 24–25, 27
Training
   effect on O_2 uptake and realization of potential. 109–110
   effect on sports performance. 184–186
   for required weight categories. 145–146
   of young participants. 140–141
   problems of. 137–138
   recent developments. 140–142

Violence
   in sport. 5–22, 27
   self-discipline, and control by referees and governing bodies. 192–194

Weight factors
   in boxing and judo. 145
   in karate. 160–161
Women and sport
   body image. 44–45
   comment. 49–52
   encouragement for girls. 52
   equal opportunities. 52
   female performance. 117–127
   leisure: availability and use. 35–39
   particular problems of women. 34–35, 49–52
   sex tests. 49–50, 177
   social aspects. 33–47
   social expectations. 41–44

Young performers
   communication of moral issues. 188
   drug-taking. 164, 172
   early opportunities. 139–140
   encouragement for girls. 52
   experience of failure. 64
   parental attitudes. 51, 52
   particular needs in sport. 93
   role of the coach. 70
   selection at an early age. 134
   sex roles and influence of schools. 41–42, 50–51, 52
   vulnerability to injury. 162

Southern Methodist Univ. fond
GV 706.8.B5 1980
Biosocial aspects of sport :
3 2177 00271 9605

WITHDRAWN